CORNUBIA

The Life and Times of a Hayle Steamship

Peter Joseph

Published by Peninsula Projects

Printed and bound by Short Run Press Ltd
25 Bittern Road, Sowton Industrial Estate, Devon EX2 7LW

978-0-9575660-9-5

Typeset, layout and design by Peninsula Projects
c/o PO Box 62, Camborne TR14 7ZN

The *Cornubia* remembered on the Mayoral medallion of Hayle Town Council.
Used with permission.

And here's to our 'Cornubia' and all her gallant crew
Who fear not the Yankee ironclads and all that the Union can do
Rough seas and Round Shot are to her never a bar
And she will always fly the Bonnie Blue Flag that bears a single star
Hurrah ! Hurrah ! for Southern Rights Hurrah!
Hurrah for the Bonnie Blue Flag that hears a Single Star

For Lisetta,

who had to listen to the story so many times when people asked me what I was currently researching.

Thanks also to my mother, Joyce, for her financial support.

Foreword

The history of the Cornish-built paddle steamer, the *Cornubia*, is one of the most interesting and exciting stories to come out of Cornwall in the 19th century. Peter Joseph's account covers subjects as diverse and varied as one can imagine: ship building by Harvey & Co. of Hayle; the transition from sail to steam; the impact on the Cornish coastal trade of the new railways, together with a valuable description of the development of those railways.

The narrative becomes truly exciting as the ship becomes involved in the American Civil War, as a Confederate blockade runner. Much has been written about that conflict, but little attention has been paid to the activities of those charged with carrying the South's cotton to Europe and bringing much-needed arms, ammunition, food and other essentials to the South's ports. *Cornubia* was one of the most successful of those blockade runners. On average, runners made about four successful trips through the Union's heavily armed blockading war ships. The *Cornubia* made over twenty successful runs into and out of the southern port of Wilmington – fourth most successful of the dozens which attempted the same journey. The part played by Captain John Burroughs, possibly a Royal Navy officer, was impressive. His outstanding skill and resourcefulness were matched only by his courage and daring. Richard Gayle, the Confederate captain who replaced him, along with his crew, followed his outstanding example.

After capture by the Union Navy, the *Cornubia* had a new career as a Federal blockader. While this new career was less prominent than her old, she had some notable moments. After the war her engines were removed and she began another life as a trader, under sail. She then travelled tens of thousands of miles between the Baltic and the United States and northern Europe. Under sail she crossed the Atlantic eight times, finally clocking up some 130,000 miles in her long career. She disappeared from the maritime record in 1878.

Peter Joseph is a researcher with very wide interests. He has a degree in geology from the University of London, and Master's degrees in mining geology (Camborne School of Mines) and industrial heritage management (University of Exeter). He is a Fellow of the Royal Historical Society and an Associate Member of the Chartered Institute for Archaeology. Peter has written several books and many articles on Cornish mining history, and here he has shown his ability to search out and explain a mass of complex maritime material. All those interested in Cornish history, maritime history and the American Civil War will find this book fascinating.

Allen Buckley, March 2015

Author's Foreword

In 2002 Clive Carter involved me in his researches on the Hayle steamer *Cornubia*. Clive never had his own access to the internet so I would get a phone call ('ere, your interweb thing, does it do this?), he would visit me and we would go off into the history of the American Civil War, albeit with frequent diversions whenever something else caught our fancy. This research resulted in his article in the Journal of the Trevithick Society in 2003. Clive was also making a model of the steamer, though this was taking place drekly (as is my own).

Clive died three years later, rather suddenly, leaving not least a great hole in my supply of insults, banter and repartee. Towards the end of 2013 I thought I would check online for any fresh resources and information on the *Cornubia*; after all, seven more years of the internet should have resulted in many changes and more research opportunities. I was astonished; many new resources were indeed available, such as the *Official Records of the Union and Confederate Navies in the War of the Rebellion*, universally known as the ORN. Apart from this resource it was possible to get help from the other side of the Atlantic to acquire images of documents held by various institutions. There was also online access to digital newspaper archives and numerous digitised books; and not least, several forums, notably Civil War Talk, which provided me with much useful information.

This is not intended to be a definitive book on the American Civil War; it is a book about a ship which took part in it. While I have devoted some space to the war's origins, most of the book merely uses the war as a backdrop. For this reason the description of the war here may be a little simplistic; certainly its origins are much more complicated and diverse than can be accommodated in a comparatively small book such as this.

Some of the information on the *Cornubia* is still rather thin, in particular the last six or seven years of her life as the *New England*. Due to the law of diminishing returns I decided that I had all of the information I was likely to get, and the result is this book (actually I 'finished' this book eleven times before finally stopping). Hopefully Clive would have appreciated the additional information that I have managed to acquire, not least the image held by the Bristol Museums Galleries & Archives. As alluded to above I have received a lot of help in acquiring the information for this book and would like to record my appreciation of the following individuals and institutions, in no particular order:

Andy Hall (Civil War Talk), Kevin Ray (University of Alabama) Malcolm Johnstone (great-grandson of John Alexander Johnstone), Catherine Robertson (Phillips Library, Peabody Essex Museum), Andy King (Bristol Museums Galleries & Archives), Bruce D. Frail (independent researcher), Hazel Stewart (National Library of Scotland), Karla Ingemann (Bermuda Archives) and Jerry Parnell (Randall Library, UNC Wilmington).

Proof-reading was carried out by Diane Hodnett, Graham Thorne and Andrew Hutcheon, to whom go my grateful thanks.

About the Author

Peter was born in London in 1956. Despite starting life as a geologist and later a geophysicist, he has spent the last 30 years researching various aspects of Cornish industry, mostly its mining and archaeology. He has also worked for a number of years surveying industrial sites in various parts of the UK, though mostly in Cornwall.

Peter's early work in geology, particularly in mineral collecting and his great interest in Cornwall, found him starting to delve into Cornish mining history in 1985. He moved to Cornwall in 1994 and became Curator of the Trevithick Society in 1999. He has been a committee member of various bodies such as the St Just and District Trust, the Royal Geological Society of Cornwall and Pendeen Community Heritage and is a former secretary of St Just Old Cornwall Society. He is currently involved with the Madron History Project and is a volunteer guide for the National Trust at Levant Mine.

To date Peter has written or co-written seven historical books, contributed to fifteen British Geological Survey publications, and written twenty-one historical and archaeological articles, mostly for the Journal of the Trevithick Society. Other books are in progress. He has also produced over 30 archaeological reports on industrial sites, once again mostly in Cornwall.

Contents

Introduction

Launched in February 1858 and in service for less than twenty years, the steamship *Cornubia's* life was comparatively brief but no less interesting for that. At that time, one of the fastest ships in the world, she plied the busy shipping lanes of the Bristol Channel. Ironically, it was probably the intrusion of the steam railway into southwest England which made her change career, and how she found herself embroiled in a fraternal conflict on the other side of the Atlantic.

As an object of study there are a few inaccuracies told, the most common that she started life as the *Columbia*, and was renamed *Cornubia* with the nickname *Lady Davis*. *Cornubia* commenced life as the *Cornubia* and was later renamed the CSS *Lady Davis*. However, she was mostly known by her original name, possibly because the Confederate Navy already had a *Lady Davis* (a gunboat) in service; as an added complication, she too was launched in 1858 and later became a blockade runner. *Columbia* is the name associated with a previous *Cornubia* which operated in the 1830s, although another *Columbia* did serve as a blockade runner. Another story is that she ran a ferry service from Hayle to St Ives, presumably a story told by someone not acquainted with the geography of West Cornwall. After 1865 she continued as the merchant steamer *New England*, though whether she actually sailed under this name seems unlikely; following the removal of her engines she sailed as the barquentine *New England* between 1871 and 1878.

The *Cornubia* led an extraordinary career; the first of the (comparatively) large iron-hulled ships built in Hayle she was the only Cornish-built vessel to serve not only in another nation's navy but on both sides in the same conflict. As a blockade runner she was one of only a handful to be owned by the Confederate Government and was the joint fifth most successful during the American Civil War. As a blockader she captured what is recognised as the last Confederate flag taken in a naval engagement. Of the British-built ships to serve on either, or both, sides in this conflict, the vast majority were built on Clydeside, with others built on the Thames, the Mersey or the Tyne-Tees area; *Cornubia* is the only British vessel known not to have been built in any of these British ports, another rarity.

The last part of her career was at a more sedate pace, though she was still one of the fastest sailing ships of her age, at the mercy of the winds. As a tramp ship she not only plied the seas on the East Coast of the United States, but also the Baltic. As the *New England* she crossed the Atlantic eight times in five years, a remarkable achievement for a comparatively small vessel designed for coastal operations. *Cornubia's* sailing career of well over 130,000 miles was surely a testament to the designers and builders of Harvey & Co. of Hayle.

Chapter 1

The Beginning: The Bristol and Hayle Packet Service

The decision to start a packet service between Hayle and Bristol was taken in February 1831 during a meeting at the White Hart Hotel in Hayle.[1] William Bolitho, the Penzance banker, took the chair and a notable attendee was Henry Harvey, proprietor of Harvey & Company's foundry. Hayle was already a thriving port, the hub of the fabled 'Cornish Copper Kingdom' and home of the 'Welsh Fleet,' the colloquial name for the once vast flotilla of sloops, schooners and brigantines that hauled copper ore to the smelters in South Wales and brought back vast tonnages of coal for the Cornish mine engines. Cornish boilers and beam engines* were built in great number by Harvey's and bought by anyone who could afford them for mine drainage and water supply. These too were moved largely by sea.

Harvey was in favour of a modern steam service which could carry goods quickly and cheaply, and passengers in comparative comfort. Fast paddle packets had been sailing between Waterford, Liverpool, Bristol and London for many years but only a few Cornish ports, such as Penzance and Falmouth, had adequate wharfage, and even then the packets did not always call in. An alternative was the small packet schooners running a fairly regular service from Truro, Falmouth and Penzance to London.

Within a month Captain John Vivian senior was dispatched to Bristol to find a suitable shipbuilder. He could not, but he then went to Glasgow where John Scott & Sons readily accepted the order to build a wooden paddler; named the *Herald*, she was launched on 30th July 1831.[2] Captain Vivian, William Bolitho and John Harvey Trevithick, the great engineer's eldest son, were some of the shareholders. Henry Harvey himself acquired 15/64ths and seems to have acted as manager for the new packet company. Francis Harvey of Copperhouse (Hayle) was purser and the Bristol agent for the Herald Steam Packet Company, as was

***'Cornish' boilers were of the type patented by Richard Trevithick in 1799. These were the very first tubular boilers, capable of producing high-pressure steam, usually sold with 'Cornish' beam engines. 'Cornish' beam engines worked on a particular cycle, which was different to that of other types of beam engine; neither had to be built in Cornwall to be given the name.**

John Harvey who ran the ticket office at the West of England Tavern.

Command was given to Captain John Vivian senior, who was a friend of Richard Trevithick. His cousin, Andrew Vivian, had helped Trevithick build the famous "Puffing Devil," the Camborne road locomotive.

The *Herald* departed on her first journey, from Bristol, on 24th September 1831,[3] and was described as a "superior Vessel, with Engines of 100-horse power", just arrived from Greenock. She soon became a highly popular and profitable vessel, though the astute Henry Harvey wrote to J. E. Blewett of Plymouth regarding the wages and conditions expected onboard a packet. Blewett was the uncle of his ex-partner, and manager of the packet *Brunswick.*

The new vessel ran a weekly service sailing from Hayle on the Wednesday tide, commencing at the beginning of October and returning the next Saturday with moderate fares.[4] A cabin cost £1 10s, including services of the steward, deck passage cost 11s while children under ten travelled half fare.

All packets included in their adverts the clause *Liberty to Tow*, warning passengers that passages might be delayed if the vessel were called upon to serve as a salvage tug in bad weather. On 11 January 1832 Captain J. T. Short recorded that the *Herald* steamer towed into harbour a schooner with foretopmast gone.[5] In the early summer of 1832 the *Herald* ran what must have been the first tourist trips to the Isles of Scilly which was again noted by Captain Short on 12th April 1832. However, she could not escape the danger of early navigation, and on Christmas Eve 1832 she ran aground on Hayle Bar, but got off unharmed.

Harvey's foundry at Hayle; St Ives is in the distance.

In January 1835 the ship's boilers were replaced and her route was temporarily occupied by the *Talbot*, commanded by Captain John Vivian junior, and the *Nautilus*.[6] Captain Vivian is also credited with creating the big export of spring greens from West Cornwall, after Bristol was deprived of fresh vegetables by spring frosts in 1837. He, or what seems to be more likely from later reminiscences, the packet's steward Mr Dupen, took up a small shipment of fifty broccoli which were so popular that the Hayle service was to open up a vast market for the market gardeners.[7]

The packet company continued to be highly successful and the other shareholders began urging Henry Harvey to acquire another vessel before a rival appeared on the run. Harvey remained deeply reluctant, even knowing he would get the contract to build her, as for some reason he had always declined to build a steamship complete with machinery. He finally relented in the autumn of 1840, but agreed only to make the paddle engines, while the wooden hull was built by Thomas & John White of East Cowes and then towed to Hayle for fitting out. The new packet was named the *Cornwall* and her listed owners included many of those who held interests in the *Herald*. Captain Vivian junior became her master.[8]

The *Cornwall* had her sea trial in April 1842; William West, the St Blazey engineer, congratulated Henry Harvey that he was "glad to hear of such a satisfactory trip you had in the *Cornwall* on Saturday last and I hope that she will beat every other Boat in the North Channel". She entered service on the 29th.[9] and should have replaced the elderly *Herald* but, as the shareholders had feared, Henry Harvey's intransigence had opened the way for a rival, the *Brilliant*. On one day in May the *Herald*, Captain Vivian, arrived at Hayle from Bristol while the *Queen*, Captain Vivian, departed that port for Bristol.[10] It was not until 1848 that the *Herald's* hull, masts, spars and sails were put up for sale.[11]

Captain Short's diary recorded that on 16 March 1842 the *Brilliant* steamer arrived from London; she was an ex-Thames River paddler, launched by Fletcher, Son & Fearnall at Poplar in 1832.[12] Although she was a river boat plying from the City down to Gravesend, she was sturdily built of English oak with an African oak keelson with iron diagonal fastenings and wooden stringers, while her engines of 120 hp were made by Seawards of Blackwall. This may have been a trial run prior to purchase and during the next few months she was seen at Padstow and ran an excursion to Scilly. She may have already been spoken for by Vivian Stevens, a St Ives merchant, whose son Vivian junior became her captain, and by early summer the packet was on the Bristol run.

The *Brilliant* was a popular excursion ship and on 21-22 June 1842 made her first excursion to Scilly, staying overnight.[13] Her first of many mishaps came

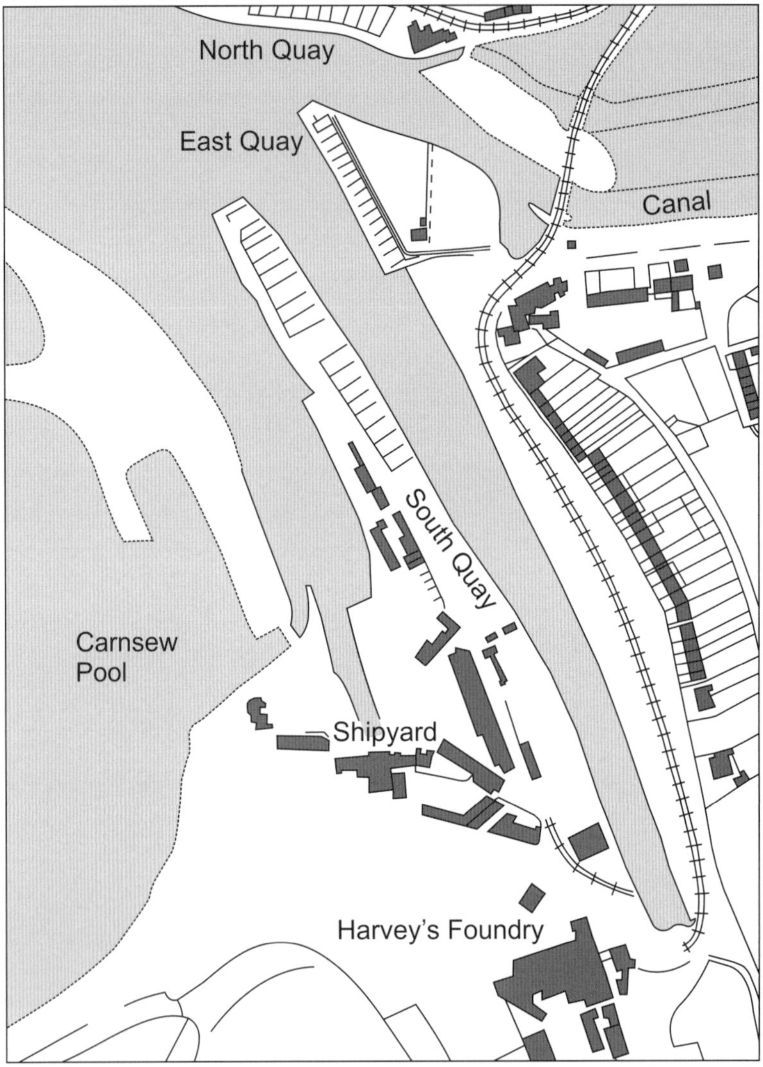

Harvey's foundry and shipyard in Hayle as shown on the 1842 tithe map.

that November while heading for Bristol on a wet and dark morning, when she steamed under the jibboom of the West Indiaman *William Miles*. Captain Stevens, who was on watch on the paddle bridge, was almost killed as the clipper's stay chains and dolphin striker swept the decks. Three passengers and four of the crew were flung overboard but were rescued by a boat which also retrieved Mate White, who was clinging to the clipper's bows. She had left her figurehead, a likeness of William Miles himself, lying on the foc'stle, glaring up at the shaken crew of the packet, which managed to reach Hayle only a few hours late.

There was the inevitable rivalry between the two companies which resulted in the *Brilliant* company offering a £20 reward for information on who was removing labels from luggage marked *per Brilliant*.[14] There were still fist fights on the quay, while the two horse buses, each bearing the name of a rival packet, pounded wheel hub to wheel hub, exchanging whip blows as, to the terror of the passengers, they raced up the high road from Penzance.

In March 1843 both packet captains were heavily fined at Bristol when, over-anxious to be first away, both sailed without asking the permission of the Quay Warden. There were endless arguments over which was the fastest packet, as in May 1843 when for a stake of £5 they raced from Hayle to Bristol, the *Brilliant* beating the *Cornwall* by 27 minutes; the next month she again beat *Cornwall* on an excursion to Jersey and Guernsey. The *Cornwall* was obviously the lesser vessel and in 1845 she went back to her builders at Cowes where she was lengthened by nearly 17 feet and her tonnage increased to 120. She was able to reduce passage time down from Bristol to 14 hours though she had to be re-boilered the following summer. The *Brilliant* was herself re-boilered and refitted in November 1847, and was back on station for 17th December.[15]

Early in 1848 the Original Cornwall and Express Steam Company was reorganised as the Hayle & Bristol Steamship Company.[16] with Edwin Ley, auctioneer of Penzance, William Pascoe of Tregembo, and William Hitchens of St Ives as trustees. They also acquired the new iron paddler *Express*, launched by Ditchburn & Mare of London, which proved popular, though not quite as fast as the *Brilliant*.

Her sister packet *Cornwall* had her own share of alarms, the first in early March 1848 when she sailed from Bristol at nine o'clock on a breezy and clear Friday morning. By early afternoon a storm was threatening and Captain Vivian had the packet battened down off Lundy Island. By dusk a full north-north-east gale was blowing and at midnight he turned back for the shelter of Lundy. The packet spent the Saturday snugged under the high cliffs until at 10 pm Captain Vivian again resumed the voyage. Again he was forced back to Lundy; by noon on the Sunday all the food had gone and the longboat manned by twelve sailors failed to reach the landing beach. To feed his hungry and cold passengers Captain Vivian broke into the cargo; they paid 9d a pound for bacon and a shilling for 10 pounds of bread, reinforced with some seed potatoes boiled in the galley. The voyage was resumed that evening with the *Cornwall* so short of coal that she made most of the passage under sail until she crossed Hayle Bar forty-eight hours late.[17]

That October the *Brilliant* was in serious trouble when, towing the Penzance barque *Mecca* over Hayle Bar, she was caught in a strong tide and heavy ground seas. The tow was cut away but the packet grounded by the weirs, and the tide

Hayle harbour in 1905. The shipyard is in the right background with the slipway to the right of the stack on the right-hand side of the viaduct.

carried her across the Lelant channel. She flooded out, and at low tide, during the night, her cargo and some of her own machinery was unloaded, though she was not refloated until four days later. She had taken considerable pounding and spent several months alongside Harvey's Foundry, where the hull was newly planked and fastened while her engines and machinery were thoroughly overhauled, "as were necessary in the advancing state of marine engineering and still further to increase the speed and efficiency which she has been celebrated for, her engines having always been admired for their superior finish and construction ... the saloon and cabins have been newly decorated; the *papier maché* panelling of the saloon which has become soiled, has been removed; the panels are chaste and delicate and the fittings are very appropriate".[18]

Her worst voyage was probably that in July 1851 when, soon after leaving Bristol on the evening tide, she encountered a violent summer gale. She was forced to cross over the Bristol Channel and shelter in Penarth Roads until that night. Her passage down was still very rough and tragically a lady passenger (Mary Melling) died of exhaustion as the packet entered St Ives Bay.[19] By now the *Brilliant* had seen ten years hard service, and in January 1852 she was being offered for sale at Hayle.[20] Her replacement was the *Queen*, a robust iron paddler, launched for £12,000 by Stothert & Slaughter of St Philip's Yard in Bristol.[21] She was commanded by the *Brilliant's* former master Captain William Spray, an excellent mariner so highly regarded in the town that on the day of his funeral in November 1873 all businesses in Hayle closed as a mark of respect.

The *Queen* soon exceeded all expectations and in December 1852 did the whole voyage to Bristol in thirteen hours. To ensure such schedules, loading and unloading had to be swift and there was often so much pushing and shoving that a police constable had to be stationed on the quay. The *Queen* was sufficiently speedy to outrun the Cornish gales but the congested approaches to the Bristol Channel, especially the River Avon down to Bristol, remained hazardous. She left Hayle at 5.30am on 5th March 1855 and by 4.30am next morning she was closing the Flat Holms light in increasing thick weather. Captain Spray reduced to half speed, occasionally stopping and sounding his whistle until 7am when the fog, being now dense, he anchored in Kingsroad. An hour later the screw steamer *Avon* loomed out of the murk and rammed the *Queen* squarely on the foreside of her starboard paddlebox, carrying away the springbeam and deck house. The *Avon* reeled away with her bows crushed but two days later the *Queen* returned to Hayle in her usual time of thirteen hours.[22]

The SS *Ramleh* being built in Harvey's shipyard in 1891, the largest ship ever built in Cornwall. This was the last ship built by Harvey & Co. and the shipyard closed in 1893. Kressen Kernow image.

The *Queen* continued to outpace her rivals, as in July 1856 when she made Bristol in 12½ hours and discharged 500 baskets of potatoes, several tons of tin from the Mellanear smelter and some general cargo. After cleaning down, coaling up and loading a cargo of general goods she sailed at 7.30am on the Saturday morning and reached Hayle at 9pm. On board was a 'Hayle gentleman' who had come down from Liverpool and so reached home in 22 hours.[23] In January 1857 she was sent up river to the Copperhouse Foundry where ‘new boilers of the best construction were fitted and her engines have been overhauled and repaired,’ all regardless of cost, to give her an extra two knots. The *Queen* was temporarily replaced by the “Powerful steamer *Emerald* John Wallace Commander” until she returned to service on 16 February 1857.[24]

Chapter 2

A New Ship for the Packet Service

Just four days before the *Queen* sailed again on 11th February 1857, the "keel of the new iron steamship, intended to run from Hayle to Bristol in the place of the *Cornwall* was laid on Wednesday when a dinner was given to the workmen by Messrs. Harvey".[1] The new packet would bear the name *Cornubia*, the Romano-Latin name for Cornwall, and the Hayle & Bristol Steam Packet Company Ltd. was reorganised to raise the £18,000 to pay for her. The *Cornwall* would be sold at a guaranteed £2,000 and the shareholders were almost the same as before, John Harvey Trevithick, William Hitchens and William Bazeley, both from St Ives, William Pascoe of Tregembo, William Harvey the iron founder and Edwin Ley of Penzance.

This would be the second *Cornubia* afloat, there already being a brigantine with that name. While comparatively small, this vessel was making journeys around Europe and to the Mediterranean. Occasionally she went further afield; in June 1860 she arrived on the Thames with tea and silk from Shanghai.[2]

The *Cornubia* would be the first big iron paddler built in Cornwall, or by Harvey's, and alongside her on the building slip was the schooner *Henry Harvey*, built with especially wide hatchways to carry Cornish boilers. The designer of the *Cornubia* was most likely Jebus Bickle, one of the many excellent engineers who learned their skills in the Harvey foundry. He was born in 1822, the son of a Tavistock blacksmith, who had migrated to Hayle via the St Austell mines in the early days of the foundry. He went to work at the age of eight in the wheel-wrights' shop then the foundry, but after having his foot burned by molten metal he entered the drawing office.

By now Jebus Bickle was Harvey's chief draughtsman, a position which gave him responsibility for the design of the *Cornubia*, long and low with the proportions of a Yankee 'Extreme' clipper. Once set up, work on the *Cornubia* proceeded at a rapid pace, though towards the end of May 1857 the workers paused in their labours to watch the launch of the *Henry Harvey* from the adjacent slipway; she would become the longest serving schooner in the Harvey fleet.

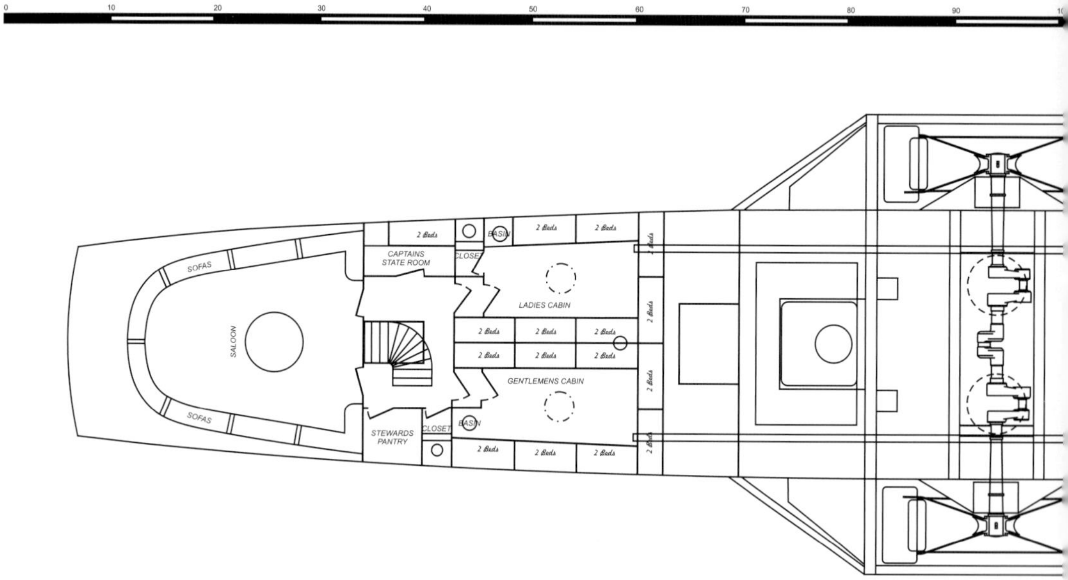
0
10
20
30
40
50
60
70
80
90
CAPTAINS STATE ROOM
2 Beds
BASIN
CLOSET
SOFAS
SALOON
LADIES CABIN
GENTLEMENS CABIN
STEWARDS PANTRY
SOFAS

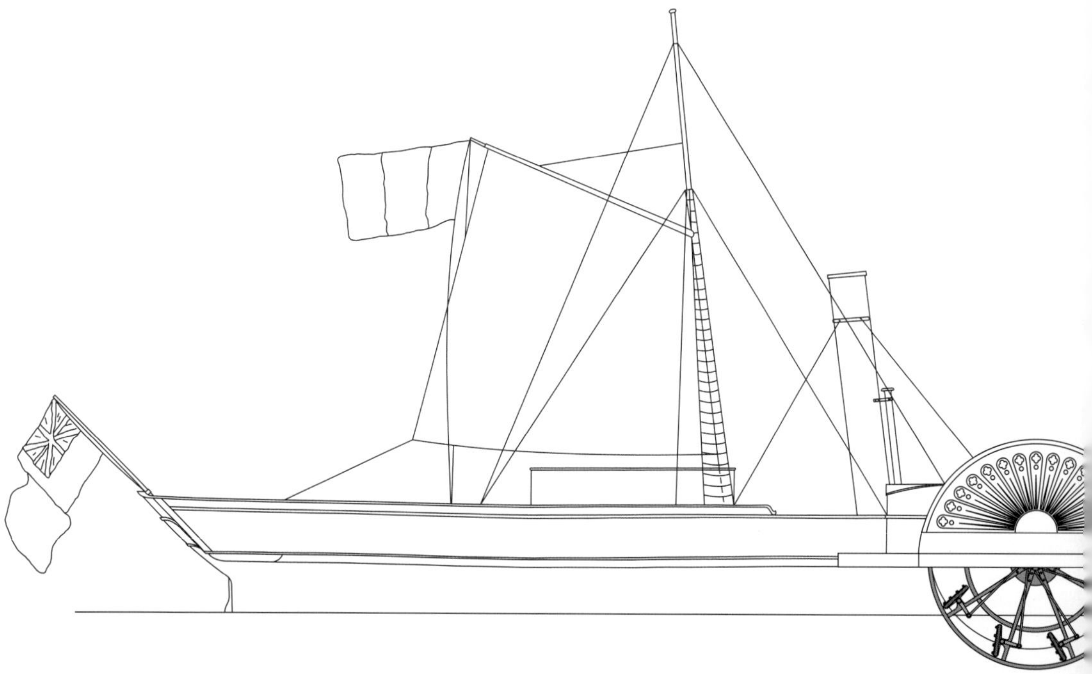

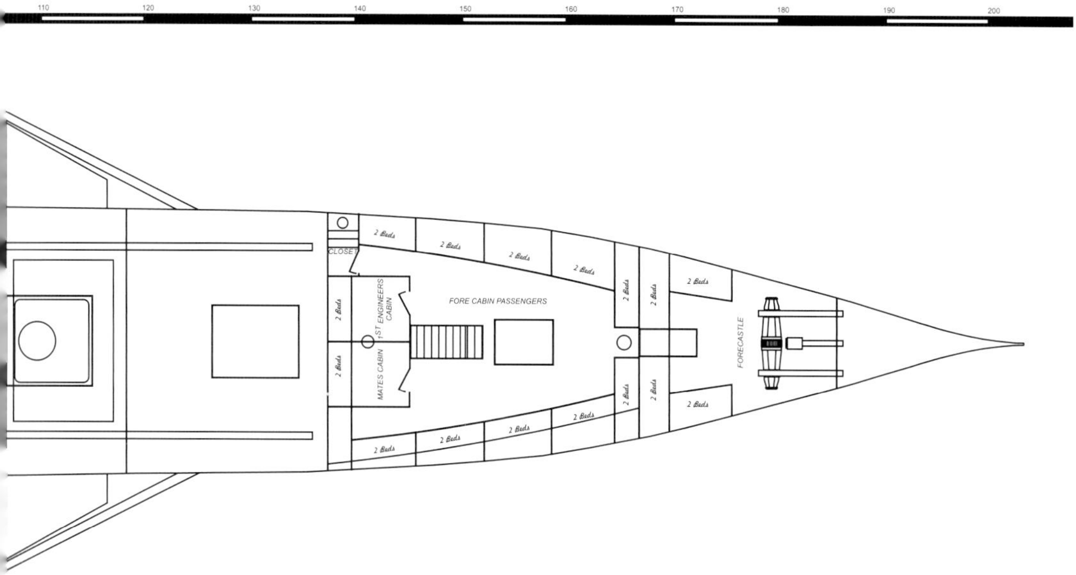

Plan and elevation of the *Cornubia*, redrawn from the original plans at the Cornwall Record Office, Truro, by the author.

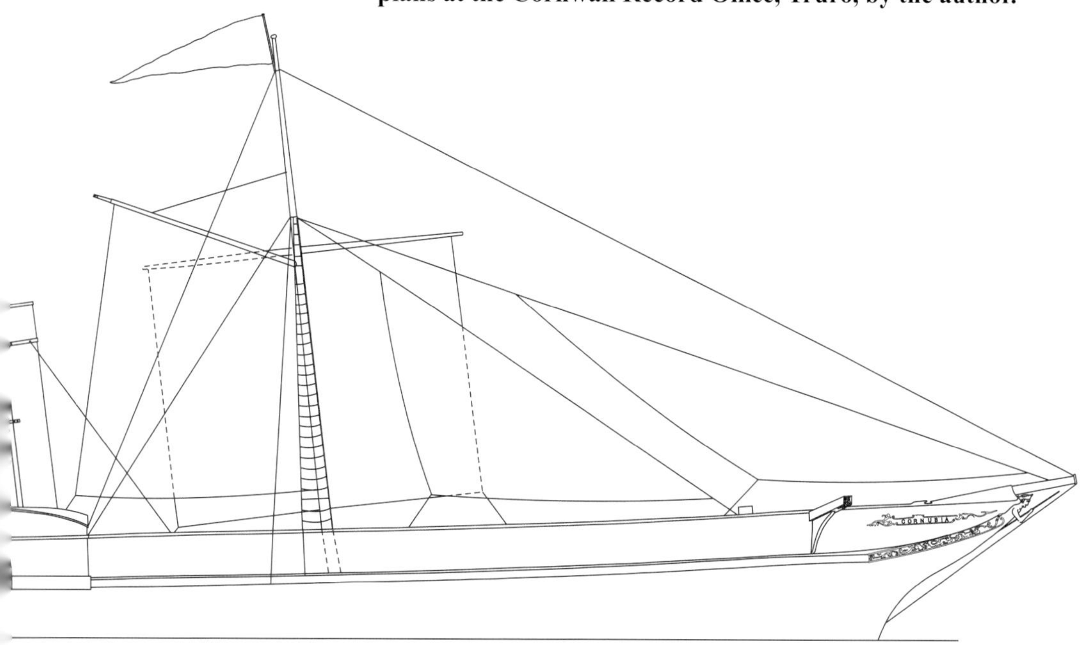

> Hayle - We learn that the new iron steamer now being built at Messrs. Harvey & Co'.s will be launched on next Saturday, the 27th instant, about 4 o'clock in the afternoon. She is to be called the *Cornubia* and will replace the *Cornwall* steamer, now plying between Hayle and Bristol. No expense or energy has been or will be spared by her enterprising builders to render her a model of perfection; and it is the universal opinion that she will prove to be a credit to her builders, and an honour to the port and county.
>
> *Royal Cornwall Gazette* 26th February 1858

In fact the launch probably exceeded the reporter's expectations. While Hayle was an extremely busy shipping port, ship launches were a rarity, and it was because of this that "a large concourse of persons" - in all 4,000 to 5,000 people - had turned up to see the launch of the only iron passenger steamer ever built in the Cornwall.[3] Not only were local people involved but many had journeyed from Penzance, Camborne, Redruth and other towns.

At 4 o'clock precisely, Harvey & Co. opened its works to the public, only partly distracted by "a smart snow-storm". The task of christening and launching was reported to have been given to the daughter of Edwin Ley of Penzance. However, the young lady was probably Susan S. W. Ley, daughter of the Edwin Ley described in the 1851 census as a steam packet fitter and in the 1861 census as a steam packet engineer. The launching was an automated process:

> Two weights were suspended over two dog shores at the bows, which formed the last link that bound the vessel to her cradles and to the land. The severing of a small rope caused the weights to fall, some levers to act on the shores, and the vessel to be free. About a quarter after four Miss Ley, a little lady of some 10 years, cut the rope, christened the vessel *The Cornubia*, and in a few seconds the large mass of iron glided slowly down the ways to its native element, amid the loud plaudits of the sight-seers. Her shape and proportions, both on the stocks and in the water, excited general admiration. She was soon moored alongside the quay at Carnsew, and will be rapidly prepared for sea - so as to be ready for June, at the latest.[4]

An hour later about fifty gentlemen sat down to a cold dinner which had been laid out in the large loft attached to the yard. Messrs. William Harvey, William Bazeley, Edwin Ley and Captain William Pascoe occupied posts of honour.

The newly launched *Cornubia* was described as having a 185 feet length of keel, 24½ feet of breadth of beam, 13 feet depth of hold, and a length of 200 feet

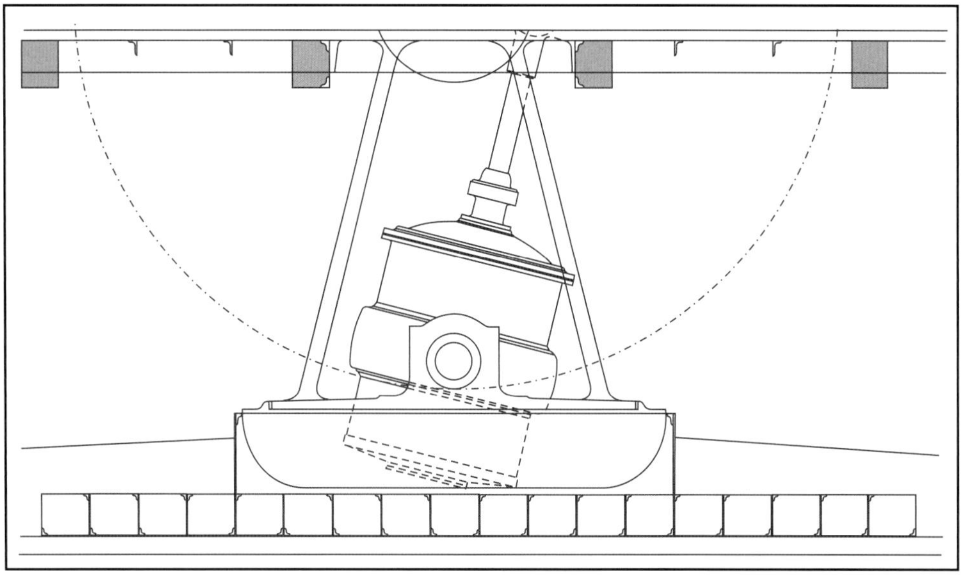

10 feet

Detail of the *Cornubia's* oscillating engines.
Redrawn from the original plans held by the Cornwall Record Office.

over all. Later she would be fitted with a pair of oscillating engines of nominal 230hp output fed by two boilers, "comprising the very latest improvements". The pistons would be steel, acting on vertically-acting paddle wheels with feathering floats. Her gross tonnage would be 400 tons Old Measurement or 500 New Measurement; her registered tonnage had not yet been ascertained. The *Cornubia* was launched on the change-over from one measurement system to another: the Builder's Old Measurement Rule was adopted to estimate deadweight from the length of keel and maximum breadth or beam of a ship. This overly simplistic system was replaced by the Moorsom System in 1854 and calculated internal volume, not weight. This system evolved into the current set of internationally accepted rules and regulations.

Cornubia's enclosed deck promenade would be about 20 feet long. Her saloon would be 26 feet by 18 feet, "very handsomely fitted up with sofas, &c. – the frames of mahogany, with maple and satin-wood panels". The total number of passengers was not given, however she would accommodate from 55 to 60 saloon passengers and a number of second cabin and deck passengers. Once *Cornubia* was in service she would replace the *Express*, which would be relegated to the Padstow to Bristol route.

Cornubia would have looked very smart: her hull was black, the upper parts of the paddleboxes white, with natural timber superstructures and black

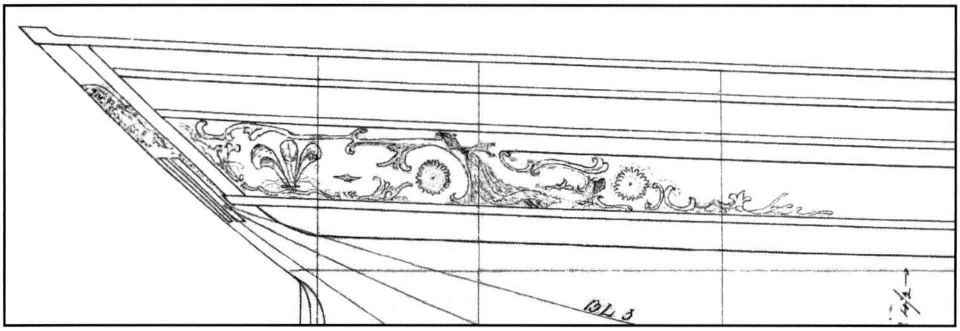

Detail of the *Cornubia* showing the mouldings on the stern.

funnels. The Duchy shield with fifteen bezants was painted on the centre of each paddlebox; about this the design radiating around the paddlebox was a deep blue. On each bow and on each side of the stern were traceries of flowers, which may have been picked out in colour paint or gold leaf. Either side of the stern the traceries included the Duchy's plume of feathers. On the stern were windows although these were probably false and only put on for decoration; usually these were painted gold. The figurehead was a female figure holding a bunch of daffodils, another Cornish connection; this would have been coloured. While modern paintings and the Harvey & Co. model show a bridge spanning the two paddleboxes this is incorrect; one was never fitted during her life (in fact this is where the word 'bridge' comes from; it literally bridged the two paddleboxes to allow greater visibility for the captain).

It took just under four months to fit out the new ship and her first trial run was on 11th June. The trip under Captain Vivian senior was a success, *Cornubia*

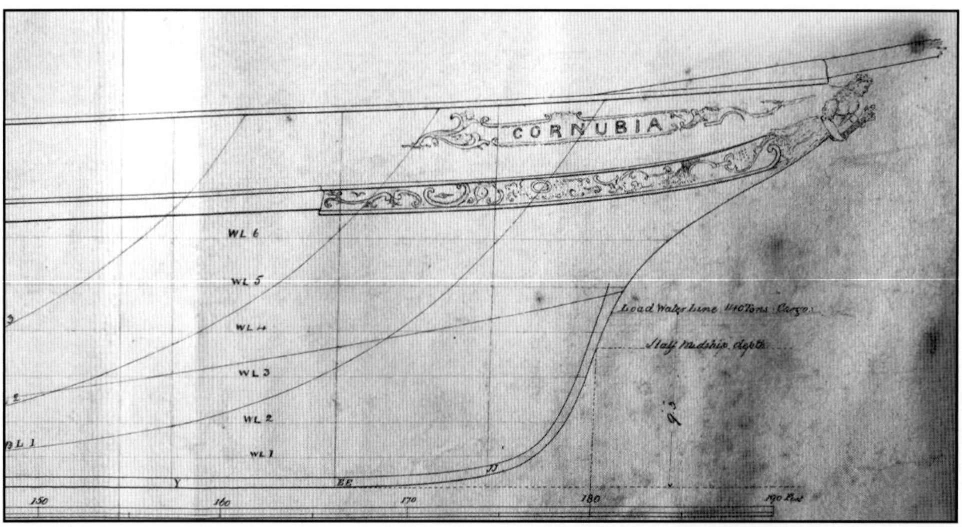

Detail of the *Cornubia* showing the figurehead and the mouldings on the bows.

reaching 15 knots despite using inappropriate coal. She was, however, under-loaded, carrying only 50 tons of ballast and 30 tons of coal.[5] Her seaworthiness having been proved, her cabins would be finished with all speed for her new passengers.

Just under a month later the Hayle & Bristol Steam Packet Company Ltd. announced the commencement of the new service of its "Splendid new iron steam ship *Cornubia*, W. Gill Commander".[6] Unfortunately, almost nothing is known of William Gill except that he was born in 1815, possibly in St Agnes, was captain of the *Express* from February 1854[7] and, possibly, the *Stucley* prior to this. He must however have been well thought of to have been given such a prestigious command.

While *Cornubia* was ostensibly steam powered she could also use the wind. Her two masts were fore-and-aft and she had a gaff rig. The former meant that the sails were aligned parallel with the keel, rather than at right angles. The latter meant that the sail was four-cornered, controlled at its peak and, usually, its entire head by a spar (pole) called the gaff. This would undoubtedly add a couple of knots, or more, to her top speed.

On Monday 5th July the *Cornubia* ran a short trip from Hayle to Lands End and the Lizard.[8] She had brought a "large company" from Hayle Bar to Penzance pierhead in two hours fourteen minutes, then steamed on to the Lizard, where the passengers dined, and continued on to Falmouth. This may have been in part a flag-flying trip to show Harvey's new ship at Cornwall's largest port, and she returned to Hayle that evening at a speed of 16 miles per hour.

Cornubia's schedule for July was trips to Bristol on the 8th, 15th, 22nd and 29th (Thursdays), with return trips to Hayle on the 13th, 20th, 27th and August 3rd (Tuesdays) and 3 to 4 round trips per month were a regular feature of the packet service.[9] The departure for the 8th however, was described a "trial trip," and no account of the *Cornubia* leaving harbour was made, despite the importance of the event.[10] It seems likely that the ship was not carrying passengers or goods on the Bristol leg of the trip. The return trip was somewhat different.

The trip from Bristol to Hayle on July 13th and *Cornubia's* lines and behaviour were commented on by a reporter from the *Bristol Mercury*; he seems to have been quite excited:

> We have an especial liking for a "trial trip," whether it be across the Menai Straits, the Wye at Chepstow, the viaduct at Crumlin, or the Atlantic in the Leviathan. We, therefore, hailed with pleasure the announcement that the *Cornubia* was about to start from Bristol on her first down voyage to the land of fish, tin, and potatoes, id. est. Cornwall; and in company with our

better half (for man is never complete without that portion of himself), we took a run from the muddy waters of the Usk in the taut little screw steamer *Severn*, and in due time reached the quay at ancient Bristowe, where the good ship *Cornubia* was awaiting her cargo and passengers.

Truth to tell, our recollections of the old Cornwall, and her predecessor the *Herald*, sank into unpleasant ideas when our eyes rested on the majestic, two-funnelled *Cornubia*. She was indeed a stately ship – taut, beautifully modelled, and light and graceful.[11]

As soon as he could, the reporter made himself known to Captain William Gill, who he described as "a bluff, hearty, son of Neptune" and Mr (William) Husband, who was responsible for building the ship. From the latter he learned that *Cornubia* was 260 feet long, which was a slight exaggeration, even including the bowsprit. On prior trips, once again with presumed light loads, she had

By The Lords of the Committee of Privy Council for Trade.

CERTIFICATE OF COMPETENCY.

MASTER

OF A

HOME TRADE PASSENGER SHIP.

To William Gill

Whereas it has been reported to us that you have been found duly qualified to fulfil the duties of MASTER of a Home TRADE PASSENGER SHIP, we do hereby, in pursuance of the Merchant Shipping Act, 1854, grant you this Certificate of Competency.

Given under the Seal of The Board of Trade, this Fourth day of May 1855

By Order of the Board. Officers of the Marine Department.

Registered.

Entered at the General Register and Record Office of Seamen, on the Fifth day of May 1855.

William Gill's master's certificate.

averaged 16 and 17 miles per hour. *Cornubia's* passenger-carrying capacity was given as 120 "luxuriously accommodated and provides well for ninety second cabin ditto: and two hundred and eleven deck ditto"; this total of 421 seems far too large and one wonders if it has been doubled. For this journey she was carrying sixty-four passengers; her cargo weighed 100 tons.

Cornubia left Bristol at 7.30 on Tuesday evening, the gates of the Cumberland Dock having been "flung open"; once again several thousand spectators were on hand lining the banks of the Avon to see her go. Unfortunately, while time and tide waited for no man it was soon discovered that *Cornubia* could have waited on both; once into the River Avon there was insufficient water "and there we lay ingloriously, as if it was intended to exhibit the proportions of our majestic ship, just on the west bank of the new river". But then there were more problems:

> At length, the word was given, and we were away. But just then, at an ugly bend in the tortuous river, a Frenchman brought his ungainly craft athwart the tide, and, after much difficulty, escaped only by having his bulwark chipped into a thousand fragments by the sharp iron plates of our paddle-wheel. A few more "bends," and their concomitant danger - few good-bye hailings to the friends on board the saner [seiner?] *Taff*, from Newport, and other "local" boats, and we were clear of Pill, and steaming away towards our haven in the far west, at the speed of sixteen miles an hour.

On the deck of the *Cornubia* was "a capacious house, with plate-glass windows tastefully designed, afforded two entrances to the cabin stairs". In the cabin below were a dozen mahogany velvet-covered sofas along the sides of the room with velvet-covered chairs to match. The ceiling panelling was white with chased gold mouldings, the side panels were of maple, mahogany and satin wood with more gold mouldings.

Back on deck it was noticed that the *Ely*, "a beautiful steamer, and which has the reputation of being one of the fastest class, was speedily distanced and left far away behind, looking like a mere speck upon the tide". Shortly afterwards the *Cornubia* passed the Usk lighthouse, with views of the Cardiff gas lights in the distance to the north, then past the Flat Holms light, beyond Weston-super-Mare and Burnham-on-Sea. Past Weston the Bristol Channel broadened and the sea became heavier; the wind was from the southwest with a heavy ground sea against the steamer. Following brandy and cigars on the quarter deck, the last of the male passengers went below.

At half past midnight many of the passengers were awakened by a noise; this turned out to be a float breaking off the port paddle wheel, possibly damaged by

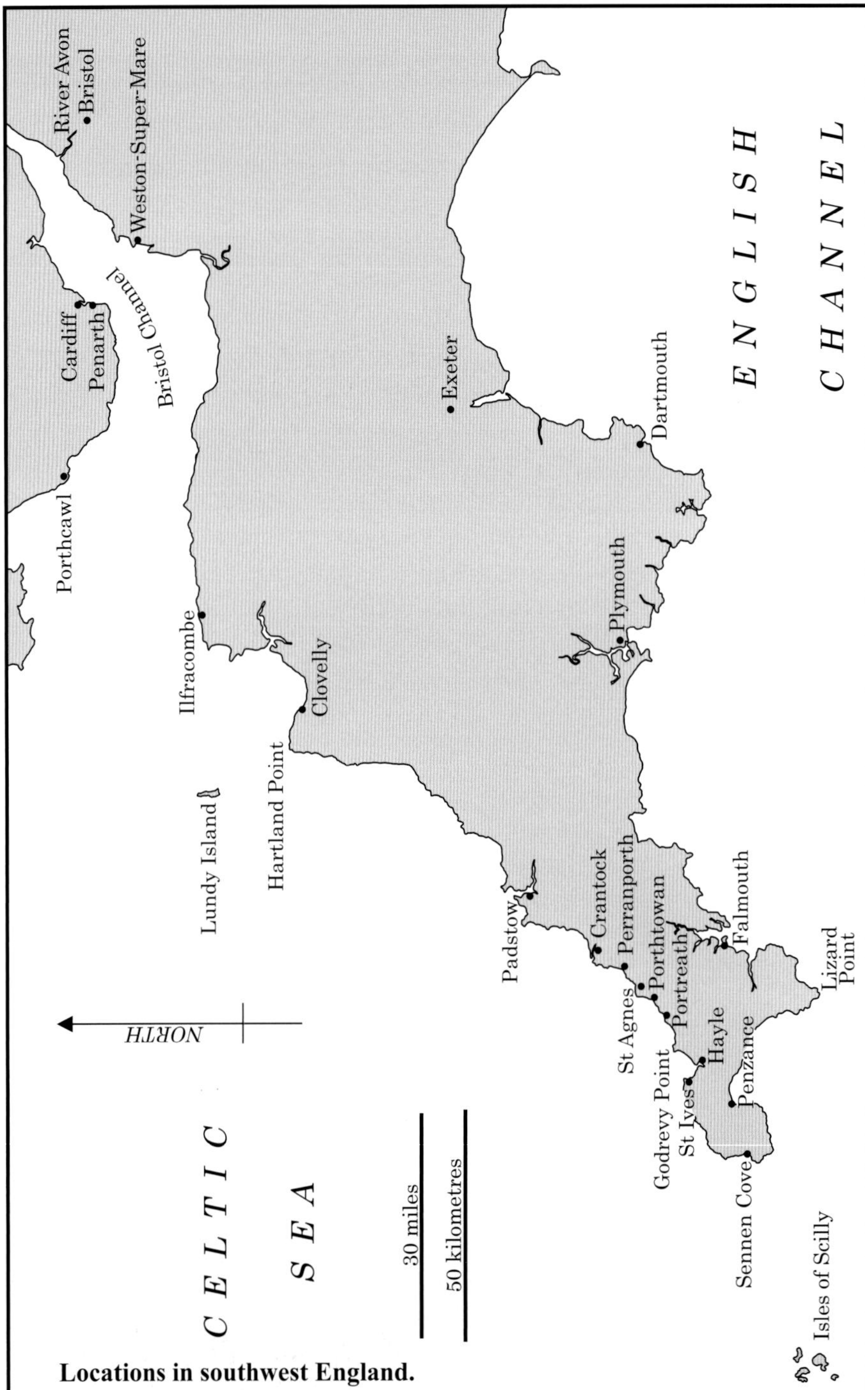

Locations in southwest England.

touching the river bank at Bristol or the collision with the French ship. *Cornubia* was now eight miles below Ilfracombe but because of the heavy sea running, Captain Gill decided to bear away to Lundy Roads. There the broken parts of the wheel were removed and she left at 3am, now running two hours late. Coming back with the tide some time was saved, and *Cornubia* sailed across Hayle Bar and arrived at the quay at 9am to the cheers once again of some thousands of people.

It was also reported that the first voyage took 10½ hours, being about two hours less than the previous best time.[12] On her down trip at the end of July (29th) she carried 64 passengers and 100 tons of cargo. Her speed was said to have been 15½ miles an hour "against a strong head wind and tide".

The *Cornubia* had a crew of approximately two dozen. The only list, dating from 1861 (see Appendix III), gives the crew as Master, 1st Mate, 2nd Mate, 2 engineers, 9 firemen, 2 coal trimmers and 7 seamen.[13] A purser is not mentioned, though one was certainly present on board *Cornubia*. The engineering crew allowed two shifts of one engineer, 4 firemen and 1 coal trimmer each. The additional fireman was probably the fireman/passer supervisor and a replacement back if someone were injured or hurt.

At the same time the *Royal Cornwall Gazette* reported that the "*Express* steamer was laying at the bay [at Wadebridge], and her presence at Wadebridge will be quite an era in the history of the town. We understand, that in future she will not go to Hayle, but trade exclusively to Padstow and Wadebridge".[14] The report noted that a number of sheep were onboard, destined for the cattle market in Bristol. As well as miscellaneous casks and boxes the ship

Hayle and Bristol Steam Packet Company Limited.

"CORNWALL" STEAMER FOR JULY, 1858.

From Hayle to Bristol.	*From Bristol to Hayle.*
Thursday 1st, 6 afternoon.	Tuesday 6, 12 noon.

SPLENDID NEW IRON STEAM SHIP

C O R N U B I A,

W. GILL, Commander.

JULY, 1858.

From Hayle to Bristol.	*From Bristol to Hayle.*
Thursday 8, 12½ noon.	Tuesday 13, 7 evening.
Thursday 15, 7 evening.	Tuesday 20, 12 noon.
Thursday 22, 1 afternoon.	Tuesday 27, 6 afternoon.
Thursday 29, 5½ afternoon.	AUGUST.
	Tuesday 3, 10 morning.

"E X P R E S S,"

JOHN P. LOWTHER, COMMANDER.

From Wadebridge to Bristol, calling at Padstow.	*From Bristol to Padstow & Hayle.*
Tuesday 13, 6 evening.	Friday 2, 9 morning.
Thursday 29, 5½ evening.	

From Padstow to Bristol.	*From Bristol to Padstow and Wadebridge.*
Thursday 22, 1½ afternoon	Monday 19, 11½ morning.
	Monday 26, 6 evening.

Information of the sailing of these Vessels may be always obtained from the County Newspapers and principal Hotels.

FARES, STEWARDS' FEES INCLUDED.

	Saloon.	*Fore Cabin.*	*Deck.*
To or from Bristol and Hayle......	16s.	9s. 0d.	5s. 0d.
To or from Bristol and Ilfracombe.	8s.	7s. 0d.	5s. 0d.
To or from Ilfracombe and Hayle.	12s.	7s. 6d.	4s. 6d.

CHILDREN UNDER TWELVE YEARS OF AGE, HALF-PRICE.

Family Carriage, £2 2s.; Phaeton, 30s.; Gig, 25s.; Horses, 25s.; Dogs, 3s. each.

Return Tickets, available Twenty-eight days, by either of these vessels.

	Saloon.	*Fore Cabin.*	*Deck.*
To and from Bristol & Hayle.......	22s. ...	12s. ..	7s.
To and from Bristol and Padstow..	22s. ...	12s. ..	7s.

NOTICE.—All Goods intended for Shipment by this Company's Vessels must be accompanied by a Shipping Note, and be on the Wharf AT LEAST two hours previous to the appointed time of Sailing—otherwise the Company will not be responsible to forward them the same day.

Agent in Bristol, H. H. CUNDY, No. 86, Broad Quay. JOHN VIVIAN.

Hayle, June 27th, 1858.

Timetables for the *Cornubia* and *Express* steamers, *Royal Cornwall Gazette*.

also carried oil, possibly fish oil, from Port Isaac.

A letter regarding the reported top speeds of steamers appeared in the *Royal Cornwall Gazette* at the end of July. Speeds of between 17 and 20 miles an hour had been heard of, however, by dividing the distance between Hayle and Bristol, 138 nautical miles, by the time taken to travel it, 11 to 11½ hours, the writer demonstrated that this would only give an average speed of about 12.5 knots.[15] Unfortunately he did not convert the nautical distance to statute distance; this would give an average speed of 18½ miles an hour.

On 1st December 1858 the *Cornubia* arrived at Hayle after surviving a "fearful" gale the night before. Damage had been sustained, including the loss of the fore-companion, which had been washed away, and the fore-part of the fore-cabin skylight, which had been stove in. Despite this she was back at Bristol on the 9th.[16]

On March 31st 1859 the *Cornubia* left her mark – literally – on a steam tug while travelling east on the River Avon.[17] At about 4am the *Cornubia* was moving towards Bristol on her correct track, to the south of the centre of the river. Ahead of her lay a steam tug belonging to the Cardiff Steam Towing Company. This tug, the *Pilot*, appears to have been out of position and should have been on the north (Broad Pill) side of the River. Seeing the *Cornubia* coming towards her she moved to starboard (north); unfortunately this put her completely astride the *Cornubia's* course, making her a much bigger target and therefore much harder

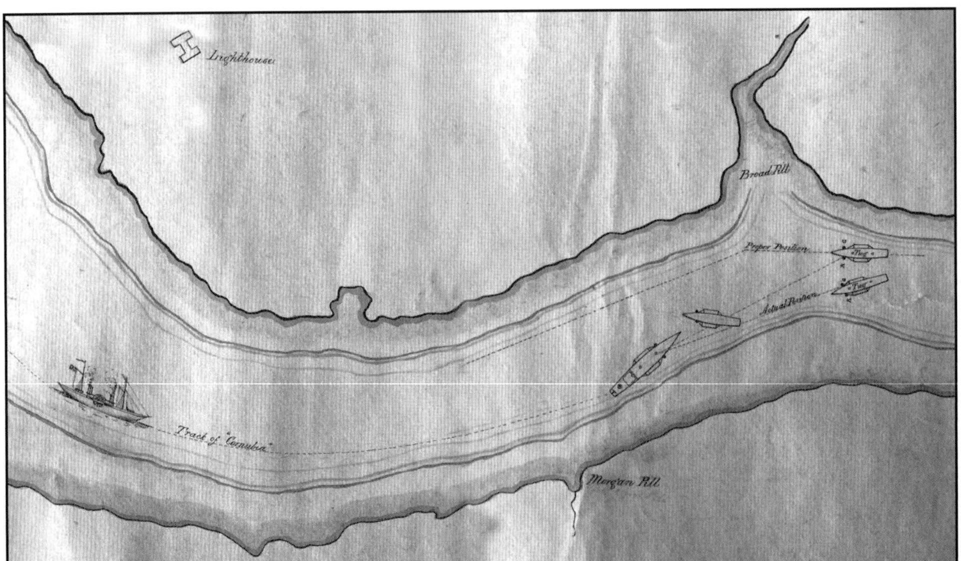

Map showing the route and positions of the *Cornubia* and the steam tug *Pilot* with which she collided.

to miss. Just north-east of Morgan Pill the *Pilot* was struck amidships, the sharp bows of *Cornubia's* iron hull stove in her port side, entering her engine room and completely disabling her. She was later towed to Bristol for repairs, the *Cornubia* sustaining "but trifling injury".

On her arrival in Bristol, *Cornubia* had carried the largest cargo of broccoli and radishes ever imported there – 1,000 baskets – in addition to 38 tons of tin and some general merchandise. She had been making good time despite the recent heavy gales.[18]

The *Pilot* was a year older than the *Cornubia*, having been built by Marshall & Co. of South Shields. She was 96½ feet long and 18 feet wide, of 111 gross registered tons; despite having an iron hull herself she was unable to take the mass and momentum of *Cornubia* all on one point. After the incident she continued to work as a tug and was eventually sold for breaking in 1873, but rebuilt as a screw-powered barge the following year; she was wrecked on Tusker Rock, Porthcawl, in 1881, while in ballast from Portreath to Cardiff.[19]

In September 1859 action was taken against the Hayle & Bristol Steam Packet Company by Thomas Bryant, a St Ives fish dealer, to try to recover £8 10s 1d.[20] Mr Treseder of St Ives appeared for plaintiff and Mr Hichens junior of St. Ives appeared for the defendants; the case occupied some hours. The *Cornubia* was advertised to sail from Hayle on Wednesday, 27th April, at 11 o'clock in the morning. On the previous day the plaintiff had sent 16 baskets of fish by a boat from St Ives to Hayle, and they were taken on board. Fish were generally kept on deck, but on this occasion the steamer had an extraordinary number of cattle to carry, 39 large oxen, as well as 36 pigs and 10 sheep, besides 600 baskets of mackerel, cargo, and passengers.

As there was no accommodation below for cattle, the deck was necessarily occupied by them, and the fish were placed in the fore-hold as it was cooler than the after hold, directly under the hatchway, and one or more compartments of the hatchway were kept open at all convenient times. Unfortunately, the *Cornubia* could not sail on Wednesday as a storm came in. The cattle were then landed to enable them to be fed, and some of the fish was brought on deck, while the whole hatchway was open throughout the day.

At 11 o'clock on Thursday the cattle were re-shipped, and the steamer sailed. That day proved one of the hottest on record for the month of April. The *Cornubia* arrived at Bristol at 2 am on Friday morning, when the cattle were first landed, and the fish followed. These were now in a sad state, most of them stinking and unsalable, and Bryant had to sell his 16 baskets for £7 19s in total, instead of about 32s per basket, which the next week's fish realised. He contended that the owners had overloaded their vessel, giving no notice to the fish-dealers of the extraordinary influx of cattle; the defendants stated that they had to accommodate all as far as possible, and that the storm and hot weather, not their stowage, spoilt the mackerel. His honour took this view, and gave a judgment for the defendants.

More bad weather was recorded in October that year. A tremendous north-easterly gale blew between 6 and 7am on the morning of the 25th, forcing the *Pearl* of Hayle to be beached by her master at Hayle.[21] The crew all got ashore safely. But for one of the crew having been there previously, she would have come ashore at Porthtowan where there would have been little chance for her, and the crew would probably have been lost. The *Pearl* had been making a great deal of water when she came ashore and the men describe it as being a most terrific night of weather. Four or five vessels had sailed from Cardiff with them, all bound for Hayle and St Ives; one went aground at Perranporth and another was said to have been seen going ashore at Crantock, not far from Newquay; nothing was known about these crews. Crantock is probably a misidentification as it cannot be seen from the sea, though it is on the River Gannel and not far from the north coast.

Photograph of a model of the *Cornubia* as a packet ship, taken in the 1960s at the UBS Harvey showroom in Hayle. The model has several inaccuracies: the paddles are incorrect and the vessel never had a bridge.
Unfortunately the model was destroyed in a fire in 1969.

A large ship was also seen in the offing, labouring hard, and for a time there were concerns whether she would clear The Stones off Godrevy. Somehow she did and started making her way up the Bristol Channel; the *Cornubia* was now coming down, and was expected to render assistance if required. On the morning of 21st December the *Cornubia* was herself again in trouble when she grounded

The eastern end of the packet route - Bristol, showing the 'floating dock' (known in Bristol as the 'floating harbour'); the *Great Western* can be seen on the right (1882).

on a spit of Hayle Bar on entering the river.[22] She was still there on the 23rd despite attempts to float her off.

In January 1860 a reduction to the fares of both the *Cornubia* and the *Queen* were announced.[23] This was probably in response to competition from the railway companies which were ever advancing to the south-west. The Great Western Railway Company (also known as God's Wonderful Railway)* had been founded at a public meeting in Bristol in 1833 and was incorporated by Act of Parliament in 1835. Isambard Kingdom Brunel, then 29, was appointed engineer. The first 22½ miles of the line, from Paddington Station in London to Maidenhead Bridge Station, opened on 4th June 1838. On 1st July 1839 it reached Twyford, then Reading on 30 March 1840. Work on the Bristol end commenced that year, with a connection to Bath opened on 31st August.[24]

On 17 December 1840, the line from London reached a temporary terminus at Wootton Bassett Road, west of Swindon; the section from Wootton Bassett

***On 20 September 2015 First Great Western Trains was rebranded as Great Western Railway (GWR) and introduced a green livery in recognition of the former Great Western Railway. The new brand was first rolled out when first class HST interiors were refurbished, on sleeper carriages and Class 57/6s locomotives.[25]**

Road to Chippenham was opened on 31st May 1841, as was Swindon Junction station where the Cheltenham and Great Western Union Railway (C&GWUR) to Cirencester connected.[26]

That was an independent line worked by the GWR, as was the Bristol and Exeter Railway (B&ER), the first section of which from Bristol to Bridgwater was opened on 14 June 1841. The GWR main line remained incomplete during the construction of the 1.83 mile-long Box Tunnel, which was ready for trains on 30 June 1841, after which trains ran the 152 miles from Paddington through to Bridgwater. In 1851, the GWR purchased the Kennet and Avon Canal, which was a competing carrier between London, Reading, Bath and Bristol. The South Devon Railway was completed in 1849, extending the broad gauge to Plymouth; from 1859 the Cornwall Railway took it over the Royal Albert Bridge and into Cornwall, eventually reaching Penzance in 1867, over the old West Cornwall Railway. Rail travel was indeed mass transport, allowing far more people to travel at any one time and at lower prices.[27]

In June 1860 it was reported that the Cornish fishermen had had a success "without parallel".[28] On Tuesday the 29th the mackerel landed at Lands End, possibly Sennen Cove, were taken by cart to Penzance where they were put on the 1.45pm train. On the following night the fish caught were so large that only 46 filled a pad or basket instead of the normal 66; these fish were put on a special train on Thursday. On the same afternoon the *Cornubia* sailed at 1pm, calling in at St Ives Bay to take on a consignment of fish from that port, which was of a "considerable quantity". However, over 100 tons were sent using the West Cornwall Railway on at least three special trains, another demonstration of the steam packet's limitations. On the 22nd of the month however, it was announced that there would be an increase in the number of trips made by the *Cornubia* "to afford greater accommodation to Potato growers and others".

On 9th February 1861, during heavy seas, one of the *Cornubia's* gigs was returning with a passenger in St Ives Bay.[29] Struck by a heavy wave while crossing a sand bank at the entrance to St Ives harbour it capsized, throwing all occupants into the sea. Luckily the accident was observed from the shore and several gigs immediately pushed off; all of the men were rescued, though some were exhausted by the time they were picked up.

At the Easter Petty Sessions held on 27th March 1861, James Bryant, a lodging house keeper of Hayle, was charged with stealing two tin ingots, the property of Williams, Harvey & Co. (owners of the Mellanear Smelting Works at Hayle).[30] Richard H. Daniell, watch maker and jeweller of Copperhouse, was charged with receiving the same. The ingots had been transported on the *Cornubia* The trial report is quite extensive; it is also useful in that it does name some members of the ship's crew. These are John Rosewarne, chief mate, James Hill, second mate and Richard Russell, a sailor, working as porter at *Cornubia's* quay.

The evidence against Bryant was regarded as being of "the slightest description" and he was quickly acquitted by the jury, as was Daniell. On leaving the court however, Daniell was cautioned by the Chairman "now, Daniell, be extremely cautious in future," to which the latter replied "I shall never buy any more tin".[31]

On 27th April it was reported that the *Cornubia* had made her quickest journey to date, 174 miles from Hayle to Bristol in just under twelve hours.[32] It was also noted with "wind, tides, and weather being all in her favour".

On Tuesday 15th October the *Cornubia* left Bristol with the "old" steamer *Express* in tow.[33] According to the schedule printed in the newspapers *Cornubia* was due in Hayle on the 17th; however she was back at Bristol on the 18th and left again on the 22nd, her scheduled departure day. It is not clear where the *Express* was taken; certainly the *Cornubia* could not have done the return trip to Hayle in that time with another ship in tow. Possibly the *Express* was taken to another port, or even handed over to another ship for tow, but at the present time this is conjecture. She had apparently been sold to a company in London after being re-engined; she operated as a packet until 1889.[34]

The *Cornubia* continued to sail regularly between Hayle and Bristol but between 1st and 22nd August she was laid up at Hayle for repairs.[35] During the period January 1st to July 4th she had made 27 return trips from Hayle to Bristol, averaging 5½ days per round trip.[36] The exception to this was her 7th trip, which started at Hayle on February 12th and finished there on the 26th; possibly the ship had some problems but these are not recorded. Remarkably her 22nd to 26th trips (5th-26th June) took between two and three days, half the average duration. It is possible that these were show trips, as a notice in the *Royal Cornwall Gazette* regarding the proper labelling of goods brought into Bristol by rail, stated that "The *Cornubia* will sail this month as follows, unless Sold in the meantime".[37] In fact, the sale of the *Cornubia*, along with the *Express*, was confirmed two weeks

NOTICE.

THE CORNUBIA STEAMER having been Sold, NOTICE IS HEREBY GIVEN that she will cease to run between *Hayle* and *Bristol* from the present time.

T. POLKINGHORNE,
Secretary.

Dated Hayle, 6th Nov., 1861,

later.[38] Two "Fast Sailing Vessels" had been acquired until a screw steamer could be found to replace the two.

Cornubia had been acquired by Thomas Sterling Begbie, an early 'wheeler and dealer' of the American Civil War. Begbie, living in London, was a business partner of the ship builder John Scott of Greenock, and eager to make a fast buck from the Civil War.[39] One method was to buy a comparatively cheap steamer and have it overhauled, to be passed on at a profit, in this case to the Confederate Navy; comparisons with modern used-car salesmen are inevitable. Following an inspection of the *Cornubia* while in Bristol by his technical manager, E. S. Paddon, Begbie clinched the deal that November; the ship was re-registered on the 32rd November. This greatly pleased him and he wrote: "*Cornubia* is mine the best buy of the lot or I'm very much cheated!"[40] However, her appearance on the other side of the Atlantic was to be by a very circuitous route.

There was nothing particularly dubious regarding the reasons for selling the *Cornubia*; her departure from Hayle coincided with the decline in the Bristol trade and there was mutual merger of convenience between the two packet companies. The old *Express* was unsuccessfully converted to a brigantine, and was later re-engined with a propeller and served as a collier for another forty years.[41] The *Cornwall* suffered a similar fate as, despite the optimism, no buyer could be found for her until Harvey's converted her to a barquentine on their own account. Commanded by Captain Thomas Shugg, she had her maiden trip under sail to Cardiff on 6th August 1859, and, thereafter sailed regularly as a collier for the foundry. Like the *Express* she was lacking under sail, and after her voyage to Cardiff on 19th December 1861 she was laid up until scrapped by Harvey's early the next year.

The paddle steamer *Queen* kept up the Bristol service and was still called to save lives and ships during the Atlantic gales. The steam clipper *African* of Liverpool, bound from Cardiff to Smyrna, via Malta, was caught in what became known as the *Royal Charter* Gale off Godrevy on 25th-26th October 1859.[42] The gale, during which the winds actually reached Force 12, was named after the steam clipper *Royal Charter*, which was wrecked on the north-west coast of Anglesey on the 26th. Of the 493 passengers and crew, 454 lives were lost, the highest death toll of any shipwreck on the Welsh coast.

Huge seas knocked off *African's* funnel and bridge, cleared the decks and swept overboard her captain, chief engineer, carpenter and two sailors. Utterly helpless she was taken in tow by the *Queen*, and by supreme seamanship Captain Spray held on to her for the next fifteen hours, until, late on this stormy autumn afternoon, they made Stepper Point outside Padstow. Washing around them was wreckage from the Yankee clipper *Favourite*, wrecked close by with all hands lost, and to leeward the schooner *Sultana Selina* lay in the surf. The tide had begun to ebb but Captain Spray manoeuvred the crippled *African* onto the 'Ketch' of the Doom Bar, where she lay, partially sheltered by Stepper Point until the pilots could get her up river. It was a pretty piece of salvage that would bring the *Queen* a very handsome salvage award.[43]

She did occasional excursions, and she was often chartered for special work. In August 1860 she brought the guns and ammunition for the new St Ives Battery from Devonport, with a special detachment of gunners from Raglan Barracks. The Copperhouse Foundry hired her to tow a caisson they had built to Falmouth docks in October 1862. Incredibly the caisson was treated as an extemperore excursion vessel, and an astonishing 300 people crowded onto the great iron tank which floated barely clear of the fortunately calm seas. One wonders what modern health and safety regulations would have to say about this! The *Queen* steamed off at a good rate of knots, in a freshening north-west breeze "so that many passengers who never before had been on the briny deep.....complained of feeling queerish and others who did not complain looked queer".[44]

The *Queen* reached Falmouth around midnight, providently without losing a single excursionist, and most of them appear to have returned home by road. The *Queen* served as a tug again a year later, when she was hired by Harvey's to tow home their barque *Glencairn*, which had been crippled by a heavy south-west gale off the Bishop Rock. The packet was herself lost when, coming down the Bristol Channel on a foggy night, she struck a rock off Hartland Point at midnight on 29th March 1866. She backed clear but was leaking so badly that Captain Spray turned about and ran her ashore near Clovelly; forty passengers and crew were landed and later several valuable horses but the old packet was a wreck. She was replaced by the iron paddler *Albion*, which resumed the service to Bristol, calling at Ilfracombe and with a weekly trip to Swansea. Yet the heyday of the Hayle paddle packets was over, sunk by the rapid expansion of Brunel's GWR.

Chapter 3

A Time of Transition

Cornubia was out of the news until 15th June 1862 when it was reported that she had arrived in Queenstown (Cobh) from Glasgow.[1] On 8th July it was announced in various newspapers that she had sailed from Southampton for Vigo and under her new master, Captain Davidson.[2] She was now working for the South Western Steam Packet Company. This company was incorporated in 1843 "to convey Passengers, Merchandize and Goods by means of Steam Packets between the Port of Southampton and the Port of Havre in the Kingdom of France and any other Ports in any of the Islands in the British Channel".[3] In 1842 the company had purchased seven ships from the defunct Commercial Steam Packet Company, a competitor on the same service. In late 1846 a new company, the New South Western Navigation Company, was formed with the object of co-operating with the London and South Western Railway Company; it took over the South Western fleet. Development of the sea link continued to be bound up with the railway services; the London and South Western Railway Company became the dominant partner, and in 1862 took possession of the New South Western's fleet under the terms of a mortgage entered into in 1848 and 1849.

In the missing half-year, it seems likely that the *Cornubia* was completely overhauled; where this took place is not known, however, given Thomas Begbie's connection with John Scott's shipyard on the Clyde, this seems a reasonable place. Whilst operating on the Hayle-Bristol route she was rarely, if ever, out of sight of land; her new route would take her through the Bay of Biscay and potentially much rougher seas than she had ever faced before. The route had previously been operated by the Peninsular and Oriental Company, but that company had abandoned the route following the withdrawal of the Peninsula mail contract.

Her voyage of July 7th was the first on the new London-Southampton-Vigo-Lisbon route, carrying ship's mail, 38 passengers and a large cargo.[4] Interestingly she was described as being able to carry 85 saloon and 58 fore-cabin passengers, a great reduction from that noted in the *Bristol Mercury* of 1858. She would be followed by the screw-steamer *Tartar*, 559 tons burthen and 120 horse-power and the *Mangerton*, 535 tons burthen and 130 horse-power.

Almost certainly by coincidence, as the *Cornubia* was leaving Southampton, the Federal sloop-of-war, the USS *Tuscarora* was entering.[5] Under Captain Tunis Augustus Macdonough Craven she had a 'roving commission,' visiting such diverse ports as Glasgow, Kingstown, Liverpool and Queenstown, on the lookout for vessels leaving Britain to join the blockade of the southern American states. The *Tuscarora* was commissioned on 5th December 1861 and sailed for England later that month, under orders to capture or sink the cruiser CSS *Nashville*.[6] The *Nashville* had run the blockade on 21st October and docked at Southampton after crossing the Atlantic, becoming the first vessel to show the Confederate flag in English waters. She finally weighed anchor and departed on 3rd February 1862, but *Tuscarora* was unable to pursue her as English law required that two belligerent vessels leave port separated by not less than 24 hours. Disgruntled, Craven sailed for Gibraltar where, upon his arrival on 12th February, he found anchored the raider CSS *Sumter*, Commander Raphael Semmes in command.

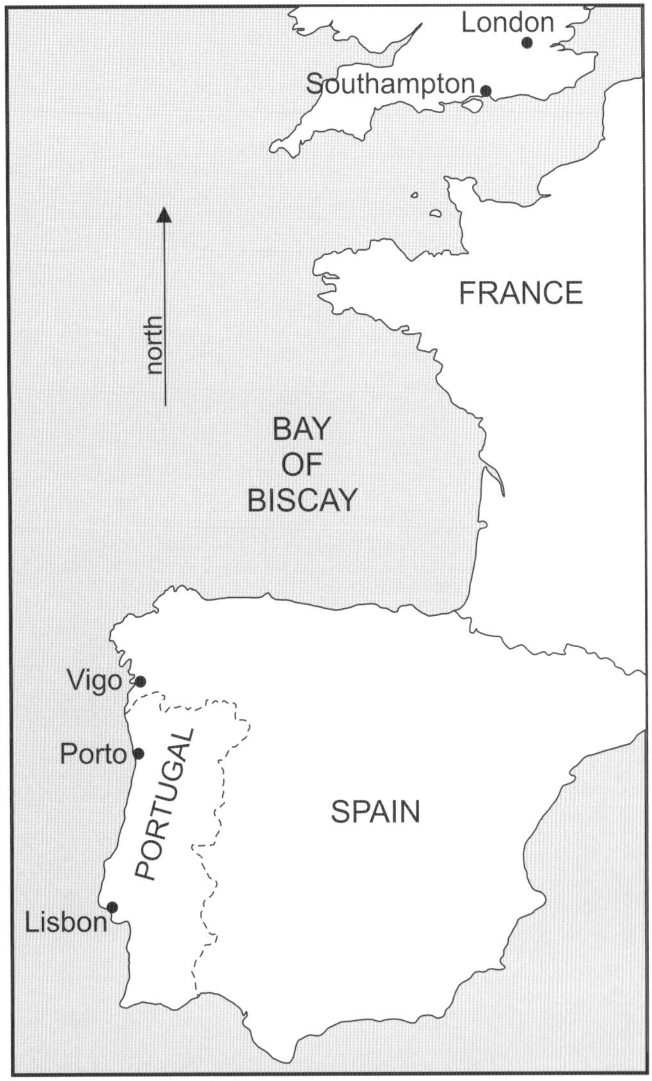

The cities on the Britain-Portugal route of the South Western Steam Packet Service.

For almost two months, Craven and Semmes exchanged verbal broadsides with each other and the British authorities. Semmes then cleverly feigned preparations

The USS *Tuscarora* was laid down on 27th June 1861, launched on 24th August 1861 and commissioned on 5th December 1861, her first captain was Commander Tunis Augustus Macdonough Craven. She is seen here at the Mare Island Naval Shipyard, California, in the early 1870s.

NHHC image NH 93243

for departure, only to abandon *Sumter* in port on 11th April. *Tuscarora* remained at Gibraltar until relieved by her sister ship the USS *Kearsarge* on 12th June. The *Tuscarora* will rejoin this story later.

On 23rd June 1862, *Tuscarora* received orders to sail immediately for England and to deploy off the coast in search of the recently launched Confederate raider CSS *Alabama*. The *Tuscarora* reconnoitred the southern coasts of England and Ireland and scoured the Irish channel without finding any trace of the vessel. She returned to Spanish waters in September and cruised off the Azores during October, but again found nothing. On 1st December 1862, the *Tuscarora* was ordered to remain off the European coast and to protect American shipping. On 15th March 1863, she reported that she had no intelligence that Confederate vessels were operating in her area. She returned to the Philadelphia Navy Yard later that month.

On her return from Lisbon, *Cornubia* brought back 13 passengers, two packages of specie (coins) to the value of £600, 188 chests of lemons, 8 baskets and 291 boxes of onions, 197 boxes of eggs and 21 packages of sundries, quite a change from the fish and farm animals moving between Hayle and Bristol.[7] She had been detained at Vigo for six hours.

On July 16th an accident occurred onboard the *Cornubia* at Thomas's Yard in Southampton.[8] While in the yard some spars were being unloaded; three were being lifted by a chain which broke, the spars falling onto John Dolphin, one of the crew. He suffered a compound fracture of one leg and thigh as well as damage to his spine, and later died from these injuries. The chain had been used several times before and was considered to be in good condition, resulting in a verdict of 'accidental death'.

On her next trip, 7th August, an extra stop was announced at Oporto (Porto).[9] Three months later she was on her way across the Atlantic to run the blockade for the Confederate States.

It seems likely that there was an ulterior motive behind *Cornubia* sailing to Lisbon. Many putative blockade runners were sailing from Liverpool via Funchal in Madeira, the Portuguese-ruled island lying some 650 miles or so south-west of Lisbon. In fact so many ships were passing that the USS *Tuscarora* was on almost permanent station there when not checking out various British ports. Possibly

Commander Tunis Augustus Macdonough Craven, date unknown. NHHC image NH 79201.

she was to be observed by one or more of the Confederate agents operating in Europe, who may even have sailed on her to judge her worthiness. Certainly the *Cornubia* was to be one of only four ships owned outright by the Confederate States government and it certainly seems to have been the intention of Thomas Begbie to sell her on as quickly as he could.

It is interesting also to compare the journeys: the distance from Southampton to Vigo is entirely comparable with the distance she would be required to run the blockade to Wilmington or Charleston from Bermuda.

Cornubia's journey across the Atlantic was somewhat odd. On 13th August it was reported that she had caught fire shortly after leaving Dartmouth on the 12th;[10] while this port was not an unreasonable port to leave for Madeira it seems odd that she did not leave directly from Southampton. On the following day she arrived in Queenstown, under Captain Davidson;[11] once again this is a rather odd direction to head in order to cross the Atlantic at this time as the blockade runners tended to cross via the Azores. As a complication, the London Standard reported that another steamer called *Cornubia* had left from Dartmouth, bound for the West Indies; these are the same vessel. An article in the *Southern Reporter and Cork Commercial Courier* stated that

> RUNNING THE CHANCE
> The very handsome, and elegantly clipper built paddle steamer, *Cornubia*, commanded by Captain DAVIDSON bound, as would appear per orders, from London to Havanah, under the British flag, put into Queenstown yesterday morning to fill up coal. Her cargo is report to be machinery for refining sugar and molasses, though we have an opinion of our own what the same "machinery" means. But we must add that Captain Davidson is as gentlemanly and seemingly as excellent a seaman as we have ever met with, and if anyone can do the business he is entrusted with he will be found to be "the right man in the right place"; and, probably, events will bear us out in our judgement.[12]

The reporter here seems to be hinting at slightly dubious activities, not just with regard to the 'machinery' but also by including the word 'running' in the title of the piece. On 16th August the same publication printed another interesting report:

> THE *TUSCARORA* ON THE WATCH
> We have reason to believe from information received at Queenstown yesterday, that the Federal man of war steamer *Tuscarora* is lying in wait off the harbour, with a view to the capture of the beautiful steamer

Cornubia, Captain Dawson [sic], now lying near the Custom House Quay, beside the slip of Messrs John Dawson and Co. The *Cornubia* is likely to keep quiet, and give the Tuscarora something else to do than playing the detective towards her.[13]

John Dawson & Co. was a shipping agent based at Lynchs Quay.[14] The company also acted as "consuls & ship & insurance agents", George B. Dawson being the US consul in the town; this address was also that for the Dutch Consul. In April 1864 John Dawson was the defendant in an action to recover the price of a cargo of coals supplied to the USS *Kearsarge*, which had been in Queenstown the previous November.[15]

On 22nd August the *Cornubia* left Queenstown for Glasgow; it is not known if this was a pre-arranged stop-over or a ploy to avoid the *Tuscarora*.[16] On the 26th it was reported that: "the *Cornubia* screw steamer, from London, for Havana, put in (to the Clyde) for repairs to machinery".[17]

In October the *Bristol Mercury* recorded the death, on the 9th, of George Burt, aged 59, former engineer on the *Cornubia*. This appears to have been from complications following a "severe operation" on the 7th.[18]

Unfortunately *Cornubia's* movements, and that of various other ships, had been noted and a message was sent out by Acting Rear-Admiral Samuel Phillips Lee, US Navy, to Commander Scott, regarding suspicious vessels:

U. S. Flag-Steamer *Philadelphia*,

Hampton Roads, Virginia, October 31, 1862.

Sir: Enclosed herewith are extracts from consular correspondence relative to the character and movements of the following vessels suspected of intentions to violate the blockade or otherwise give aid and comfort to the enemy: Steamer *Lloyds*, with description, and *Cornubia*; the Clyde steamers *Neptune*, *Iona*, *Pearl*, *Ruby*, *Eagle*, and *Thistle*; the sailing vessels *Morton Castle*, *Honor*, and *Nina*, and two ironclad gunboats being built by the Messrs. Laird at Liverpool. Distribute these extracts by earliest opportunity among the commanders of the blockading vessels, and impress them with the necessity of becoming familiar with the character and movements of these vessels. Respectfully, yours,

S. P. Lee,

Actg. Rear-Admiral, Comdg. North Atlantic Blockading Squadron

Commander G. H. Scott,

Commanding U. S. S. *Maratanza*, etc., off Wilmington, N. C.[19]

Cornubia was back in Queenstown on 3rd November to re-coal; she had come from Greenock and was bound again for Havana.[20] This time she was described as being in ballast, so whatever "machinery" had been on board was presumably removed whilst on the Clyde so that the *Tuscarora* could not interfere with it. Her preparations prior to departure had been watched with great interest by John S. Prettyman, the US Consul in Glasgow for 1861-62.[21] Prettyman lodged a formal request that the *Cornubia* should be stopped from sailing and searched for war contraband by local customs officers. This request was rejected by the Board of Commissioners of Customs in London, with the final comment, "we see no ground to interfere in the matter".

Unfortunately the weather was very bad and *Cornubia* was back in Queenstown on the 11th; the *John and Elizabeth*, bound for Galway, had also put back, having lost her topsails.[22] *Cornubia's* stay was brief however and she sailed again later that day, with the steamer *Antonia*, both bound for Bermuda.[23] On 12th December both the *Cornubia* and the *Tuscarora* were at Fayal (now Faial, in the Azores); the latter, "on a cruise" had been at Liverpool which she left on 23rd November, the third time in eight days. Presumably she had been on the lookout for the *Cornubia*, which had given her the slip in the Irish Sea.

Chapter 4

The Origins of the Blockade

> Nobody here would believe at first that a great war was before us. South Carolina seceded first, and improvised a navy consisting of two small tug boats! North Carolina followed suit, and armed a tug and a small passenger boat! Georgia, Alabama and Louisiana put in commission a handful of frail river boats that you could have knocked to pieces with a pistol shot. That was our navy!
>
> Captain John Newland Maffit[1]

The American Civil War commenced with the first shots fired by the Confederates on the Union troops occupying Fort Sumter, in Charleston harbour, on 12th April 1861. Just five days later, President Abraham Lincoln declared a blockade of the six states which then constituted the Confederate States of America: South Carolina, Alabama, Florida, Georgia, Mississippi and Texas, under the leadership of President Jefferson Davis. Eight days later Lincoln issued a second decree, extending the blockade to cover North Carolina and Virginia; these two decrees became known as the First and Second Anaconda Plans. The entire blockade extended some 4,000 miles, from Cape Henry in the north to the Mexican border in the south.

The 'Anaconda Plans' were originally credited to General Winfield Scott; these envisaged the construction of a tight blockade of all Confederate ports, ultimately leading to closing down all trade. A second component of the plan was the creation of a shallow draft river force capable of dominating the numerous waterways which allowed transports to carry troops and supplies with much less time, effort, and expense than carrying them overland. River gunboats were essentially floating forts that could bring a concentrated amount of force to bear where needed to open choke points or to harry an enemy's flank to facilitate a troop advance or retreat. Scott's ideas were sound but were ridiculed at the time because they could only be established gradually.[2]

Scott was the United State's longest serving officer, with 53 years in post. In the majority of his pictures he has an astonishingly grumpy appearance. How-

General-in-Chief, Winfield Scott, U.S. Army c1863. NHHC image NH 45875

ever, when the American Civil War began Scott was 74 years old and suffering numerous health problems, including gout, rheumatism, and dropsy. He was also extremely overweight and unable to mount a horse or review troops. He died in 1866 and is buried at Arlington Military Cemetary.[3]

The outbreak of hostilities found the Southern States in the worst position, with the North having more manufacturing, arms production and industrial power. The Confederate States Navy comprised just a handful of revenue cutters, seized from Federal port authorities in the seceding Southern states; its personnel mostly comprised 237 Southern officers who had resigned their commissions in the United States Navy. Because of its lack of resources, the South was forced to look to Europe. The already strong links from the cotton trade, made Liverpool one of the obvious choices for organising supplies and aid for the Confederacy. It was also important to keep open the supply line for cotton upon which the South and the Lancashire cotton mills depended. A fleet of Confederate blockade-runners and naval cruisers was built on the Clyde and other British ports to keep this vital supply line open.

The United States Navy had problems of a different kind. For various reasons, at the outbreak of war it had a nominal strength of 90 vessels and about 9,000 officers and sailors.[4] Unfortunately, of the 90 vessels, some 48 were out of commission through lack of funds for repairs and upkeep. Over half of its 42 operational vessels were obsolete sailing ships. Worse, nearly every Navy vessel that could make sail or steam was off protecting American interests in foreign ports. At the start of hostilities, Lincoln had only three proper warships at his

The South's response to the so-called Anaconda Plans to strangle the Confederacy.

disposal. However because of the North's greater potential for productivity nearly every company which could provide materials – hulls, masts, sails, engines, etc. – was busily manufacturing them.

Clearly, both sides needed many more ships than they had, to fight any sort of war. Most of all they needed ships to attack the enemy where he was most vulnerable. One of the Union's strongest points, and, paradoxically, one of its greatest weaknesses, was its huge merchant fleet, second in tonnage only to Britain. There were far too few warships to defend these against any possible attack from commerce raiders.

The two governments quickly put their war plans into practice and declared their strategies in the first naval-policy statements of the war. In an effort to hire a navy whilst trying to build one, on April 17th, just four days after Fort Sumter surrendered, Jefferson Davis published an announcement inviting ship-owners to apply for Confederate letters of marque and reprisal.[5] These licences, much like others issued by belligerent nations in the past, notably Britain, authorised the

THE BLOCKADE ON THE "CONNECTICUT PLAN".

A cartoon ridiculing the Federal government's early efforts to overhaul and augment a somewhat outdated Union fleet to blockade Southern ports and effectively defend against Confederate privateers and blockade-runners. Navy Secretary Gideon Welles of Connecticut is disparaged as two Union vessels - essentially wooden washtubs armed with small cannons - try to block the path of a sleek Confederate steamer, the *Nashville*.

bearers to become privateer. Acting as Navy vessels they could capture Union merchantmen to sell for their own profit as contraband of war. The Confederate Government also vowed to pay the privateers 20 per cent of the value of any Federal warship they destroyed.

As part of Lincoln's second blockade decree he issued a warning against Davis' call for privateers; he stated that any private party caught in possession of a Union merchantman would be tried, convicted and hanged for piracy. This was reversed when the Confederate Government stated it would treat Union privateers in the same manner.

However, both blockading and privateering brought their own problems. Davis believed that the European powers would concede the Confederacy's right to practice privateering. Both England and France had signed the 1856 Declaration (or Treaty) of Paris,[6] which disavowed privateering as a form of warfare but the United States had not; Davis held the view that this fully justified his own decision to use privateering against the Union. Lincoln was against this, believing that the states were not only united but were indivisible and, therefore, that the Confederacy was not a separate sovereign nation. Confederate privateers he therefore considered pirates, on the ground that Davis had no authority to license privateers, as legitimate nations might if they

Gideon Welles, Secretary of the United States Navy.

had not signed the Declaration of Paris.

The blockaders trod a very narrow line. The vessels were weaponless, because any form of armed resistance, even a single pistol shot, would revoke their neutral status.[7] Any British subjects found onboard under these circumstances would be branded as pirates and were liable to be hanged under international law. However running under the Confederate flag meant that a captured crew was regarded as belligerent and treated as prisoners of war, in which case they could be expelled as undesirable non-combatants.

It is generally regarded that the decision to create the blockade, and to encourage Lincoln into accepting it, was taken by the US Secretary of State, William H. Seward. Gideon Welles, the fiercely bearded Secretary of the US Navy, had advised Lincoln against proclaiming a blockade and was furious with Seward for invoking it: the very proclamation would, by implication, grant the Confederacy the status of nationhood.

Welles had tried to persuade Lincoln that he should close the Southern ports by executive order instead. Although Lincoln had agreed with Welles's view, there was a strong argument against

William H. Seward, US Secretary of State.

it. For example, the British Minister in Washington, Lord Richard Lyons, had made it clear that the British government would refuse to respect an executive order closing the Southern ports.[8] Hence there were concerns that port closure might encourage the Royal Navy to become involved. As a belligerent nation, the Confederacy would have the right under international law to buy arms in Europe, to float loans there, to conduct business abroad subject only to the regulations of the countries involved, and to raid enemy commerce not as pirates but as a legitimate national navy.

All of these manoeuvres from both sides came about because both Lincoln and Davis wanted to establish the legality of their actions in the eyes of the world. The approval or disapproval of the European powers could have an enormous effect on such practical matters as trade, credit and material aid, and could even bring about foreign intervention in the American war.

There was however one advantage to declaring a formal blockade: it would confer on the United States the right under international law to stop and search neutral merchant ships on the high seas and to confiscate contraband of war bound for Confederate ports. Lincoln came to the sensible decision to decline to challenge England, and he decided on the blockade.

When the war broke out, the Union Navy's interference with neutral shipping arising from its efforts to enforce its blockade was one of the two major issues which caused friction between Britain and the US. Ostensibly at least, Britain pursued an official policy of strict neutrality, which was largely a naval matter, practised and enforced off the coast of North America and, to a lesser extent, between Portugal and the Azores. Admiral Sir Alexander Milne was appointed Commander-in-Chief of the West Indian Station on 13 January 1860 and it fell to him and his successor, Admiral Sir James Hope, to carry out this policy of neutrality while at the same time protecting British seaborne commerce.

A *Memorandum on Blockades for the Officers of the Navy* issued confidentially to Milne by the Admiralty on 11th May 1861 emphasized the requirement for sufficient force and the need for public notification to neutral ships in order for a blockade to be enforced. Mere declaration of a blockade without adequate naval force was not enough. In order legally to capture violators of a blockade, it had to be conclusively verified:

> That the blockade, by an adequate force on the spot, was actually in existence at the time of capture.
>
> That the captured ship knew of its being in existence; and,
>
> That she knowingly and designedly endeavoured, or attempted by some outward acts to violate it, after she knew of its existence.

On 1st June 1861 Milne was instructed by the Admiralty that the United States and the Confederate States were to be considered in a state of war. Both were to be allowed to visit and search British merchant ships for contraband on the high seas but, because neither side had signed the Declaration of Paris they could not seize British ships or British goods which were not contraband belonging to either side. Contraband of war was to be defined by each of the belligerents and the validity of the blockade was held to be dependent on its efficiency.

Milne referred to blockade running as "this fraudulent trade" in defiance of Britain's neutrality. His policy towards what he called "these doubtful vessels" was to have as little to do with them as possible.[9] He "was extremely annoyed with the authorities at Bermuda and the Bahamas, when they . . . allowed blockade-runners to use these islands as depots and bases". On 20th August 1863, for example, he expressly ordered Captain Glasse at the Bermuda Dockyard not to

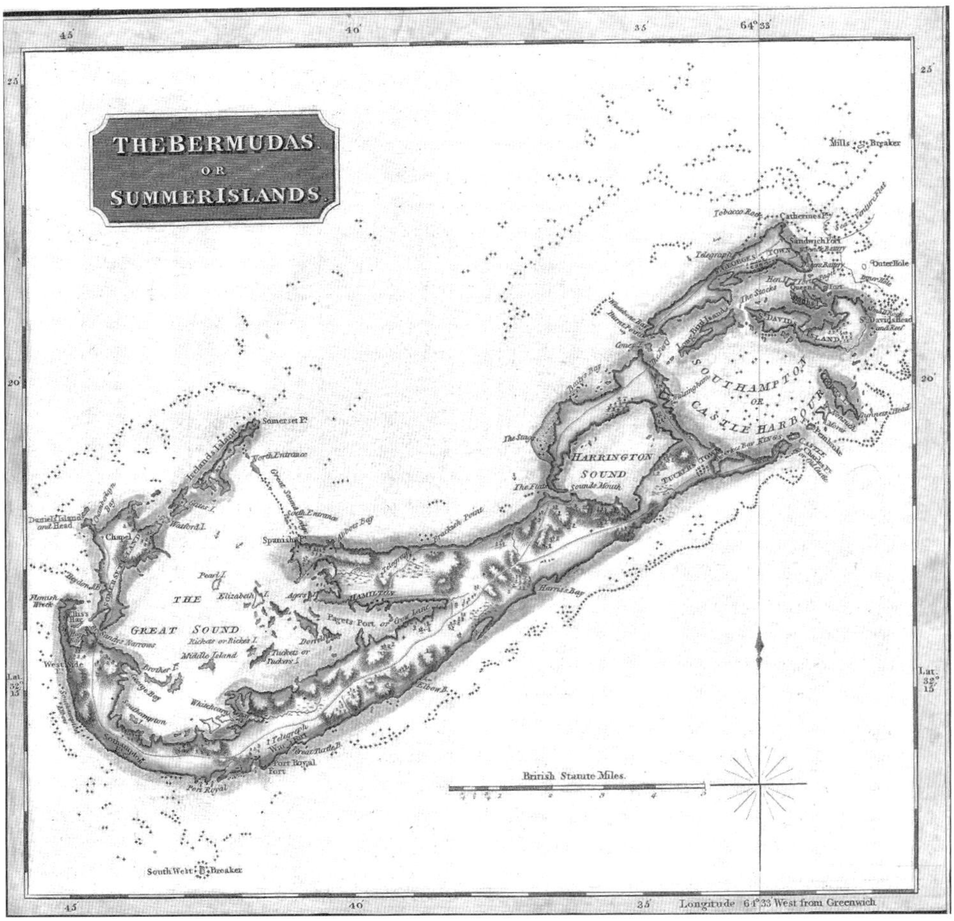

1818 map of Bermuda showing the natural harbours.

give coal or assistance to blockade runners.

There were four centres for the blockade runners: Matamoros in Mexico, serving Victoria and Galveston; Havana in Cuba, serving Galveston, New Orleans and Mobile; Nassau in the Bahamas, serving Savannah and Charleston; and St George's, Bermuda, serving Wilmington and Charleston. It would be the latter route that the *Cornubia* was to ply.

Bermuda lies 568 miles east of Cape Hatteras, the closest point on the coast of the United States. Ironically, at the beginning of the American War of Independence the island supported the rebel colonists, particularly as many islanders had important trade connections with them. Bermuda regularly supplied the rebels with ships, salt and gunpowder; however towards the end of the war economic realities caused the Bermudians to re-assess their situation and they turned to sending privateers against them.[10] Throughout the period of the war Bermuda was built up as a fortress and the harbour at St George's was improved. This was to make the facilities for the Civil War blockade runners ideal for their work and made the island an ideal staging post for materials being shipped to and from the Confederate States and the UK, with the exception of facilities for repairing and maintaining marine steam engines.

In Britain and elsewhere, people refused to see why the Confederates should be branded as "rebels" or "pirates". The "stone" blockade by the Federals (sinking stone-filled ships in or near harbours to affect Confederate shipping), the harsh treatment of captured crews, and, most of all, the high-handedness displayed in the *Trent* Affair all served to intensify the feeling against the North.

The *Trent* Affair was an international diplomatic incident that took place on 8th November 1861, when the USS *San Jacinto*, commanded by Captain Charles Wilkes, intercepted the British mail packet RMS *Trent*.[11] Wilkes removed, as contraband of war, two Confederate diplomats, James Mason and John Slidell. The envoys were bound for Great Britain and France to press the Confederacy's case for diplomatic recognition and financial support for the Confederacy in the name of King Cotton. To make matters worse, the incident took place in international waters, in direct contravention of the Declaration of Paris. The two were eventually released although no official apology was ever given; Wilkes was eventually court-martialled and dismissed from the US Navy even though there was much support for him both inside and outside of the service; indeed he was feted for some time by both public and press.

The *Trent* Affair marked a peak in the danger level for the United States as both Britain and France were both outraged by the behaviour of the US Navy. In fact this was just the situation that the Confederate government must have prayed for, with two major powers on the verge of declaring war on the United States;

James Mason and John Slidell being removed from the RMS *Trent*, left, and taken to the USS *San Jacinto*. *Illustrated London Daily News.*

however it was not to be.

As soon as Lincoln proclaimed the blockade, the Confederates ridiculed it, not least because it covered a coastline of some 4,000 miles, including inlets, rivers and numerous small islands. It was also assumed that Britain owed nothing to the North, which was its industrial and mercantile rival. On the other hand the South was an important customer for British manufactures and shipping services. Most significant, the South produced half of the world's output of cotton, so important to the northern part of England, and to Lancashire in particular.

Since Britain had abolished slavery, there was some British support for the Union's antislavery stand. However, the most influential parts of British society were sympathetic to the Confederate cause.

Somewhat ironically the man put in charge of stopping the blockade, or at least part of it, was Samuel Phillips Lee who, in September 1862, was put in command of the North Atlantic Blockading Squadron with the rank of Acting Rear Admiral. His flagship at this point was the USS *Philadelphia*.[12] He led this force for over two years, during which it was responsible for the blockade of the North Carolina coast and operations on North Carolina and Virginia inland waters, all areas of very active combat between Union and Confederate forces. In

Acting Rear-Admiral Samuel Phillips Lee of the North Atlantic Blockading Squadron.

October 1864 he was transferred to the command of the Mississippi River Squadron, which he led to the end of the Civil War.

Born in Fairfax County, Virginia, he was third cousin to Robert E. Lee who, in June 1862, was appointed General commanding the Army of Northern Virginia. He was appointed a midshipman in the U.S. Navy in November 1825 and saw extensive service at sea, including combat action during the Mexican–American War and exploration, surveying and oceanographic duty. At the outbreak of the American Civil War he held the rank of commander and was captain of the sloop of war USS *Vandalia* in the East Indies. He sailed her home on his own initiative to join the blockade of the Southern coast. Commander Lee commanded the new steam sloop USS *Oneida* during the New Orleans campaign and subsequent operations on the Mississippi River in the first half of 1862.

Lee's relationship with his cousin could be problematic; once, when questioned about his loyalty, Lee famously replied "When I find the word Virginia in my commission I will join the Confederacy".[13] This quote is often referenced by historians in contrast to the actions of his cousin Robert to show how the war divided families. Reverting to his permanent rank of Captain after the Civil War, Lee served extensively in the Washington. He was promoted to Rear Admiral in 1870 and retired from active service in February 1873.

Chapter 5

British Shipbuilders and the Rebels

Though with the North we sympathise
It must not be forgotten
That with the South we've stronger ties
Which are composed of cotton[1]

It was presumably through the Lancashire cotton connection that James Dunwoody Bulloch, a Confederate naval officer, arrived in Liverpool on 4th June 1861.[2] Bulloch had orders to buy or have constructed six steam vessels suitable for use as commerce destroyers against the Union, to be delivered, unarmed, under the British flag at any Southern port. In addition, he was to purchase and run the blockade with armaments for the cruisers. He was assisted by Fraser, Trenholm & Company (including Trenholm Brothers and Fraser & Co. with branches in New York and Charleston), foreign bankers to the Confederacy.

James Dunwoody Bulloch was a Confederate Naval Officer and Agent in England, while his half-brother Irvine Stephens Bulloch was the youngest officer on the CSS *Alabama* (*see below*).

Bulloch's first contract was with Fawcett, Preston Engineering, founded in 1758, by George Perry, as the Liverpool branch of the Coalbrookdale Foundry at Ironbridge.[3] It became an independent Liverpool company and built up an international reputation, particularly for sugar machinery. In the early days its marine engines were also world famous, and these included those of the first Mersey steam ferry *Etna*, in 1817 and the *President*, the largest ship in the world, in 1840. It was also a noted supplier of guns. The near-neighbour of Fawcett, Preston Engineering was W. C. Miller & Son. Fawcett, Preston Engineering was asked to subcontract for the hull and fittings of the new ship, for which Miller & Son was building the engines. This vessel would become the steam sloop CSS *Florida*, which was completed later that year.

The commerce raider CSS *Florida* running past the USS *Oneida* into Mobile Bay. Painted by R. N. Floyd, NHHC image NH 1319.

The work of the blockade runner did not change very much during the war, but it did get much harder. While the US Navy had a number of commerce raiders they were not employed in stopping the runners. That job was given to the blockading fleets which were arranged in defensive units around the various ports. The runners from Bermuda had a (usually) quiet journey of nearly three days to get to the coast of North Carolina. Once there it was often necessary to sail at full speed, often faster than was actually safe, to run into Wilmington. The advantage here was with the runners; there is a gentle and regular slope in the level of the sand out to sea and the hard-pressed runners could often run along the outer edge of the breakers without a big risk of grounding; the blockaders, usually having deeper drafts, had to keep further out from the shore. The return journey was the opposite. Darkness and fog were the runners' friends.

In many ways the runners suffered from the law of diminishing returns. Each new runner arrived with a new, inexperienced captain, and it was often down to luck if the two survived their first run. On the other hand the blockaders gained in experience day-by-day; in addition training was given to officers and men, often on the spot, while there was no equivalent for the runners. Runner captains were lucky if they could experience one or two trips under another captain before they started their own runs.

The desperation of organisations and individuals to run the blockade is shown by the fact that steam ships were being sold for up to £10,000 over their actual value. An enormous naval industry therefore evolved which brought great profits for shipbuilders, shippers and suppliers alike. It had been estimated by the US Consul at Nassau, Samuel Whiting, that each blockade runner would make at least two voyages, there and back.[4] He estimated the profit of these voyages at:

One voyage outward cargo, say	$100,000
One voyage expenses etc	$15,000
Total	$115,000
She returns with 1,300 bales of cotton, weighing an average of 400lbs per bale, equal to 45 cents per lb, or	$234,000
Leaves profit	$115,000
From which deduct cost	$119,000

At this time there were 28 vessels at Nassau; these would therefore make a combined profit of $6,664,000 for two months work.

The second contract was signed in July 1861 with William Laird & Son, experts in building steamships with iron plate hulls.[5] The first of these vessels was number 290, later named the *Enrica*. On 29 July 1862 the *Enrica* sailed to Anglesey for trials with various dignitaries on board, and after putting them off on a tug, quietly sailed off for the Azores to take on armaments and ammunition from the *Agrippina*, to begin life as the CSS *Alabama*.

Raphael Semmes. NHHC image NH 45785.

The *Alabama* had a mostly British, mainly Liverpudlian, crew; after leaving Liverpool in great secrecy, most of her Liverpudlian crew signed on for the Confederate Navy. Captain Raphael Semmes took command of the *Alabama* on the 13th August, and from that time until June 1864, she captured and burned fifty-five Union merchantmen, worth $4,500,000, and bonded ten others to the value of $562,000. Semmes was yet another former US Navy officer; he had resigned in 1861, his letter, accepted on the day it was written, stating:

Sir: I respectfully tender through you to the President of the United States, this, the resignation of the commission which I have the honor to hold as a Commander in the Navy of the United States. In severing my connection with the Government of the United States, and with the Department over which you preside, I pray to you to accept my thanks for kindness which has characterized your official deportment towards me.[6]

Even busier was Clydeside, the principal area for Civil War ship-building, where by 1864 some twenty-seven shipyards were busy at work building ships such as the *Giraffe*, *Lilian*, *Havelock* and the *Advance*.[7] The importance of this industry to the local economy is testified by the fact that 25,000 men were employed.[8]

Unfortunately for the Scottish ships and crews they were inadvertently insulted by the newspapers which supported the North, being invariably described as English or British, invariably followed, at least in the case of *Harper's Weekly Magazine*, by the word 'pirates'.

It was not pure sympathy with the South that caused British sailors, and those from other countries, to volunteer to run the blockade; the financial rewards could be very remunerative. Details of employment conditions for Confederate States personnel were given in a letter from Josiah M. Seixas, War Department Agent, dated 27th June 1863.[9]

Wilmington, N. C, June 27, 1863.

After the 1st of July, proximo, the wages of the officers and crews of the steamers of the War Department will be as follows: Officers will be required to sign agreements for six months and their pay will be continued for full term of engagement, or imprisonment, if captured. Being in the Confederate service they are entitled to be exchanged as prisoners of war.

Assignments of pay to their families or representatives can be made through the agent here.

The voyage begins and ends here or in Charleston, but one half of the wages, as far as they have accrued in reference to date, will be paid, if desired, at Bermuda, before completion of the voyage.

Payment of the wages will be made here, by an order given on the Confederate States agent at Bermuda, but the Government reserves the right to pay the bounty either at this agency, or by order on the Confederate States agent at Bermuda, or in currency.

Bounty will be earned on the completion of the voyage:

On 19 August 1864 the CSS *Alabama* met the USS *Kearsarge* off Cherbourg, France, and after a spectacular, but rather short – not more than an hour long – battle watched by thousands of people on the French coast, the *Alabama* was sunk.[10] Fortunately the steam yacht *Deerhound* (another Laird-built ship), owned by Englishman John Lancaster, saved a number of crew including Captain Semmes and a number of his officers, who were given a hero's welcome when they arrived back at Southampton.

The commerce raider CSS *Alabama*.

In 1873 the United States Government's demand that the British Government should pay compensation for the damage caused by the Confederate ships was settled.[11] This became known as the *Alabama* Claims, because she had caused the most damage. Together with the CSS *Florida* and the CSS *Shenandoah*, they accounted for half of the total number of Union vessels captured; this resulted in the British Government paying about £3,000,000 ($15,500,000) compensation for allowing the Confederate Government to purchase the ships in England and allowing them to use British ports. The claim had actually mentioned eleven cruisers by name but the tribunal in Geneva, where it was held, decided that Great Britain was only responsible for losses to the *Alabama*, *Florida* and *Shenandoah*.[12]

The loss however could have been much, much more. It was originally estimated at about *£8 billion* and the categorical refusal of the British government to even consider this sum, along with the United States' opinion that Britain should pay it, brought both countries to the brink of war. With the potential for conflict looming ever nearer, many European countries sold US bonds, stocks and shares, with the effect that the value of the dollar dropped dramatically. This in turn reduced the potential value of any money received from Britain; eventually cooler heads were involved and the situation resolved itself.

Ironically it was also noted during this case that a number of American ships had been transferred to the British Red Ensign to avoid capture whilst running the blockade.[13] In 1861 it was 126; 1862, 135; 1863, 348 and in 1864 106.

Bulloch ordered several more ships from the Lairds including the so-called "Laird's Rams".[14] These took their name from an iron piercer which protruded six to seven feet from the prow and was used for striking opposing vessels below the waterline. In October 1863 the Royal Marines raided these ships during construction forcing off the workmen and their equipment. In addition a gunship, HMS *Heron*, was deployed to the area to prevent the half constructed ships from leaving the port. Following this turn of events Bulloch commissioned a shipbuilder in France to construct the *Stonewall*, another armoured ram.

John Laird then sued the British government for impeding his construction. At the time Laird was an MP and must certainly have been aware of the intricacies of international relations between the UK and both belligerent sides during the Civil War. It is likely that he had contacts in the South through his connections with the sugar trade. In 1903 William Laird & Son merged with Johnson Cammell & Company to form Cammell, Laird.

Major Josiah C. Gorgas, head of the Confederate Ordnance Bureau.

Major (later General) Josiah C. Gorgas was the man charged with breaking the blockade.[15] Gorgas was a West Point graduate who, prior to the war, had worked in the United States Ordnance Bureau and had served in most of the arsenals in the United States. While working in the south, like many other military officers, he became sympathetic to the secessionist movement and eventually sided with the Confederacy, becoming the head of the Confederate Ordnance Bureau. He liaised with Charles Prioleau, who ran Fraser, Trenholm & Co's Liverpool office, arranging for the shipping of arms and other supplies to the Confederacy. During the summer of 1861 Gorgas stockpiled supplies and prepared his first load of cargo while the Trenholm company procured a suitable ship for the voyage. A 1,200 ton iron-hulled steamer, the *Bermuda*, was chosen to make the voyage.

Beneath Gorgas, to coordinate the business and the buying of weapons and supplies in England, were Captain Caleb Huse and Major Edward C. Anderson.[16] Huse served under Gorgas as an arms procurement agent and purchasing specialist. He became well known for his successful acquisition of weapons contracts with various European nations, including the UK and Austria, among others. Anderson was also sent to aid Huse and check on his activity.

Caleb Huse long after the end of the war.

Huse's principal supplier of arms in the UK was the London Armoury Company,[17] formed in 1856. Ironically, its first Civil War sales were for 16 Kerr revolvers to the US Army; two years later Messrs. Huse and Bulloch contracted for all the rifles and revolvers that the Armoury could produce. The British company Willoughbe, Willoughbe & Ponsonby played a prominent role in the blockade running of these shipments to the south. The Confederacy became the London Armoury Company's principal client and it manufactured and by February 1863 had shipped more than 70,000 rifles and about 7,000 revolvers (out of a total production run of about 10,000) to the South. Just how many of these weapons actually reached the South is not known; however the Confederates regarded the Armoury's guns as the best weapons made in Britain.

Almost completely dependent on sales to the Confederacy, the London Armoury Company only survived for a year after the end of the war, dissolving in the spring of 1866. However, most of the gunsmiths and staff went on to form the London Small Arms Company Limited the same year.

Huse was also owner of several seagoing steamers used in blockade running and made several trips to Europe and back aboard these vessels. While in Europe he represented the Confederate War Department and Ordnance Bureau throughout the entire war and also arranged for credit and the shipping of supplies when funds were short. Huse and Bulloch also acted as liaison with Charles Prioleau in Liverpool. Through him they would procure the ships and arrange for the shipment of these goods to the Confederacy. Bulloch also worked in close correspondence with Confederate Secretary of the Navy Stephen Mallory in the procurement of several British-made blockade running vessels.

Captain John Newland Maffit junior.

Another of the principals was Captain John Maffitt junior who, on 11th April 1862, was appointed acting agent in Nassau for the Confederacy by George W. Randolph, the new Confederate Secretary of War.[18] Maffitt was an officer of the Confederate States Navy, previously with the US Navy, and a notorious privateer with a long success record; he had been particularly successful in catching slave ships. Nassau was one of several offshore stopover points for shipments coming into or leaving the Confederate States. Maffitt's duties were broad: "You are authorized to take entire control of all vessels loaded with arms and munitions for the Confederate States".[19] His duties included selecting ports of entry and discharging and replacing officers and crews as needed. His only condition was that he would first confer with Louis Heylinger, Confederate agent in Nassau. Maffitt, a Scot born at sea during a gale, would later be given command of the CSS *Albemarle*.

The Confederate Government was keen for more ships. On 14th November Captain John Wilkinson of the Confederate States Navy wrote to Alexander Collie & Brother, dealers in various commodities including cotton.[20] In the event of the steamer *Giraffe* (later the *Robert E. Lee*) being sent back to England with a cargo he would be glad to take charge of her and dispose of the cargo on account of the Confederate Government. If a further supply of boats or other articles be required from England, he would place his services, for the purchase and shipping of said goods, at the disposal of the Government.

The US Consul in Liverpool reported, between 8th and 21st November, on the huge number of ships sailing for Havana and Nassau via Madeira.[21] These included:

> The *Julia Usher* has not yet sailed. She took on yesterday 3 more large cases containing guns, 12 cases shells, and 4 other cases, contents unknown. She will sail from this port direct for Havana.
>
> The bark *Intrinsic* sailed yesterday, having cleared on the 14th instant.
>
> The *Monmouth* cleared for Nassau on the 18th instant.
>
> The steamer *Thistle* cleared for Havana and Nassau, via Madeira, on the 18th instant and sailed on the 19th instant. On the day she cleared she took on board a large number of cases containing guns.
>
> The bark *Severn* cleared for Nassau yesterday and will sail to-day. Her cargo is a valuable one, consisting of arms, shot, shell, and military goods.
>
> The steamer *Julia Usher* is ready for sea, and will sail most likely tomorrow.
>
> The steamer *Gladiator* entered to load on the 19th instant.
>
> The brig *Peep of Day* is bound for Charleston, but will most likely clear for Nassau. Description: *Peep of Day*, brig, late *Ella* and previously *Ella Fleming*, 196 tons; hull painted green; square stern; small top gallant forecastle deck; masts, mastheads, yards, and bowsprit painted black. The bark entered to load for Nassau on the 19th instant; 354 tons; hull painted black; square stern; small bust painted white for figurehead; masts, mastheads, and jib boom bright.
>
> The steamer *Giraffe*, which sailed from Glasgow, has important dispatches and documents.
>
> Within the past few weeks the following fast steamers have been purchased in England to run the blockade: *Iona*, *Pearl*, *Thistle*, *Antonia*, *Giraffe*, *Eagle*, *Havelock*, *Princess Royal*, *Northumbria*, *Nicolai I*, *Douglass*, *Perley*, *Britannia*, *Wave Queen*, and *Justitia*. Of these the *Iona* has been seen off Greenock.
>
> The steamer *Cornubia* recently sailed from Glasgow.
>
> The *Justitia* sailed last week. The papers of this week report that a very

fast and valuable steamer called the *Daylight* has been purchased this week either by the rebels or their sympathizers here for the Confederates.

The steamer *Giraffe* has just left the Clyde to cross the Atlantic, with a view to run the blockade. She is schooner rig, with paddle wheels of medium size. She is unquestionably loaded with munitions of war.

On 21st November 1862 the USS *Tuscarora* was off the Azores overhauling British vessels suspected of conveying stores to the south. Fayal (now Faial) was the main port for coaling prior to crossing the Atlantic. Commander Craven, was looking for the *Pearl*, en route from Liverpool; shortly after leaving Funchal the *Tuscarora* ran down on the *Cornubia*, which was boarded off the island of Faial.[22] Her hatches were all opened and "the coal turned all on one side of the ship," which was minutely searched. The *Cornubia* then travelled on, bound for Trinidad "but it is alleged she is bound for the American coast". The report below of her being "low in the water" suggests she was heavily in ballast; possibly she was carrying reserves of coal in her holds. Craven later stopped and boarded the steamer *Thistle*; doubtless Commander Craven must have been convinced that this fast paddle steamer, also heading west, was bound for the blockade. Following this, HMS *Leopard* tried to stop the *Pearl* but the latter chose not to oblige. It appears that the *Tuscarora* and *Cornubia* were both at Fayal at the same time; presumably the *Tuscarora* was unable to inspect the ostensibly neutral vessels in a neutral port.[23] Several newspapers report that the *Tuscarora* was at Bermuda while waiting for the *Pearl* but this is incorrect.

STOPPAGE AND SEARCH OF A BRITISH MERCHANT SHIP BY AN AMERICAN MAN-OF-WAR.

THE THISTLE & THE TUSCARORA.

(From the Scotsman.)

ST. THOMAS, WEST INDIES, DEC., 1862.

As an account of the stoppage and search of a British merchant ship in the Atlantic by an American man-of-war may not be without interest to your readers, I subjoin the particulars of such an event which happened to the vessel in which I was a passenger, on Saturday, the 29th November last.

The Thistle is a screw-steamer of 206 tons register.

News of the *Tuscarora's* activities from the *Liverpool Mercury*, 3rd January 1863.

Report of Commander Craven, U. S. Navy, commanding U. S. S. *Tuscarora*, of the boarding of two suspicious vessels, the *Cornubia* and *Thistle*

U. S. S. TUSCARORA,

Madeira, December 1, 1862.

Sir : I have the honor to advise you of two suspicious steamers recently boarded by this vessel.

The *Cornubia*, of London, boarded on the night of the [21st] November off

Fayal, was in ballast; a side-wheel steamer of about 600 tons, schooner rig, with short bowsprit; two smoke pipes, one standing forward of the other; of light draft, and very low in the water.

The *Thistle*, of Glasgow, was boarded off Funchal, November 29; is from Liverpool with an assorted cargo for Nassau; no goods contraband of war on board; is an iron-built screw steamer of 400 tons; schooner rigged, with light foretopsail; no bowsprit; stem raking and without billet head or scroll; has a wale, or fender, of oak, along the water line; her stern elliptical; smoke pipe remarkably high; draft, 9 feet; vessel said to be good for 15 knots.

From the general character of the above vessels I have no doubt they may attempt running the blockade.

I have the honor to be, sir, your obedient servant,

T. Augs. Craven,

Commander[24]

A total of 485 blockade runners was eventually supplied, mostly from Britain, during the war; these shipped 8,250 cargoes worth $2,000,000 and the Confederate States paid for these with 1,250,000 bales of cotton (Wise gives the much lower figure of 400,000).[25] This was an act regarded by the Federal Government as "virtually tantamount to a participation in the war by the people of Great Britain", though this would be more correct had it stated the "businesses of Great Britain" as the ordinary man or woman in the street probably had little to say on the matter.[26]

Chapter 6

Enigma: Captain John Burroughs

The cunning of a fox, the patience of a Job, and the bravery of a Spartan warrior

Attributed to a veteran blockade runner

The surprise of being overhauled and boarded aside, the *Cornubia* reached Port St George's, Bermuda, on 1st December, her journey from Madeira having taken ten days.

On 9th December, Captain Edward C. Stiles wrote to Captain John Burroughs on the *Cornubia*. The previous day Burroughs had written to Stiles to tell him that the *Cornubia* was "coaled, stored, and ready to take in the cargo".[1] A crew had been procured – possibly the one that came from Britain was to return – and an agreement had been made with them "that in case of capture or loss of steamer they are to be sent to England at the expense of the Confederate Government, and their wages paid up to the time of arrival in Great Britain. Once Stiles had received an inventory "of stores, furnishings, fixtures, &c" he was ready to receive the ship "in the name of the Confederate States Government".

Little is known about John M. Burroughs, the first master of the blockade runner. A John Burroughs is mentioned in the *Register of Officers of the Confederate States Navy, 1861-1865*, which states that in February 1862 he was a carpenter and also in the Provisional Navy in June 1864. Apart from his command on the *Cornubia* between 1862 and 1863 he was stated to be on special duties in 1864. His age and origins are not given and, assuming that the Register has not confused at least two people in the description, there must be some strange underlying story why he was given command of several runners whilst holding a comparatively lowly position. This person is therefore unlikely to be the person of interest.

In addition, two other John Burroughs were noted in the official records. One was the superintendent of the government shipyards at Norfolk, and the other a Confederate Government official working in London. John Burroughs appears to have caused problems for some time. Writing in 1910, Walter Brownell Hayward commented

> Conspicuous among the merchant captains were the mysterious John Burroughs - a naval officer, some called him, master of the *Cornubia, North Heath*, *Gertrude* and *Pevensey*...[2]

John Burroughs had arrived in St George's in command of the *Justitia* the day before the *Cornubia* arrived.[3] The *Justitia* had come from London and was carrying "Government goods and general merchandise" for John T. Bourne. *Cornubia* had been commanded on her trip to Bermuda by Captain Holmes; Holmes in turn took the *Justitia* back to England on 8th January 1863.[4] Passages were £20-25 and she carried 87 tons of stores for the government as well as 26 packets of merchandise. Holmes was back at St George's on 25th July with the *Miriam*, again from London, which voyage he repeated several times.[5] Each trip to St George's was to bring in goods for J. T. Bourne. *Cornubia* was privately operated and still owned by Thomas Begbie. Burroughs, in these early days was described as 'British,' although many other blockade runner crews were also described as British even though they may not have been. British citizenship was sufficient to ensure that a crew was not imprisoned by the US Government.

It was a not an uncommon practice in the Royal Navy to allow its officers to serve in other navies to gain experience. Also, Royal Navy officers, when not in regular service, were on half-pay, so service in another navy would help with their income. In December 1863 C. F. Adams wrote to Lord Russell on behalf of the US government stating

> Ralph Carter is engaged in violating the blockade of the insurgent ports of the United States, under the assumed name of Peterson. I am further instructed to express the belief that other British naval officers are thus engaged.[6]

James Sprunt later stated that the captain of the *Venus* blockade runner was Captain Murray-Aynsley, better known as Captain Murray, a Royal Navy officer on a leave of absence.[7]

The fact that the Confederate States Navy officer Richard Gayle eventually took command of the *Cornubia* implies that Burroughs was not a CSN officer (Gayle's warrant was issued by the Confederate Government). If this is the case he is almost certainly not the person, or one of the people, mentioned in the Register of Officers and is more likely to have been a Royal Navy officer, though there is no one of this name listed at the British National Archives.[8] It is also possible that he was working under a *nomme de guerre*.

Certainly Burroughs was a successful runner captain with at least twenty-six completed runs to his credit. While in charge of *Cornubia* she completed ten successful runs. He was also master of the *Stag* (two successful runs), the *North Heath* (at least eight successful runs) and the *Pevensey* (possibly four successful runs).[9] The *Pevensey* seems to have been a temporary command; shortly after the *North Heath* left St George's on 29th April 1864 she was found to be leaking badly and returned to harbour, to be grounded in Mullet Bay.[10] Burroughs took the *Pevensey* out of St George's, presumably as a replacement, on 7th May.[11] The *North Heath* was sailed to Bermuda by Burroughs from Cardiff, while some of the journeys he made were to Halifax, Nova Scotia. These were likely to have been to bring coal supplies to the island. The ship was chased and run aground by Federal ships on 9th June, following which her boilers were deliberately exploded, destroying her mid-section. After unsuccessful attempts were made to pull her off, a boat was sent from the USS *Dacotah* to plunder her. Unfortunately the boat was loaded so deeply that it was swamped by the surf; everything in it was lost and the officer in charge, Acting Master's Mate Farrar, was drowned.

James Sprunt was a well-known figure of Wilmington life from the time of the Civil War to the Roaring Twenties.[12] After the war, using five bales of cotton that he had managed to buy with his blockade running profits, Sprunt and his father launched Alexander Sprunt & Sons; its headquarters and warehouses were part of the present Cotton Exchange in downtown Wilmington. The Sprunts traded cotton and naval stores (tar, pitch and turpentine) to more than 50 agencies across Europe and also dealt in sugar, nitrates and cement. At one point, they were the largest cotton brokerage firm in the world. As a teenager, Sprunt served on the *North Heath* with Burroughs, as well as on the *Lilian* and *Susan Beirne*. He was so impressed with Burroughs that he later wrote:

James Sprunt, probably circa 1920.

> I believe that under God, Captain Burroughs, by his fine qualities as a cool and capable seaman, saved this ship from foundering at sea when we ran into a hurricane shortly after our departure from St. George, Bermuda, bound for Wilmington. For two days and nights we were in imminent danger of our lives — tossed upon a raging sea, every man of our crew

> of 48 except those at the wheel was lashed to the vessel, while we bailed with buckets and [with] the use of hand pumps the flooded fireroom of our sinking vessel. For an entire night she wallowed like a log in a trough of mountainous waves, which broke over us in ever-increasing fury. I can never forget this frightful scene. It seems photographed upon my memory in all its fearsome details.
>
> The water had risen in our hold until every one of our fourteen furnaces was extinguished. There was no steam to run our donkey boilers and steam-power pumps. Lashed to one another, in the blackness of darkness, relieved only by the intermittent flashes of lightning which illuminated the giant waves towering around us and threatening to overwhelm and sink the laboring, quivering fabric, we held on in despair until morning, when we began to gain on the leaks until our steam pumps could be used in relieving the boiler room, and our brave captain got the ship under control. Then we succeeded in putting her about and headed back to Bermuda.[13]

The *North Heath* was another ship operated by Thomas Begbie and it is possible that Burroughs was employed directly by him or one of his various associates and is more evidence that Burroughs was indeed British. Begbie was also the manager of the London-based Albion Trading Company,[14] which, along with various other companies, had been set up purely as an outlet for Confederate cotton. The company owned the blockade runners *Ivanhoe*, *Lady Sterling*, *Marmion* and *Talisman*, the latter two operated by Begbie himself. The *Helen*, also operated by Begbie, was owned by the Universal Trading Company.[15] Begbie is considered to have operated more blockade runners during the war than any other owner.

An interesting comment appeared in the *Houston Tri-Weekly Telegraph* in September 1863. This states:–

> Blockade running goes on swimmingly. Mr. T. S. Begbie, of this city, boasts that his steamers are all successful, and the port they run into is Wilmington. One of his commissioners is Capt. Burroughs, a grandson of the notorious Stephen Burroughs (a well-known counterfeiter and jail breaker) and he has run the blockade of Wilmington twelve times – six times in and six times out.....He has been chased repeatedly and fired at; but none of your blockaders can catch him. Will some of your Rip Van Winkles put more steam on and capture this fellow?[16]

This familial connection appears to be completely false – it has not been possible to relate John with Stephen – and the reason for publishing this can

The *Pevensey* being run ashore on 9th June 1864, at Pine Knoll Shores, by the USS *New Berne*. In the background the *Lilian* is being captured. To prevent capture of the supplies on board, the *Pevensey's* crew exploded the ship's boilers before escaping to shore, where they were captured and taken to Fort Macon.

only be conjectured. Possibly the paper was trying to add some colour to John Burroughs (if that were actually needed) but it seems slightly insulting to associate him with a criminal, even one so good at his trade as Stephen Burroughs.

There is a certain amount of confusion as to who brought the *Cornubia* to St George's; this has previously been assumed to be Burroughs, but this is incorrect (see next chapter). *Cornubia's* master on arrival at Queenstown on August 13th was Captain Holmes.[17] Later reports from the *Cork Examiner* and the *Daily Post* also state that the *Cornubia* was under the command of Captain Holmes after her departure from Queenstown and Fayal.[18] In addition the *Liverpool Daily Post* and *Bermuda Royal Gazette* both state that Holmes was in command on arrival at St George's.[19] However it has also been reported that *Cornubia* went to Queenstown under the command of her South Western Steam Packet Company's master Captain Davidson,[20] and then on across the Atlantic, minus his mysterious "machinery". However, whether Davidson was Holmes is a question not yet possible to answer.

On 20th February 1863 the "armed privateer" *Georgiana* arrived at Nassau, under a Captain Davidson.[21] Davidson, with his Mate Wilson, later arrived in New York on another vessel, apparently en route for Liverpool, where a "more formidable cruiser than any yet in service of the rebels awaiting them"; this would be the CSS *South Carolina*. Meanwhile back in Nassau the *Georgiana* suffered a name change when the last two letters of her name were painted out. Needless to say, this caused a certain amount of diplomatic correspondence. It is possible that the two Davidsons are the same person, though this is conjecture; however if they are the same it shows the involvement of even more British companies in attempting to break the blockade. A Hunter Davidson was promoted to Commander on 10th June 1864 for gallant and meritorious conduct in command of the torpedo boat *Squib* in passing through the enemy's fleet off Newport News on the night of 9th April 1864, and attacking the steam frigate *Minnesota*.[22] His connection with Captain Davidson also cannot be proven, however he would have been a captain before his promotion.

Chapter 7

Runner! The *Cornubia* and the Blockade

> Now the real excitement began, and nothing I have ever experienced can compare with it. Hunting, pig sticking, big-game shooting, polo - I have done a little of each - all have their thrilling moments, but none can approach 'running the blockade'; and perhaps my readers can sympathise with my enthusiasm when they consider the dangers we encountered, after three days of constant anxiety and little sleep, in threading our way through a swarm of blockaders and the accuracy required to hit in the nick of time the mouth of a river only half a mile wide, without lights and with a coastline so low and featureless, that as a rule the first indication we had of its nearness was the dim white line of the surf.
>
> Thomas E. Taylor, blockade runner (*Banshee*)[1]

On 10th December Captain Edward C. Stiles formally wrote to Josiah Gorgas that he had:

> Received from Thomas Sterling Begbie, Esq., of London, by the hands of Captain John Burroughs, the British Steamship *Cornubia*, complete in masts, spars, rigging, machinery, boilers, boats and all stores, appertaining to the said *Cornubia*, as per agreement in London.[2]

Charles Maxwell Allen, the beleagered US Consul in St George's.

During a court case regarding the ownership of the *Mary* (ex-*Alexandra*) in June 1869 Edward Copeland Stiles stated that he had been a midshipman in the US Navy and had been in Vienna when the war broke out (it has been stated that he was actually the US Consul).[3] On returning to America he entered the Confederate Navy in May 1863 and was appointed Lieutenant for the War on 1st

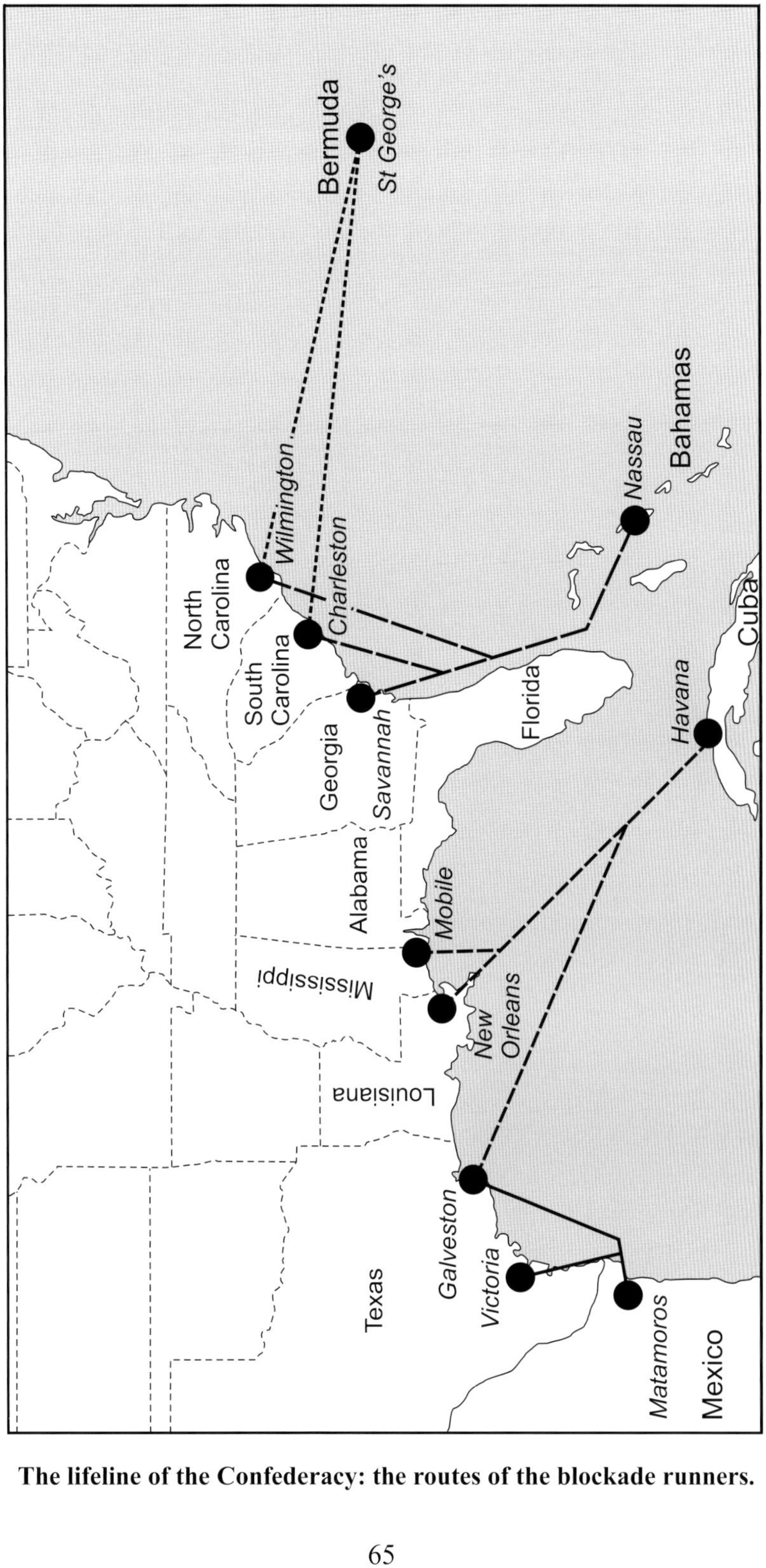

The lifeline of the Confederacy: the routes of the blockade runners.

January 1864.[4] He had been ordered to Bermuda and then to London, which he reached in October. While Stiles titled himself Captain, this seems to have been as a potential commander of a naval vessel. A letter to him from Josiah Gorgas on 24th December stated:

> Captain – Having been appointed by the Secretary of War to carry out certain instructions from this bureau, dated Dec. 24, 1862, you are hereby assigned the pay and allowance of a captain of artillery on ordnance duty, while on duty with this bureau, in executing the functions assigned to you in the said letter.[5]

A postscript also stated that he would be paid at the same rate from 1st November, "or from date of taking charge of steamer *Justitia*". With Burroughs in command of the *Cornubia* she was allowed to keep her British registry. The following year James Bulloch explained to Secretary Mallory:

> I would suggest that as fast as the ships are paid for, Navy officers be put in command as a general rule," adding that such vessels "ought to be kept registered in the names of private individuals, otherwise serious embarrassment may arise, as Lord Russell has stated in the House of Lords that if it could be shown that the steamers trading between the Confederate States and the British Islands were owned by the Confederate States Government, they would be considered as transports and would be forbidden to enter English ports, except under the restrictions imposed upon all men-of-war of the belligerent powers[6]

The following day a number of blockade runners was reported at St George's:

> steamer *Antonia*, bark *Hero*, steamer *Bonita*, steamer *Pearl*, steamers *Adelaide* and *Victoria*, steamer *Melita*, steamer *Justitia*, steamer *Leonidas*, two ironclad steamers ready to sail from Newcastle-upon-Tyne; ship *Louisiana*, steamer *Eagle*, French schooner *Georgetta Amelie*, two sailing vessels *Severn* and *Queen of the Usk*, steamer *Thistle*, sailing vessels *Digby*, *Intrinsic*, *Ellen*, *Jenkinson*, *Pepita*, and the steamer *Nicholas III*.[7]

The *Cornubia* was regarded by US Consul Charles Maxwell Allen as well adapted to run the blockade and "undoubtedly faster than any vessel previously here".[8] He also noted that her colour had been changed "from black to a light lead color" since arrival.[9] The "light lead" colour was also known as 'Hatteras Grey' and would later be called 'battleship grey,' a dull light lead grey colour that

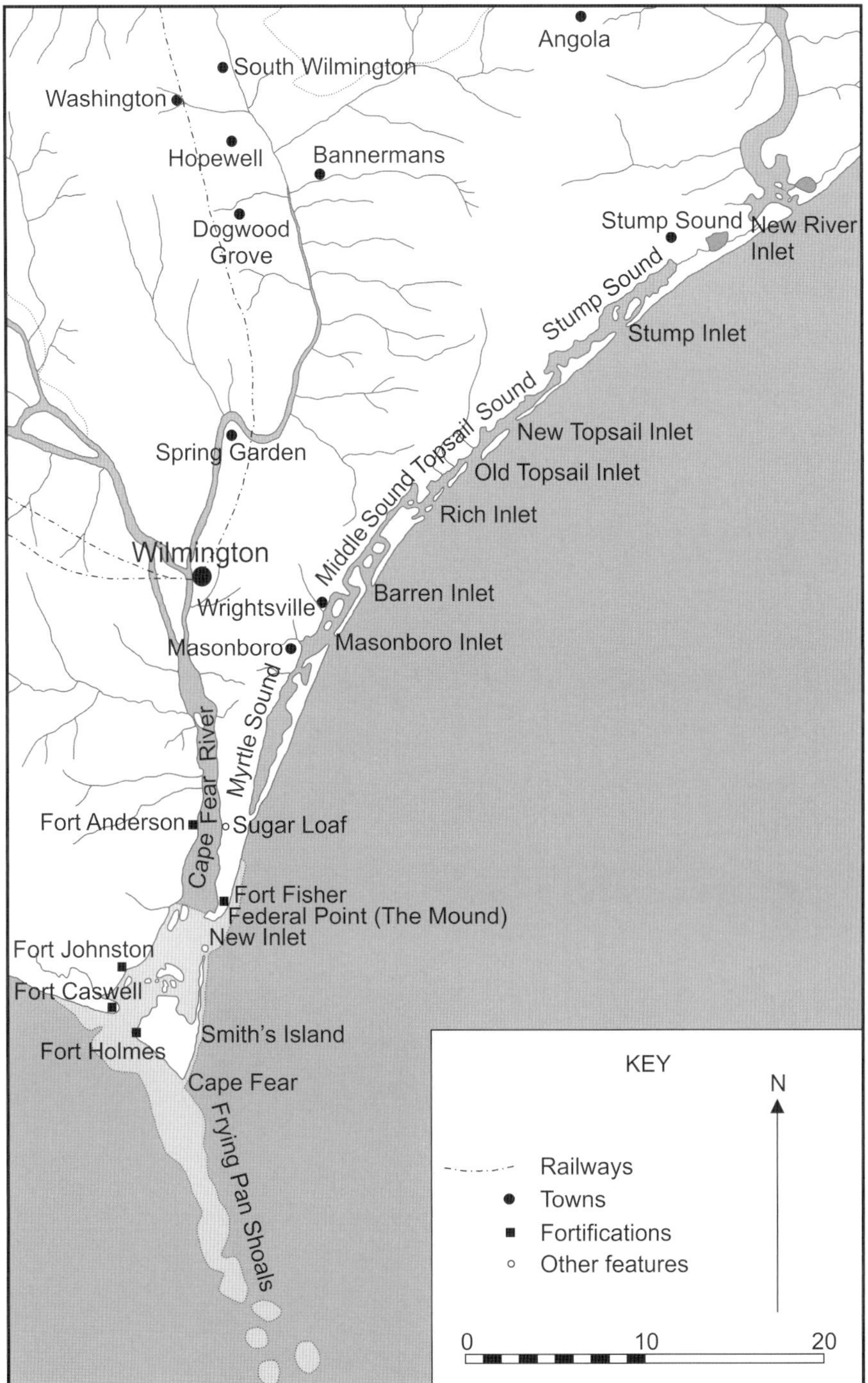

The dangerous approaches to Wilmington.

would hide her from Union lookouts amid the fogs and thick weather off Cape Hatteras. Repainting in Bermuda was a necessity, not least because had it been done before crossing the Atlantic it would have tipped her hand to the *Tuscarora* and her crossing would never have been allowed.

On the very day Allen wrote, 13th December 1862, the *Cornubia* had cleared for Charleston loaded with 525 bales "containing general merchandise" from the steamers *Harriet Pinckney* and the *Justitia* with a Bermudan pilot onboard, promising to return him in a month.[10] The full name of the former was actually the *Harriet Pinckney Huse*, named for the wife of Caleb. Edward Stiles was also aboard and he too had been described as a Charleston pilot, though he was also stated to be her supercargo (that is, a person employed on board a vessel by the owner of cargo carried on the ship).

Despite the fact that the *Cornubia* was destined for Charleston, and later to Wilmington, as were all blockade runners, their official destination was invariably Nassau; this applied to many vessels leaving British ports, though some were said to be going to Havana. Typical of this is a declaration from the Controller of Customs and Navigation Laws, in the Island of Bermuda:

> Whereas the Ship of Vessel called the "Cornubia"
> whose Master is John Burroughs
> is about to sail from the port of St Georges Bermuda
> on this Fifth day of June in the Year
> of our Lord 1863
> and thence for Nassau
> and other places beyond the Seas, with Thirty Seven
> Persons on board including the sail Master.[11]

Henceforth the name *Cornubia* would increasingly appear in the dispatches of both the North and the South. General Beauregard himself applauded her exploits in bringing in desperately needed munitions to the army of Virginia. Writing on 19th December Beauregard noted that the *Cornubia* had arrived in broad daylight, the "blockaders not molesting her".[12] Consul Allen continued to chronicle her successes and she was fast becoming familiar to the Union cruisers trying to bottle up the Confederate Atlantic ports. Like Consul Allen they too had a thankless task; too few in number, often short of coal and manned by 'green' crews they patrolled through the gales and fogs, but by the time the *Cornubia* appeared the Union blockade was getting better organised which made her daring and successful runs all the more galling.

While Allen's posting may have looking idyllic he was fairly well resented by the locals for his attempts to interfere with the lucrative blockading trade and he suffered from a good deal of harassment. One morning in March a group of "colored blockade running seamen" took their revenge by loudly singing Confederate songs beneath his window.[13] On another occasion his office was broken in to and some of his correspondence stolen.

On the 13th December the schooner *Golden Eagle* was seized by the USS *Penobscot*, under Lieutenant-Commander J. E. de Haven.[14] There then followed a letter from Captain John MacKenzie, master of the *Golden Eagle*, claiming compensation for seizure and detention of his ship as well as for property pillaged while detained.[15] De Haven replied to the claim:

> In my report of the 14th of December last I made known the circumstances under which it was deemed necessary to detain that vessel, and in compliance with your instructions of 26th of same month, released her.
>
> The claim for provisions consumed can not, I think, be sustained, as the officer and men detailed for her were provisioned from the *Penobscot*.
>
> The claim for property pillaged I have no knowledge of, there having been no complaint made to me on the part of Captain MacKenzie or his crew of that character; therefore I must conclude that the accusation made is altogether without foundation.
>
> The movements of the schooner at the time of her seizure were suspicious, showing a desire to evade the blockading vessel on the coast of North Carolina by standing to the southward and eastward when the wind was fair for vessels bound for the port of Beaufort, N. C, and distant from that port about 20 miles.
>
> I will, at the earliest moment, forward instructions to the officer who was placed in charge of the schooner, Acting Ensign S. K. Luce, to report in full regarding the matter.[16]

On 17th December the *Cornubia* arrived at Wilmington with her cargo of "chiefly quartermasters' and medical supplies, which are really most needed here".[17] It was said to have proved too dangerous for her to get into Charleston, and Captain Burroughs had opted for the former port instead, sixty miles up the Carolina coast and one of the busiest of the blockade ports, despite having no pilot. She had entered in broad daylight, without interference from any of the blockading ships.

Almost six hundred miles from Bermuda and lying twenty miles up the Cape Fear River, Wilmington was an almost impossible port to blockade without a large fleet. While some ports had several shipping channels, Charleston at one time had seven; Wilmington was unique in having two separate entrances. The traditional entrance was at the Western Bar, between Bald Head and Oak Island, known as the Old Inlet. The other entrance, New Inlet, lay seven miles to the north, just below Confederate Point (formerly called Federal Point, it was renamed Confederate Point in 1862, being within the Confederate States but all US Navy reports, not surprisingly, continued with the old name). Near the tip of Confederate Point the currents from two inlets converged and formed an area of turbulence and shifting shoals known as The Rip. New Inlet was guarded by the guns of Fort Fisher and the Old Inlet by those at Fort Caswell. On leaving the port the runners had an advantage over the blockaders in that the blockading squadrons and their dispositions could be seen and the exit with the best chance of success chosen; usually this was New Inlet.[18]

On arriving upriver Captain Burroughs found five runners already there, including the *Britannia*, a Clyde paddler built especially for blockade running.[19] Once discharged the *Cornubia* shipped 300 cotton bales and slipped away quietly. Prior to departure Edward Stiles had received orders from James A. Seddon, Secretary of War, that he was to take charge of the *Cornubia* for the trip back to Bermuda. Once there he was to proceed to Liverpool "and communicate with Major Huse, relative to the purchase of a vessel such as you and he may think suitable for the purpose of carrying freight from Bermuda and Nassau to the ports of the Confederate States".[20]

A potential complication for the blockade runners occurred in January 1863 when a proclamation was published prohibiting the export of arms and ammunition.[21] However it was also stated that no such law had actually been sanctioned by the Home Authorities, and that it was only ever intended for the Governor and Council to act in the case of hostilities with Britain.

Cornubia's arrival at Wilmington was somewhat garbled by the *Memphis Daily Appeal*, which stated that the vessel had been built on the Clyde in 1860 and was known for her great speed "under the name of the *Giraffe*". Doubtless this would not have won any approval in Hayle![22]

In broad daylight on 14th January 1863 the *Cornubia* left for St George's. Stiles was allegedly carrying a note of credit for the equivalent of $200,000, for the purchase and outfitting of the putative new steamer for the Confederacy.[23] She was initially spotted by several vessels close inshore and chased without success. However, having shaken off his inshore pursuers, Burroughs was then sighted and chased the following day, in a heavy gale, by the USS *Vanderbilt*. Compared with the *Cornubia*, the *Vanderbilt*, the largest full-rigged steamer in the blockade service, was huge: 331 feet long and 47 feet 6 inches broad, displacing 3,360 tons. After being turned over to the Union Navy on 24 March 1862, she was

The USS *Vanderbilt* photographed in about 1872. NHHC image NH 42188.

fitted with a heavy battery of 15 guns, comprising two 100-pounder Parrott rifles, twelve 9-inch Dahlgren smoothbores and one 12-pounder gun, at the New York Navy Yard during the summer of that year.[24]

In a manoeuvre reminiscent of Thomas Cochrane's frigate being run down by two French ships of the line, Burroughs turned the speeding *Cornubia* directly into the teeth of the wind and heavy seas, forcing the *Vanderbilt* to bear away

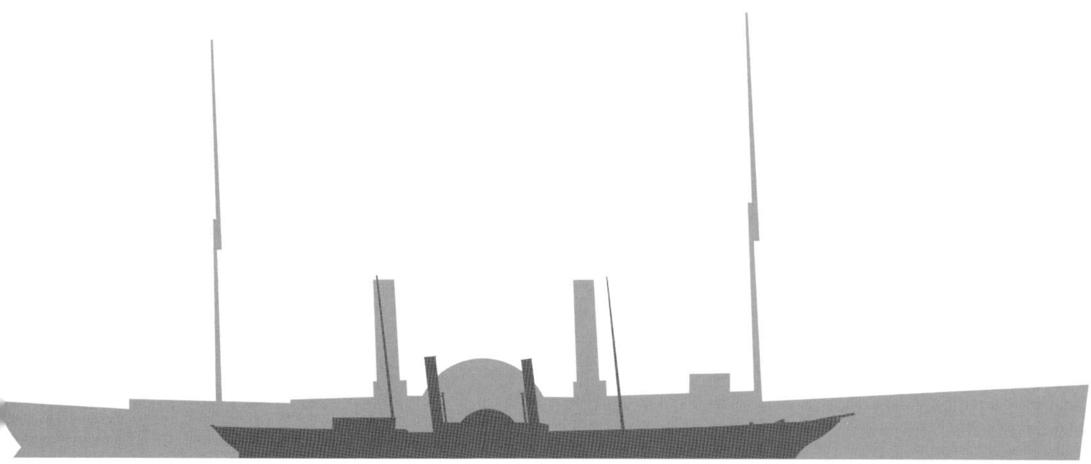

David vs Goliath: the USS *Vanderbilt* compared with the *Cornubia.*

to take in her sails (otherwise she might have lost sails, spars, or even masts to the wind). In this way he "dropped the big one in five hours" and made his escape.[25] Thomas Begbie took some satisfaction that her passengers reported that "there was not a craft out there can look at her for speed, especially in a heavy sea," even though "they put very little on her to keep her at this". Burroughs reached Bermuda on the 19th, at the same time the real *Giraffe* came in with 900 bales in her hold and on deck; *Cornubia's* cargo consisted of 300 bales of cotton, some tobacco and 80 barrels of rosin and turpentine. A number of bales had been thrown overboard during the chase to lighten her load.[26]

The *Vanderbilt* had only recently left Hampton Roads after receiving orders to conduct a much longer and more thorough search for the CSS *Alabama*; she had made a more desultory search during November and December the previous year. This year-long cruise took the vessel to the West Indies, eastern coast of South America, Cape of Good Hope, St. Helena, Cape Verde, the Canary Islands, Spain and Portugal. While the *Official Records* do report that the *Vanderbilt* had experienced a heavy gale there is no mention of her encounter with the *Cornubia*.

Back in St George's the *Harriet Pinckney* had discharged her own cargo and was now taking in *Cornubia's*, to go to Liverpool.[27] On 26th January *Cornubia* left for Wilmington with a cargo of "Blankets, Boots and Shoes, clothing, etc" from the *Justitia*, *Merrimac* and *Harriet Pinckney*; she may also have carried up to 5,200 Enfield rifles.[28] Wilmington was reached on the 30th.

> The Iron Steamship *Cornubia* arrived safe this morning at a Confederate port [Wilmington]. She ran through six blockaders and was just eighteen minutes doing it. She brings a valuable cargo.
>
> *Wilmington Journal* 5th February 1863

On 31st January Captain W. A. Parker of the USS *Cambridge* reported on the arrival of what seems to have been the *Cornubia*, stating that early in the morning a "small two-masted steamer" was seen near Fort Fisher, inside New Inlet.[29] She had a Confederate flag at her main mast and an "English" flag at her foremast. She had apparently run the blockade during the night. A letter from 'L,' a member of the 17th Regiment, South Carolina Volunteers, to the Yorkville Enquirer remarks

> I had the pleasure of passing through the splendid English steamer *Cornubia*, then loading with cotton at the wharf. This vessel had made a number of successful trips within the last six months [a slight exaggeration], bringing

Government Stores and other useful freight (by the way, this vessel went to sea again last night).

Yorkville Enquirer 18th February 1863

On 2nd February the blockade was strengthened by the addition of the USS *Iroquois*, commanded by Captain Augustus Ludlow Case. Case had taken command of the vessel at New York at the beginning of January. The orders of Acting Rear-Admiral Lee stated:

> I desire Captain Case to be stationed on the north side of the shoals and to conduct the blockade of New Inlet and the adjacent inlets to the northward of it requiring blockade.[30]

Augustus Ludlow Case as Commander, USN, about 1860.

NHHC image NH 48014.

Lee also ordered that shortfalls in the complements of the various blockading ships were to be made up from the crew of the USS *Columbia*. The *Columbia* had run aground at Masonboro Inlet on the night of 16th January.[31] The crew had surrendered and her commander, Acting Volunteer Lieutenant Joseph P. Couthouy, twelve officers and twenty-five men, were taken as prisoners of war. The USS *Penobscot* had sent a boat into the surf in order to haul the *Columbia* off however the sea was too rough to allow the volunteer crew to board her. Going back later, "nobly and daringly", the *Penobscot* opened fire on the *Columbia*, driving off a number of Confederates who were stripping the vessel while watching over the remainder of the crew. This allowed the erstwhile prisoners (forty-five men) to escape via the *Penobscot*; half of the escapees were later transferred to the *Daylight*.

After arriving on station off Wilmington on 8th February a disappointed Captain Case reported:

> I regret to say that the speed of the *Iroquois* has been very much overrated. Under the most favorable circumstances at sea, with steam alone, I have not been able to get more than 7 knots, with 60 revolutions. With steam and a fair, fresh breeze, from 9 to 10 knots.[32]

Under "the most favorable circumstances, fresh, fair wind, smooth water, 12 or 14 knots might be obtained, but it could be kept up only for a short time" however this speed created such a bad vibration that he felt it might "strain or injure" the vessel.

Departing Wilmington on 14th February with 323 more bales of cotton 23 boxes of tobacco and two barrels of turpentine, *Cornubia* made the passage back to Bermuda in 71 hours, arriving on 19th February 1863.[33] Her departure had been problematic; leaving at 4am she had been hidden by fog but had not travelled far before she was sighted by the blockading squadron, four ships of which gave chase. Finding they could not keep up with the ex-packet they resorted to shot and shell to halt her. Fourteen shots were fired at her but only one came close "but without in any way checking her progress or chilling the hearts of the bold men in command".[34] It seems that the reason for her being noticed was a picket boat from the US steam sloop *Dacotah*. At 4am on the morning of the 14th, a quarter of a mile from Fort Caswell, the picket boat was nearly run down by a "long, low, steamer, with two masts and two smoke stacks".[35] After a brief moment of panic aboard the picket boat the anchor was raised and the tiny vessel was rowed out of the way of the oncoming vessel. On coming abreast of

USS *Iroquois*, date and location unknown. NHHC image NH 43839.

the picket boat the steamer's engines were briefly stopped, and then she steamed ahead at top speed. Acting Master William Earle was able to send up a red rocket to alert the blockading fleet. According to Earle, the runner had not been visible for more than two minutes, though an exciting two minutes.

The bad penny of the boarding of the *Thistle* the previous November, came back to bother Commander Craven of the USS *Tuscarora*. The US Navy Department had received a communication from the British minister in Washington complaining of the way the *Thistle* had been stopped. It was stated that the Tuscarora had followed the *Thistle* out of the port of Madeira to a distance of between 3 and 4 miles from land, fired two guns at her, and after bringing her to and searching her returned to the port she had just left. No mention was made of her stopping and boarding the *Cornubia* however.

Gideon Welles, Secretary of the US Navy, finished:

> Your report of December does not mention these circumstances. If they are correctly stated, you have, perhaps without being aware of it, furnished ground for the complaint which has been made. It is not proper to make a convenience in any manner of neutral territory for the purpose of exercising the belligerent right of search or capture. A capture of a neutral vessel, made after standing off and on a neutral harbor or mouth of a river, or lying in wait within it for the purpose, although actually made beyond the neutral jurisdiction, would not be recognized as valid, and the right of search cannot properly be exercised when it is known previously that, whatever the event of the search, the capture would not be lawful.
>
> You will make a further and more detailed report to the Department of the facts in this case. I am, respectfully,[36]

On 25th February, having discharged one cargo and loaded a new one, "a large quantity of arms and ammunition", *Cornubia* sailed again from Bermuda for Wilmington. The cargo this time comprised:

> Imported per *Justitia*, London, value £10,000: 130 bales and 25 cases manufactured merchandise, 50 barrels saltpeter, 100 boxes tin, 100 pigs lead, 100 ingots tin
>
> Imported per *Gladiator*, value £4,500: 111 cases hardware, 72 boxes combustible merchandise, 178 boxes combustible merchandise
>
> Imported per *Delta*: 1 package wearing apparel
>
> Imported per *Merrimac*: 600 barrels gunpowder

> 4 cases stationery, £50.0.0, 45 cases brandy from John T. Bourne's warehouse[37]

She returned from Wilmington with another cargo of cotton, making the return journey in 66 hours, departing 18th March and arriving on the 22nd. On 26th February Josiah Gorgas wrote to Caleb Huse:

> MAJOR: We have retained the *Giraffe* for running the blockade, and the *G.* and *C.* will now run regularly to B. and N. One or two more are highly desirable. Has Stiles made any purchases? If we can get two more like the *Cornubia* and *G.*, we shall be beyond casualty, or we can afford to lose one occasionally.[38]

During February the defences at New Inlet, notably at Fort Fisher, were strengthened. Four casemated batteries had been constructed and a fifth partly. The old light house at Confederate Point had been taken down to provide building materials. The dangers of the defences around the Cape Fear River were demonstrated on 23rd February when the USS *Monticello* (ex-*Star*), under orders from Captain B. F. Sands, opened fire on a steamer which had grounded on The Rip.[39] The nearby guns of Fort Caswell replied and the Fort's fifth or sixth shot struck the wrought-iron band of the 30lb Parrott gun. This mortally wounded Acting Master's Mate Henry Baker and slightly wounded second-class boy William J. Fergusson in the back. The *Dacotah* then stood offshore and Baker's

USS *Monticello*. NHHC image NH 59555-KN.

body was committed to the deep. On 17th June a shot from Fort Fisher struck the USS *State of Georgia*, wounding three men.[40]

The US Navy's battle with the pilots of the runners was demonstrated in March when a list of the names of a number of pilots was sent on the 1st of the month to Acting Rear-Admiral Lee by Lieutenant-Commander Braine of the USS *Monticello*.[41] Many of these pilots worked locally, boarding the vessels close to Wilmington but only guided the runners through the local shallows. Braine was able to name twelve men: George McIthen (or McKithen), John McKinsey, -- Carroll, -- Dennis, -- Fowler, George Walker, John Marshall, Joseph Springer, Captain Fritzinger, Thomas Lockwood, Archd. Guthrie and Benson. His letter ended with "I would suggest that these parties be looked after".

On 2nd March an "English steamer" – once again the *Cornubia* – made her way into New Inlet despite the presence of, and attempted interference by, five blockaders.[42] She had arrived the previous day but just too late for the tide; because of this she went back out to sea and lay-to in a fog bank at about 9am, in theory an opportunity for the crew to rest. Unfortunately the fog bank cleared rather suddenly after only about half an hour later; lookouts aboard the USS *State of Georgia*, part of the North Atlantic Blockading Squadron, spotted her very quickly. The *Cambridge* and *Daylight*, both of whom had been patrolling nearby, then joined the chase. The USS *State of Georgia* had also signalled the USS *Mount Vernon* to converge on the trio. Acting Volunteer Lieutenant Trathen (born at sea off the coast of Maine, but quite possibly of Cornish extraction, just like his intended prey) of the latter ordered all sail to be set and as much steam as possible; having closed on the *Cornubia*, he ordered his crew to open fire but the shot fell short by about half a mile. About this time lookouts aboard the USS *Iroquois* also saw the smoke and she too took off after the *Cornubia*.

Cornubia had only just managed to get under way before shots started falling around her. *Cornubia* built up to full speed, with the *Mount Vernon* on her stern. John Burroughs must have been terribly disappointed to have been discovered so close to his destination. Determined to escape, he ordered the crew to throw some of the heaviest cargo overboard. A number of the 600 kegs of gunpowder were disposed of, left like bobbing corks in the *Cornubia's* wake. Despite their value, most of the 100 lead ingots onboard were also disposed of since this was the easiest way to lose weight quickly. Several tons lighter, the steamer surged ahead of the *Mount Vernon*. While Trathen was initially surprised to see the *Cornubia* put on a burst of speed, the debris floating in the latter's wake soon showed him where it came from (Trathen later described it as "a field of some 300 barrels, which seemed to be powder barrels"). Trathen then ordered "a quantity of condemned pork and a half barrel of pitch" to be thrown into the

The sand hills of Fort Fisher; the guns were positioned between the mounds. Most of the site has now gone, the sand eroded by the sea.

fire boxes of the boilers in an effort to increase speed.[43] While he used "every exertion to overhaul the chase" the effort was insufficient; although Trathen managed to keep *Cornubia* in view until sunset he realised that the chase was over and gave up before his engines did. By this time he and his ship were 140 miles from New Inlet, the wind and sea were both deteriorating and his ship was beginning to struggle.

The *Iroquois* remained with the chase for some five hours without being able to gain on either vessel.[44] There was sufficient wind for the ship's sails to be set and she was able to make 11 or 12 knots. The *Mount Vernon* was occasionally giving off great gouts of black smoke (doubtless from the unusual forms of fuel being used) and Commander Augustus Ludlow Case, captain of the *Iroquois*, believed that he was chasing two runners. Case abandoned the race at 3.30pm and returned his ship to its station off New Inlet.

The *Cornubia* steamed on through the night and arrived unscathed at Masonboro Inlet early in the morning; it was not until 9am on the 2nd that she reached her position of the previous day, "all hands knocked up and only a few tons of coal left".[45] Approaching The Bar, *Cornubia* came in from the northeast, close along the land and under its shadow; because of her low shape she was not visible until she threw up a dense volume of smoke within a mile and a half of Fort Fisher. With the enemy fleet in sight it was resolved to abandon the *Cornubia* and blow her up; steaming "into a quiet little bay we dropped anchor, got the boats out, and prepared for a start".

However the pilot had steered *Cornubia* so close to the shore that the crew

could get word to Colonel William Lamb. A telegraph was then sent to Fort Fisher that the *Cornubia* was in danger, to which Colonel Lamb replied that he would cover her should Burroughs attempt to run her in.[46] Rather than lose his ship, Burroughs opted for the more exciting option and ordered full steam and full speed. The *State of Georgia* fired three shots from her 100-pounder, which fell far short of the steamer as she was crossing the bar.[47]

This action turned out to be one of the *Cornubia's* most successful, facing odds of five to one in the final chase. Running along the edge of the breakers the final 12 miles of the run were completed in 45 minutes. To avoid fire from the fort, the Union ships had moved out to sea at first light, and the *Cornubia* passed into the river without interference. Although the jettisoned cargo was worth about $20,000, what remained onboard was valued at many times that amount in Wilmington.[48]

Passing by the shore near Fort Fisher the crew of the *Cornubia* could see guns from the battery arranged to cover them, supported by the other guns in the fort itself. On passing over The Bar the *Cornubia* was greeted by thousands of people, many of whom had presumably seen part of the chase, with "loud and hearty cheers"; the second part of the chase by the blockaders had lasted nine hours.[49]

The five blockaders had been spread in a picket line over a distance of two miles; from north-east to south-west they were the *Cambridge*, *Daylight*, *Mount Vernon*, *Iroquois*, and *State of Georgia*. Both the *State of Georgia* and the *Iroquois* had been underway during the day to look after vessels which proved to be blockaders, the USS *Monticello* and USS *Mount Vernon*.[50]

The blockader *Cambridge* was reported to be in such a poor condition "as

Colonel William Lamb, the man responsible for the defences of Fort Fisher and incoming blockade runners.

to be of but little service, and cannot be called upon to chase except in case of emergency".* The attentions of the blockade runners had turned to the two entrances to Wilmington, and Augustus Ludlow Case, the Commander and Senior Officer off New Inlet, North Carolina urged Acting Rear-Admiral Lee to send a larger force so that both could be covered. In particular he wanted small, fast, vessels which could close in without being seen at night, or only at short distance during the day.

In fairness to the blockading fleet it seems that the ships' captains were also taken in by a ruse from some of the other runners which were safe but visible to the blockaders. Several of these ships made a feint as if to leave New Inlet; caught in two minds the blockaders were not quite quick enough to react to the *Cornubia's* dash for safety. However, as Ludlow Case later wrote:

> The boldness of the steamer coming in was based on the knowledge, obtained yesterday, of his speed being superior to ours, which he could avail himself of, if necessary, at any time. The whole attention of blockade runners seems of late to have been turned toward the two entrances to Wilmington, and I trust that you will consider it necessary to send, if possible, a larger force here. Small, fast vessels are what is wanted most, such as can lay close in without being seen at night, or only at short distance during the day. Such are the English blockade runners; the advantage of speed and invisibility is now altogether with them.[51]

Frederick W. Gregory, of the Confederate States Signal Corps, who had been on board the *Cornubia*, described the action:

> We cleared the bar successfully, with Captain Burroughs in command, and

***In common with the blockade runners, ship owners could ask what they wanted for just about anything that floated that was destined for the US Navy. In 1861 the naval officers who examined the *Mount Vernon* and *Cambridge* declared they were both unfit for recharter.[52] In particular, the machinery of the *Cambridge* was so exposed that she was labelled "valueless for war purposes" yet both were purchased and both served until the end of the war.**

C. C. Morse as pilot, and had a good voyage to St. George, Bermuda, where we unloaded our cargo of cotton and reloaded with supplies for the Southern Army. On our return trip we made the land fifty or sixty miles above Fort Fisher and coasted down to the inlet, our intention being to get near the land inside the blockading fleet, which was obliged to keep off a certain distance on account of shoal water. As well as I remember, when within fifteen to twenty miles of Fort Fisher, Captain Burroughs sent for me to come on the bridge, and asked if I had my lights ready, and if I thought I could send a message ashore, Pilot Morse in the meantime telling me that he would let me know when we were opposite the signal station on the land, where a constant watch was kept all night for our signal. We had not gone far when Morse told me we were opposite the post. We were feeling our way very slowly in the dark. I was put down on the deck, with the gangways open, my lights facing the land and a screen behind, when I was ordered to call the station. The officers and sailors were highly interested in the movement and crowded around to watch the proceedings. I had called but a few times when I was answered from the shore with a torch. I turned to Captain Burroughs and told him I had the attention of the land forces, and asked what message he wished to send. He replied as follows: 'Colonel Lamb, steamer *Cornubia*. Protect me. Burroughs'. I got the O. K. for the message from shore, and saw the corps on land call up one station after the other, and transmit my message down to Fort Fisher, miles

Some of the main armament at Fort Fisher; the muzzle has been damaged by a strike from a shell. Note the cannon balls in the foreground and the rammer leaning against the sand bags at the rear.

ahead of us, and afterwards learned that General Whiting was notified by telegraph of the arrival of the *Cornubia* before she crossed the bar that night; and when we arrived at the fort we found Colonel Lamb down on the point with his Whitworth guns ready to protect us if necessary. The success of this attempt gave an impetus to the signal corps, and from that time every steamer that arrived applied to the Government for a signal officer before leaving port.[53]

According to Captain Case, the pilot who brought the *Cornubia* so close to the beach was "Jim Burroughs (a pilot living "on the beach"; he was also pilot for the *Banshee*) who reported that she ran five miles in twenty minutes".[54] While the word 'telegraph' is used the signallers on ships used the General Service Code; the code used one flag or two torches. The flags had three colour schemes: a red square in the middle of a white background, white on black, or black on white. The flag used at any time depended on the visibility. This was also called 'wig-wag signalling' because of the waving of the signal flags.[55]

Cornubia had been carrying 600 barrels of powder which had been delivered to St George's by the *Merrimac*; the balance was now in the powder house though 60 barrels were "in a very damaged condition, entirely unserviceable".[56] *Cornubia* was therefore still carrying 280 barrels when she arrived in Wilmington.

The story of *Cornubia's* run into Wilmington was also printed in a number of newspapers. The following is from the *Liverpool Mercury* of Wednesday 22nd April 1863, though all full accounts are identical.

RUNNING THE BLOCKADE.
AN EXCITING CHASE.

News headlines regarding the *Cornubia's* success.

RUNNING THE BLOCKADE

AN EXCITING CHASE

The following is an extract from a letter received from one of the crew of the Confederate steamer *Cornubia*, a little steamer which has successfully run the blockade of Wilmington six times :—

Bermuda, March 27, 1863.

I will now give a few particulars about our narrow escape last trip. We made a fine run across from here, but were just too late for the tide, so we steamed out to sea again, and lay-to in a fog, so as to give the men a little rest. On the 1st March (a Sunday morning), about ten o'clock, the fog cleared, and there was a thundering big Yankee bearing down upon us. We just managed to get properly under way, when her shot began to fall rather close to us. Away we went, and she after us, at full speed, keeping her ground well for several hours, although each time she fired we had gained on her, and not one shot or shell hit us, we going 17 to 18 knots per hour. A fine fair wind was blowing, and as it freshened she 'cracked' on her canvas, and, being to windward of us, we could not double her, and she then began to gain on us until we had to throw cargo overboard to lighten the ship. 150 barrels of gunpowder went (I was glad to see it, for one of the Yankee's shells might have popped into it and blown us all up) and then we went ahead again, and by dark had gained 15 miles on her, and it was then we 'gave her the slip' and ran back for Wilmington.

She chased us from ten o'clock till seven, 150 miles away from the bar. It was a splendid sight to see us flying through the water with the Yankee after us, her shells cracking and faring in the water, we did not get back to the place we started from until nine o'clock on Monday morning, all pretty well knocked up, and just too late for the tide, and with only a few tons of coal left. We could see twelve blockaders lying off the port. It was then agreed we would leave the ship and blow her up, so steaming into a nice little bay we dropped anchor, got the boats out, and everything ready for a start, such a scene! I cannot describe it, but hope someday to relate it to you. We were only eight miles from the fleet. It was telegraphed up to Wilmington 'The *Cornubia* is in danger,' and the excitement became very great all through the town. They then sent some heavy guns and surf boats to land us in, as a heavy surf runs along that coast: and the commander of the fort sent word he would protect us if we liked to risk it and run in. At four o'clock that afternoon we did risk it, and steamed slowly up the coast. When within five miles of the bar, the Yankees saw us. The whole fleet slipped their cables and came in after us. What excitement everywhere! I shall never forget it. They opened fire on us just as we crossed the bar; then the fort opened fire on them and kept them off until we were safely in. Thousands were on the beach to welcome us, and greeted us with loud and hearty cheers as we steamed slowly up to Wilmington, where we met with a very warm reception, I assure you, and had a glorious night's rest. We had no trouble whatever in coming out again.

I need not tell you anything about the war, as you will in all probability hear more about it than I do. I can, however, assure you of one thing - the women and children are in a sad state of destitution; poor things, it makes one's heart bleed to see them.

Following this an order was sent out from Acting Rear-Admiral Lee to Captain Boggs to enjoin a strict watch for the return of the *Cornubia* from Bermuda.

> Exercise all vigilance to prevent this. I have sent a copy of this letter to the senior officer off New Inlet, by which the blockade breakers probably escape from Wilmington by running along the coast under the batteries. The public papers report the capture by the *Quaker City*, off Wilmington, of the steamer *Douro*, having made her escape from that port on or about the 9th instant. Let each vessel keep a tide table on her deck board.[57]

By the following day (3rd March) Acting Rear Admiral Lee was able to report to Gideon Welles that the *Cambridge* was now at Beaufort, having repairs carried out to her boilers, which "are represented to be in so precarious a condition as to be liable to fail at any moment".[58] The *Mount Vernon's* boiler was also reported to be in bad condition and in want of scaling. This was to have been done when she next went for coal to Beaufort but the work was not carried out. The machinery of the *Daylight* was also reported to be "broken down", although her Acting Master, Warren, stated that he could remain at his station until the return of the *Mount Vernon* from Beaufort, "if he had to lay at his anchors", implying that actual movement would be problematic. These vessels were to be retained in active service as long as possible with regard to safety, however if any one of them should be sent north for repairs "the blockade of New Inlet and to the northward will be left virtually to two vessels, the third being absent most of the time for coal and repairs". While there was no obvious note of complaint in Lee's reports, he must have been very frustrated at the tired condition of his blockading ships.

The *Wilmington Journal* carried an article from the *Charleston Courier* of the 5th March, a report "current here yesterday, and thought to be correct," stating that the *Cornubia* was ashore on the North Carolina coast about fifteen miles south of the Cape Fear River.[59] The origins of this rumour were not known, nor why she should have been so far south.

A letter from Major-General Whiting, of the Confederate States Army, to Major-General Hill, Confederate States Army, on 6th March outlined the value of the Whitworth guns at Forts Caswell and Fisher as a protection to blockade runners.[60] There were three guns in all, one in each fort and one about 5 miles above Fort Fisher, on the beach. These weapons were all the Confederates had that were effective. The Whitworth was a 12-pounder rifled gun extremely accurate at long range. As described by Colonel Lamb at Fort Fisher, "With these guns, we made the U. S. blockading fleet remove their anchorage from two and a half miles to five miles from the fort". The guns had originally been salvaged from the wreck of the British merchantman *Modern Greece*. They had been mounted on carriages and were hauled down to the beach by mules when required. With these he was able to help many blockade runners attempting to enter the Cape Fear River and also to drive off Federal ships attempting to capture or destroy stranded runners.

12-Pounder Whitworth breech-loading rifled gun displayed at the Gettysburg National Military Park. This is the mobile artillery used by Colonel Lamb at Fort Fisher to provide a rapid responce for the blockade runners coming into Wilmington.

During the battle between Fort Fisher and the blockading fleet the Fort's Parrott gun had burst. However, the next ship into Wilmington was the *Merrimac*. She had also been chased and had run aground but, protected by the long-range Whitworth guns, she was refloated before she could be damaged. Major-General Whiting was later to write:

> We had quite a spirited engagement as you expected, my 30-pounder Parrott burst in the engagement. The *Merrimac* brings me three splendid Blakeley guns, 8-inch rifled 30-pounders. Two of them are for this place; one gone to Mississippi.[61]

At the present time there were five steamers, four British and one Confederate, in port, daily expecting to leave and several steamers were expected to arrive. The defences had fought an engagement with the blockaders over each one of the vessels, "the enemy's sloops of war fiercely attacking the forts, while their smaller vessels attempt to cut off the steamers".[62] This had happened at both forts. Without the protection of Fort Fisher, Whiting said that the *Cornubia* would inevitably have been lost three days before. She had been chased off the coast three times and became short of coal.

On 17th March Commander Craven was finally able to respond to the accusations regarding his stopping of the *Thistle*. He stated:

> The manner in which the *Thistle* was boarded appears to have been stated to you with tolerable accuracy. I was not, however, "lying in wait," but arrived at Madeira the day before the *Thistle* sailed, and followed that vessel to sea. I was not aware that by so doing I was violating any rule of international law, or I most certainly would not have trespassed on neutral rights. The authorities of Funchal admitted that the whole matter was *pro forma*. British naval officers of high rank whom I subsequently met there told me I was performing my "duty as they always did it;" and, as a matter of interest, I enclose you a newspaper paragraph in reference to the matter, which seems to have been written by a naval officer. You will therefore see, sir, that if I erred, I have done so through falling into old practices rather than through any disregard of neutral rights.[63]

Writing to Major Huse on 21st March, Major Norman Stewart Walker in St George's was "anxiously" expecting *Cornubia's* arrival daily, though he had personal reasons this time: his wife was on board.[64] Walker was the Confederate's chief disbursing agent in Bermuda, having arrived there on the *Cornubia*. *Cornubia's* previous cargo was still waiting to be shipped, and a coaling vessel currently in harbour was to be used if Captain Burroughs had a good opinion of her.

On 23rd March Consul Allen in Bermuda reported:

> The reception the *Cornubia* received on her return here yesterday must have been very gratifying to her officers. As she came into the harbor, the shores and wharves were lined with the inhabitants who greeted her with cheer after cheer.[65]

This was doubtless a spontaneous response to the news of her successful evasion of the Federal squadron. Her cargo this time comprised 314 bales cotton, 29 cases tobacco and 2 casks turpentine.[66] Probably because of the chase *Cornubia* reached port in just 66 hours.[67] The pregnant Georgiana Walker was on board, desperate to join her husband in St George's and had approached every blockade runner in Wilmington to plead with the captains to be taken on as a passenger. Only John Burroughs took pity:

> I went to Wilmington, & the Captain of the "Cornubia" agreed to take me & my children & do his best altho he laid plainly before me the perils of the trip, saying that the last vessel which had gone out, had just been captured - that the Northern [blockading] Fleet was large & stationed for many miles out. I said nevertheless that I should go.[68]

Despite this agreement, Georgiana was visited onboard the *Cornubia* by the "Genl in command of Wilmington" (Major-General Whiting), who tried to pursued her otherwise; he was unsuccessful and she and her three young children duly made the journey aboard the *Cornubia*. Not even a tearful appeal by Varina Davis (wife of Jefferson Davis, the Confederate President) to consider the safety of her children could change her mind. The beginning of the journey, late at night or early in the morning, was recounted in Georgiana's diary:

> I took my seat on one of the sofas in the saloon, with Lillie on one side, Normy on the other and Georgie on my lap – Seeing that they were becoming very impressed by these formidable precautions, I determined to call their attention off, & to interest them in a series of stories, to which I at once applied myself, most vigorously. The Capt. was very considerable in his attention to me, & not many minutes after we were fairly off, he came down to the saloon door to say, "We have passed one blockader, Madam". Shortly after, he reported another & another, & after the lapse of about two hours I had the satisfaction of hearing that the entire fleet had been passed, & that we were, therefore, comparatively safe...[69]

The former Government House in St George's. This building became the headquarters of Major Norman S. Walker, the Confederate Political Agent. After the Civil War the house became the Globe Hotel. The property is now owned by the Bermuda National Trust to interpret the role of the Confederacy in Bermuda.

Within the remains of her belongings was a bag containing a Confederate flag and a small pouch filled with soil from Virginia. Georgiana had intended to give birth with the flag draped symbolically above the bed and the soil placed beneath to ensure that the baby was a true Virginian! Major Walker's HQ was at the Globe Hotel, a three-storey building built in 1699 as a residence for the governor; the pink-painted building was one of the oldest houses on the island; it was situated quite close to Consul Charles Allen's office. Georgiana later became known as the First Lady of Confederate

Bermuda. Dignitaries and Confederate officers were often entertained at the Walker's home, which became known as 'Banana Manor'.

The following day Allen reported that *Cornubia's* engineer "who has left her" had told him that she was owned by the Confederate Government and was not allowed to carry any goods for merchants.[70] He believed that Major Walker "had charge of her" but the engineer's reasons for leaving the ship were not revealed.

> Report of Captain Case, U. S. Navy, referring to the escape of the steamer *Cornubia*
>
> U. S. Steam Sloop *Iroquois*,
>
> Beaufort Harbor, N. C, March 26, 1863.
>
> It is quite possible the *Cornubia* escaped via New Inlet, though from the information I obtained from a contraband taken from the *Mount Vernon* on the 16th instant, and who has been in the habit of going in the pilot boats, I think it is quite probable she went the other way. He states that most have gone in of late at New Inlet and out the Fort Caswell way.
>
> This was the two-pipe, paddle-wheel steamer which passed us on that date, as reported in my Number 36.
>
> The *Cornubia* and the *Giraffe*, the contraband states, have been quite often in and out of Wilmington. "They went to Charleston until the steamers got too thick there". I hope we may yet have success in stopping them. Vessels farther from the inlet than we usually are will have the best chance. Where we lay, and where some vessels always should be, it is a dash with them, if seen, and they are soon under the batteries; if not seen, the result is of course the same. When going out, of a dark night, it is pretty much the same thing; the ground is clear for their light draft, and they have pilots who know every inch of it. Such vessels as this are visible long before we can see them, and they come, after seeing us, with a full head of steam and are by us and away in a jiffy.
>
> The officers are anxious, the men are anxious, all keep a sharp lookout, and I do not spare myself. There is but little rest for a blockader, night or day; he must be wide awake and always ready, for, independent of any desire he may have to serve his country, his reputation, life, interest, and all are at stake—reasons sufficient, one would suppose, to make him vigilant.
>
> I am, very respectfully, your obedient servant,
>
> A. Ludlow Case,
>
> Captain and Senior Officer Present

Acting Rear-Admiral S. P. Lee,
Commanding North Atlantic Blockading Squadron[71]

'Contraband' or 'intelligent contraband' was the name given to stowaways on the blockade runners, invariably former slaves. Consul Allen seems to have had a quite kindly attitude towards the contrabands and was known to have looked after them and had them shipped to New York at his own expense.[72]

Cornubia was back out of St George's for Wilmington on the 27th March.[73] Her cargo this time seems much more overtly warlike, even though few details are given: 372 cases of manufactured merchandise (presumed to be weapons), 42 casks of hardware (ditto), 150 barrels of saltpeter, 100 pigs of lead (presumably to make shot or bullets) and 350 boxes of cartridges. Last but not least were 200 cases of brandy.

Bad news was then reported in the *Bermuda Royal Gazette*, copied from the New York papers of 4th April; luckily it turned out to be false:

> THE STEAMER *CORNUBIA* CAPTURED
>
> We learn by a Gentleman from St Georges last evening, that New York papers of the 4th inst., which he saw on board the Ship *Gertrude*, mention the capture of the Steamer *Cornubia*, Captain Burroughs, which cleared at St Georges on the 27th ult. for Nassau.[74]

In April William H. Seward, Secretary of State, wrote to Gideon Welles, Secretary of the Navy, stating that:

> I entertain no doubt that with the knowledge obtained through these papers it will be proper for you to direct that henceforth British blockade violators be detained in custody, and not released, as heretofore.[75]

This was endorsed with:

> British blockade violators will be henceforth detained, and not released, etc. Any orders inconsistent herewith countermanded.

On 18th April, Consul Allen wrote in his diary:

> The *Cornubia* is expected tomorrow, as she was to leave Wilmington last Wednesday night. This is the fourth time she has been there from here, and makes her trips as regular as the Mail steamer to Halifax, having occupied

in her former trip three weeks and three days each. I have sent to New York, at my own expense, three men from the *Cornubia*, and five from the *Robt. E. Lee* and have two contrabands on hand. The men sent to New York were free people of color who shipped in the south to escape being compelled to work on the fortifications, and did not wish to return. The Contrabands stowed themselves away till after they had passed the blockade.[76]

While attempting to enter Wilmington *Cornubia* had been chased for nine hours by a US steamer and $20,000 worth of goods had been thrown overboard to lighten her; possibly because of this thc journey had lasted just 66 hours. On leaving Wilmington some "twelve or thirteen" blockaders were in sight though none gave chase; possibly their recent experiences against the *Cornubia* encouraged them to stay at anchor and wait for slower prey.[77]

St George's Harbour, Bermuda; several blockade runners can be seen.

On April 20th the *Cornubia* and the *General Beauregard* arrived in St George's with 1,400 bales of cotton between them from Southern ports.[78] The steamer *Gertrude* had arrived at Charleston and the *Britannia* was in Wilmington. According to the *Charleston Courier*, "Four steamers have arrived from Nassau since Sunday. Notwithstanding the blockade Charleston is enjoying a larger direct foreign trade than she has ever had before".[79]

This is getting to be a great depot for vessels running the blockade. There is scarcely a week but a steamer either comes in or goes out. One of them, the *Cornubia*, makes her trips to Wilmington with as much regularity as the Barss does to New-York. She is expected back to-day, from her fourth trip. The *Gen. Beauregard* is almost as regular in her trips to Charleston. I hope she has been interfered with this time. There are also the *Gen. Lee* and the *Merrimac* and others, the names of whom I do not remember. There are now about 2,000 bales of cotton here awaiting shipment to England. Officers of the *Cornubia*, whom I have seen, say the blockading squadron could have sunk her, if they had chosen, on her last voyage, but they preferred taking her as a prize and letting her escape rather than lose their prize money. I hope she may be wrecked and they lose it altogether.[80]

This is an interesting criticism of the blockading squadron. Ships captured were sold at a prize court and the money raised was distributed amongst the crews of the ships involved, pro rata to their rank. In the Royal Navy a proportion was also given to the local admiral commanding; this perk was passed on to the US admirals who also benefited financially.

It was on one of these trips to Wilmington that the *Cornubia* carried some special goods for Lieutenant William Conway Whittle II. Whittle would later be famous, or infamous, as the Executive Officer on the CSS *Shenandoah*, a Confederate commerce raider; he was the son of Commodore William Whittle, CSN. The goods, in a box, included “four pair of gloves and four pair of gaiters for his “sweet little cousin Matoaka,” a dozen toothbrushes, a sponge and six cakes of soap for two Whittle aunts, a pair of shoes for a Dr Skipwith, and 28 pounds of shot and 49 yards of calico for a Dr Harrison”.[81] These were all hard-to-get, and therefore expensive, items in a blockaded town.

THE BRITISH WEST INDIES.

The Cornubia Runs the Blockade at Wilmington—Affairs in Barbados, Demerara, Jamaica, Antigua, &c.

The Bermuda *Royal Gazette*, of March 24, has been received.

The British neutral blockade runner *Cornubia* arrived at St. Georges from Wilmington, N. C., on the 22d of March, with a cargo of 314 bales of cotton, 29 casks of tobacco and two casks of turpentine.

The British schooner *St. George* also arrived on the 23d of March, from the same port, with 145 bales of cotton, 160 bbls. of resin, and 65 boxes of tobacco.

News on the *Cornubia’s* success from the *New York Times*, 8th April 1863.

This was supposed to be the last trip under Burroughs' command, that now going to be turned over to Lieutenant Richard Gayle, Confederate States Navy, the *Cornubia* having now been bought by the Confederate Government. According to Dawson Carr, Burroughs "eventually grew tired of the intense stress and asked to be relieved,"[82] however, given his appearance later on other blockaders, as well as some of the descriptions of his seamanship above, this does not seem likely. Also, not being part of the Confederate States Navy, Burroughs would have been ineligible to command a CSN ship.

Chapter 8

Captain Richard Haynsworth Gayle

In complete contrast with John Burroughs, Richard (Dick) Haynsworth Gayle is comparatively well known. Dick Gayle was born in Alabama in 1832,[1] fifth child and second son to John Gayle, US Congressman, governor of Alabama and jurist, and his wife Sarah Ann Haynsworth. Sarah was the daughter of a prominent South Carolina family which had recently moved to Alabama; she died in 1835. His childhood was spent in Mobile, Alabama. Gayle later joined the US Naval Academy and was appointed a midshipman in 1851. His naval career did not last very long and he resigned from the navy on 27th June 1853, returning to Mobile to complete his education at Spring Hill College.

However the sea became part of his life just a few years later, and from May to December 1856 he embarked on a trip on a steamer to South America, ultimately arriving in Peru. There he obtained command of a damaged vessel, the *Rodmond*. Gayle arranged for the repair of the ship, sailed around Cape Horn, and landed in Genoa, Italy, in January 1857.[2] He next sailed to Sicily, arriving in March 1857.[3] He returned to the US by late May or early June, though not alone, having brought with him a "very tame & gentle" donkey which he had acquired in Sicily; this was a gift for his young nephew Willie.[4]

In June 1858 Gayle was nominated for the position of US Consul of the United States at Montevideo, to fill a vacancy.[5] In mid-June he sailed for South America, however Josiah Gorgas records that:–

> He has made an excellent arrangement with Durham & Co, Boston, he becomes their agent in Buenos Ayres and received 1/3d profits. Good luck go with him! He is a fine-hearted fellow & I hope will succeed.[6]

In April 1859 Gorgas was able to record that "He is exercising the functions of his consulate at Montevideo, entertaining a great many officers of the Paraguayan expedition". Despite being busy however, he was suffering a great deal from homesickness.

Gayle returned to his home during 1861; it has been said that he had joined the army around this time and then transferred to the navy at the end of the year as a lieutenant, but this is not true.[7] Also false is the statement that during the first two years of the Civil War he was an independent blockade runner for the Confederacy during the first two years of the Civil War.[8] In August, one Richard Haynsworth Gayle was appointed a captain in the Provisional Army of the Confederate States, as a Regimental Quartermaster (regiment unknown).[9] On June 6th, as Assistant Quartermaster, he was ordered to report to General G. P. Beauregard, at Baldwin, Mississippi.[10] On the 26th he was further ordered "to report without delay to Major Merriwether commanding the Pioneer battalion for duty with the battalion".[11] The following month he was sent to Tuscaloosa to purchase forage for eight thousand animals.[12]

In November, Gayle was Assistant Quartermaster at Tullahoma, part of the Army of Tennessee, Office of the Chief Quartermaster.[13] Gayle continued to travel, and in January was ordered to Wartrace where he was to establish himself in order to procure more forage.[14] Wartrace was the winter HQ of General Hardee and lost to the Federals in June 1863, following which Tullahoma was given up.[15] A month later he was ordered to Fayetteville, Tennessee, where he worked with Captain Semmes (not to be confused with Captain Semmes of the Alabama) of the Purchasing Company in that town.[16] Feed for animals was becoming crucial and his orders from Major McMicken at Tullahoma stated:

> It is absolutely necessary for the supply of the army, that these mills should be kept constantly in operation, and if necessary for this purpose you will transfer to Capt. Semmes such an amount of corn as he may deem necessary for this purpose. The corn you have on hand & what you purchase in future you will ship to Capt. Wood, at this place as rapidly as possible.

A week later McMicken wrote that he had received no corn for five days, despite the fact that Gayle was known to have good supplies.[17] "Rail Road Transportation from Fayetteville to this place has been furnished to you, as well as a sufficient number of wagons to haul the corn from the Cribs to Fayetteville. I desire no explanations but must have the corn here at once, and an ample supply for the future." The following week Gayle had taken over the responsibilities of a Captain Harris, who had obtained a "sick leave".[18] Once again McMicken indicated how serious the supply situation was:

> Push everything as fast as you can. I wish to get all the corn here that I can. As no dependence is to be placed in the rail road it may wash away any moment and in consequence the army be cut off from its source of supplies – You did right with the "Hay Man". In all cases act prudently but firmly.

> Mr Lamb will attend to the loading and shipping of all corn you get to Fayetteville – but get it there fast – faster.

In April Gayle was ordered to transfer all of his supplies, sacks and sack corn on hand, to Captain Semmes.[19] Six days later he received Special Order No.96 from the office of General Bragg.[20] This relieved him from duty at Fayetteville and ordered him to proceed "at once to Richmond Vir. via Winsboro S.C. and report to Colonel J. Gorgas Chief of Ordnance". On 6th May he was notified by Gorgas that he had been assigned to duty with the Ordnance Bureau, "with a view to taking charge of the steamer *R. E. Lee* whenever Captain Wilkinson, C.S. Navy, her present commander, resigns charge of her, the Secretary of the Navy having declared the services of that officer necessary in the Navy Department".[21] He was ordered to Wilmington to report to General Whiting, and then to Captain Wilkinson, with whom he was to gain some experience of blockade runner work. Gayle was to go to Bermuda and back, to assume command "whenever Captain W. desires to resign the charge of the ship, or the command become vacant from any cause, you will assume charge of her without further orders".

These orders were amended two days later, and Gayle was informed that, "as suggested by Captain Wilkinson", he would take charge of the *Cornubia* at Bermuda, "should it be found that Captain Burroughs does not return in her".[22] Gayle's final amended orders arrived the following day:

> Sir: For the instructions given you on the 6th instant from this office, the following are substituted:
>
> By the direction of the Secretary of War you have been assigned to duty with the Ordnance Bureau, with a view to taking charge in the future of a steamer in the service of the War Department.
>
> You will report to Captain Wilkinson with a view to acquiring special information in relation to navigation between Bermuda and Wilmington, and you will take such position with Captain Wilkinson during the present voyage of the *R. E. Lee* as he may deem most suitable.
>
> J. Gorgas[23]

Chapter 9

Under the Stars and Bars

The war at sea was beginning to escalate; out on the ocean, the privateer CSS *Florida* had captured and burnt the ship *Star of Peace*, bound from Calcutta for Boston.[1] She had also captured another American schooner and been chased by the USS *Vanderbilt* off Barbados, but escaped (the *Vanderbilt*, for all of her strengths, only had a top speed of 14 knots, a little less than that of the fastest runners, which were also a bit more agile). The *Alabama* was to burn sixty-five, mostly merchant, vessels in her career. The schooner *Mary Jane* had also been captured off Wilmington.

On 5th May 1863 the *Bermuda Royal Gazette* printed an article on the blockade runners. It gave a list of those ships which had used Bermuda and their current situation.

> We should premise that the first column gives the date of each vessels first arrival in Bermuda; the second its name, and the third its doings.

SAILING UNDER BRITISH COLOURS

1861		*Fingal*	Blocked up at Savannah
1862	March 20	*Bermuda*	Captured
	March 20	*Southwick*	Doubtful
	March 24	*Herald*	Ran the Blockade
	April 19	*Economist*	Returned
	April 19	*Stettin*	Captured
	May 6	*Gladiator*	Returned
	June 11	*Stanley*	Returned
	June 12	*Leopard*	Destroyed
	June 19	*Adela*	Captured
	June 30	*Lodons*	Captured
	July 1	*Columbia*	Captured
	July 20	*Anglia*	Captured
	July 21	*Kersonese*	Returned
	July 29	*Phoebe*	To Australia

	August 2	*Peterhoff*	Captured
	August 27	*Harriet Pinckney*	Returned
	Sept. 3	*Minho*	Destroyed
	Sept. 5	*Merrimac*	No news*
	Sept. 15	*Ouachita*	Captured
	Sept. 24	*Justitia*	Returned
1863	Jany. 12	*Cornubia*	Ran 4 times
	Jany. 12	*Gipsy Queen*	Returned
	Jany. 24	*Princess Royal*	Captured
	Feby. 28	*Miriam*	Returned

SAILED UNDER CONFEDERATE COLOURS

Nashville		Destroyed	
General Beauregard		Ran Blockade	
General Lee		Ran Blockade	
GRAND TOTALS			
Blocked in	1	Doubtful	2
Destroyed or captured	12	Ran the Blockade	4
Returned or went on		9	

*Arrived at Wilmington, N. C.

Concerns were now being voiced regarding the state of *Cornubia's* boilers, "which are said to be wearing out".[2] On 8th May Major Walker was asked by Josiah Gorgas to turn his attention to this problem and order new boilers, and other parts as required, from Liverpool if necessary.[3] It was hoped that she could be repaired in St George's; if *Cornubia* had to sail back to Liverpool a replacement

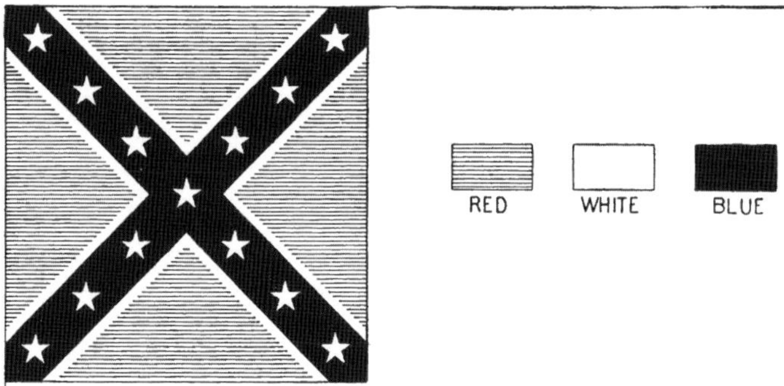

The new Confederate States Navy ensign, introduced on 1st May 1863. This is a copy of that reported by Rear-Admiral Lee to Secretary of State Gideon Welles.

Christoppher Columbus 'Kit' Morse, *Cornubia's* regular pilot.

runner would be required. However, there is no information regarding any repairs to the *Cornubia*; certainly she never went back to Liverpool for any work to be carried out; this may have come back to haunt her owners towards the end of the year. There were also concerns regarding the availability of coal at St George's as each steamer needed 160-180 tons per round trip. Major Walker only had 600 tons at St George's for which he had had to pay 45s per ton, and "was glad to get it at that price".

By about this time the *Cornubia's* regular pilot was one Christopher Columbus (Kit) Morse, a 34 year old native of Smithville, North Carolina. His father Uriah was a boat-builder and had eleven children; Kit was the first but his mother died when he was four months old.[4] One of his half-brothers, Edward Dudley, became a blockade runner captain, while another two, John and James Madison, became pilots; the former in Charleston and the latter in Fernandina, Florida. Because *Cornubia* was government-owned Morse's salary was less than it might have been on a privately-owned ship, though he earned $3,000 for piloting her at Cape Fear in May. According to James Sprunt, Morse was "counted the most skilful pilot and surfman on our coast". Quoting J. B. Smith, signalman on the *Advance*, Sprunt wrote:

> I tried to read my destiny in the imperturbable countenance of my companion, a wave of whose hand could consign me to a Northern prison, or perchance to a watery grave. As well seek to penetrate the secrets of the Sphinx as the thoughts of Kit Morse.[5]

James Sprunt reported another story of the *Cornubia*, told him by the Reverend James William Craig – 'Jim Billy' – a then a former Cape Fear River pilot, though the date of the event is not known. Jim Billy's father had been on good terms with Colonel Lamb at Fort Fisher, and had been given the duty of setting the lights that marked the channel for the blockade runners. Jim Billy did this job for the first two years of the war. While he was setting lights for the *Cornubia* to leave he was hailed by Kit Morse as she went past, who called "Don't take your lights in too soon, because if we run afoul of a blockader outside, he may run us in again, and we want the benefit of the lights". A short time later he was surprised when another steamer suddenly loomed up out of the darkness, Craig and his comrades thinking that it was a cruiser chasing the *Cornubia*.

He discovered his error when a boat was lowered over the side and he was hailed in the semi-darkness; the voice demanded to know if there was a pilot onboard. The voice proved to be that of the chief officer of the blockade runner *Orion*. The vessel had tried to run into Charleston but failed and was groping in the dark for the New Inlet Bar. The *Orion* was then brought in over the shoals and anchored safety under the guns of Fort Fisher.

During this period the *Cornubia*, still under Burroughs, left again for Wilmington on 8th May. Her cargo was more mixed this time, with cases and boxes of hardware, 250 boxes of combustible ammunition and telegraph wire as well as barrels of beef, pork and molasses.[6] To help this food down she also carried 263 cases of brandy.

The blockading squadron was strengthened again at this time with the addition of a brand new ship, the USS *Niphon*.[7] The *Niphon* was launched at Boston, Massachusetts, in February and delivered to the US Navy at Boston on 22nd April; she was commissioned at the Boston Navy Yard on 24th April with Acting

The Union blockader USS *Niphon*; the name was probably derived from 'Nippon'.

Ensign Joseph B. Breck in command. The *Niphon* is said to have been formally purchased on the 9th May 1863 but was on station off Wilmington by 7th May.

On 13th May three steamers, one paddle wheel and two with propellers, ran the blockade inward through New Inlet in the morning. They were seen from the US Steam Sloop *Iroquois* at 4:15 am but too late to chase them: the paddle steamer was at that time inside the bar and standing for the Inner Rip, one of the propeller steamers was also inside, and the other just crossing The Bar.[8] The USS *Florida*, *Niphon* and *Mount Vernon* were also nearby. The former commerce raider *Florida* had been captured at Bahia, Brazil, by the USS *Wachusett* on 7 October 1864. The paddle steamer was "very long, with two pipes not far apart and a short, light mast forward and abaft them; she appeared to be painted white. I think she is the *Cornubia*".

Acting Volunteer Lieutenant James Trathen, commanding the USS *Mount Vernon*, also reported on the chase.

> Sir: In reply to yours of this date, I have to report that at 8 p. m., on the 12th instant, I weighed anchor and stood inshore to the northward of Fort Fisher. At 8:50 I anchored in 7 fathoms water, the beach in full view, and so plainly in sight that I considered it to be impossible for anything to pass between us and it.
>
> At 2 a. m. I weighed anchor and stood down along the beach, the sky clear overhead but a mist overhanging the land. At daylight this morning we discovered three steamers inside the bar at New Inlet. At this time the U. S. S. *Niphon* fired a gun and the steamers stood up the river; Fort Fisher returned the fire.
>
> Two of these steamers were painted white, one a screw and the other a paddle steamer; the screw steamer had one mast and one smokestack; the paddle steamer had two short masts and two smokestacks. The other steamer was painted a dark color and had much the appearance of being a gunboat. She was a paddle-wheel steamer, with two masts and one smokestack, square stern, and square-rigged forward. I am, sir, very respectfully, your obedient servant...[9]

James B. Breck, commanding the USS *Niphon*, stated that his ship was on her inshore station off Smith's Island, in 4½ fathoms water, when at about daylight two steamers were discovered bearing about north by east; a third was on or over The Bar. He stood in to head them off but soon got in range of the batteries on Confederate Point. His Parrott gun fired at them but the shot fell short and the heavy guns on Fort Fisher fired on the blockaders but caused no damage. Once the steamers had crossed The Bar, the *Niphon* stood out to report to the senior officer on the station (Augustus Ludlow Case). He concluded "One steamer was of about 700 tons, three masts, two funnels, and paddle wheels; the other two were of some 300 tons, two masts, and one funnel; they were painted white or nearly so, it being difficult to tell, as the glasses furnished this ship are very bad".[10]

Cornubia was back in St George's around the 16th or 17th and had a quick turnaround, leaving again on the 19th, despite Consul Allen recording her departure having "been detained by the desertion of her engineers and a portion of her crew".[11] Given the limited space in Bermuda this seems surprising; while they may have shipped back to England on other vessels, those vessels' crews must have known who or what they were. An alternative is that they had peremptorily resigned from the ship, however under these circumstances it would have been difficult for them to get back to the UK.

In a letter dated 19th May, Consul Allen suggested that in view of the increasing traffic between Bermuda and the Southern ports, one or two "fast gunboats" posted there would have a profound effect on the "very profitable business that is now being carried on here".[12] Because of the reefs which extended around the north and west of the islands, the runners almost invariably had to make land from the southwest and then head south to get into port. A gunboat lying off the islands in that direction would be enough to keep the runners making land and, if fast enough, might capture some. However, this seems to have been a tactic never utilised by the Union forces; possibly it was too close to being a blockade of the Bermudan islands themselves, British territory.

On 22nd May 1863 *Freeman's Journal and Daily Commercial Advertiser* printed a small report entitled 'The Blockade Runners—The *Giraffe*'.

> This fine steamer, like most of our "crack" boats employed running the blockade, has been transferred to the Confederate flag; and made her debut last voyage as the *Robert E. Lee*. She has been purchased by parties, it is reported, in Wilmington, and is regularly employed running between that port and Bermuda. She has been singularly fortunate, having made over nine or ten trips to Wilmington alone. Bermuda is fast becoming as great a rendezvous for blockade runners as Nassau and Savanna, as the *R. E. Lee*, *Merrimac*, *Beauregard*, *Cornubia*, and *Columbia* make it their head quarters, trading regularly between it and Wilmington, and, in spite of the existing blockade, keeping up a regular and systematic communication between the two ports. The *Jane Gardener*, which arrived in the river on Monday, from Bermuda, brought 300 bales of cotton, being part of the cargo of one of these steamers,—*Liverpool Post*.

On 28th May the *Cornubia* was back at Wilmington with a cargo comprising 41 packages and 72 boxes of dry goods, 201 boxes of cartridges, 100 boxes of Minié rifles, 100 barrels of salt provisions, 50 boxes of tin (possibly from Cornwall), 50 pigs of lead and six carboys acid.[13] Large amounts of mail and a large number of passengers were also being carried by the runners. Returning to St George's on 2nd June in company with the *Eugenie* she carried a cargo of cotton, turpentine, and tobacco.[14] *Cornubia* left for Wilmington on 5th June with more munitions as well as 9,880 lbs of onions.[15]

Soon after Thomas Sterling Begbie had established the *Cornubia* at Bermuda, he had had her run the local measured mile; she had achieved 11 knots against a strong headwind, which was considered "not bad".[16] This was undoubtedly one of the reasons, along with the success of John Burroughs, why she was bought by the Confederate government in June 1863; Major Walker paid £10,000 (just over $51,000) on their behalf.

On 10th June Kit Morse was ordered back aboard immediately.[17] On the same day Richard Gayle was finally ordered to the *Cornubia*, though Burroughs' contract did not terminate until later that month, when he reached Bermuda, and requested to be relieved from the command at that time.[18] Gayle had presumably had a return trip with Wilkinson on the *Robert E. Lee* in the meantime. It was

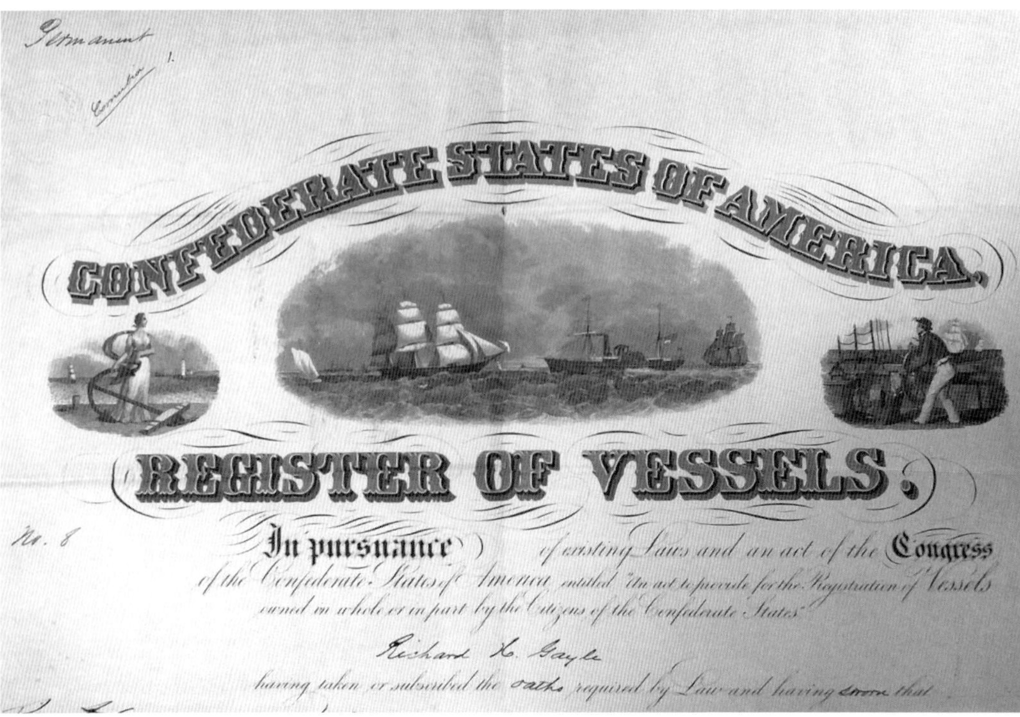

CONFEDERATE STATES OF AMERICA,

REGISTER OF VESSELS.

In pursuance of existing Laws and an act of the Congress of the Confederate States of America entitled "An act to provide for the Registration of Vessels owned in whole or in part by the Citizens of the Confederate States"

Richard H. Gayle

having taken or subscribed the oaths required by Law and having sworn that

Richard Gayle's appointment to take charge of the *Cornubia*.

thought best that Gayle should assume command at Wilmington. Burroughs had requested to accompany Gayle, "giving you the benefit of his experience and advice. He will also be able to assist you very much in retaining good officers and crew".[19] On 13th June, Gayle was given orders to "take immediate steps to change your flag and register under Confederate colors; your crew will be shipped under them".[20] Any of his crew declining to reship would be discharged and given free passage to Bermuda, to be paid up to arrival there.

On 16th June an order was sent out from Josiah Seixas (agent of the Confederate War Depatment) to Richard Gayle; the tone is rather curt but is regarding an important concern:

> Captain: I have been instructed by Colonel Gorgas to communicate the following instructions to you, which have been established in reference to the Government steamers and have been approved by the Secretary of War:
>
> No passenger or private freight shall be received aboard ship except by order of the agent.
>
> No engineer shall be employed unless with the written approval of the commanding officer of the vessel on which he is to serve.
>
> A list of the cargo, including private and public freight, shall be furnished the agent at Bermuda and at this port immediately on arrival of each steamer.
>
> An exact statement of the disbursements of each steamer will be required from the purser before clearance, and it is expected that he will obtain the bills incurred by him, and which he has to pay, properly approved by the captain and receipted.
>
> This statement must include all payments for any purposes whatever. The voyage will begin and end here.
>
> The entire ship's accounts will be forwarded through this agency. Respectfully, your obedient servant,[21]

The *Cornubia*, as owned by the Confederate government, had to be seen to be operating within the rules of the blockade, providing proper bills of lading and only carrying cargoes approved by the government.

On 20th June the *Cornubia* arrived in St George's carrying 17 bales of cotton, 20 barrels of turpentine, and important dispatches from the Confederate government to the British government. This cargo seems very light and it appears that this was all of the cotton available at Wilmington for shipment, the rest having been

The steam tug *James Gray*, later the *Lady Davis*.

destroyed by fire.[22] *Cornubia* was now officially the *Lady Davis*, named for the wife of Jefferson Davis by James Seddon, Secretary for the Confederate Navy, though she was rarely called by that name; it is possible that this was an informal change of name and not included in her registry papers.

There had already been a *Lady Davis* in the Confederate Navy, this being an iron hulled steam tug, originally the *James Grey*, which had been converted to a gunboat.[23] The *James Gray* was launched in the same year as the *Cornubia* and acquired by Governor Francis Wilkinson Pickens of South Carolina, who armed her, in March 1861. On 7th May 1861 *Lady Davis* was purchased by the Confederacy for $32,000 and commissioned in the Confederate Navy, thereafter operating along the Georgia and South Carolina coasts. For a time she served as the flagship of Commodore Josiah Tatthall's Savannah Defence Squadron,

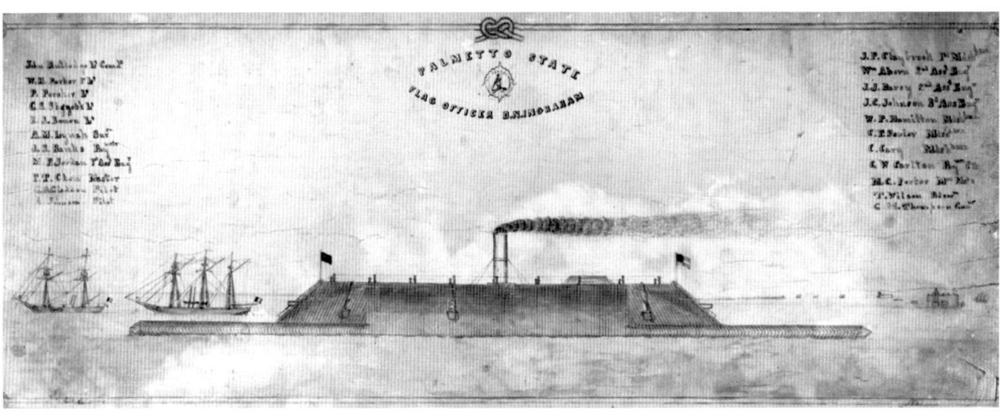

The iron-clad ram CSS *Palmetto State*. The casemate carried 4-inch armour over 22 inches of wood and she was armed with two 7-inch Brooke rifled canon and two 9-inch smooth-bore Dahlgren cannon.

consisting of the CSS *Savannah*, CSS *Sampson* and CSS *Resolute*.

Although her engines were transferred to the CSS *Palmetto State* late in 1862, well-built iron hulls were in great demand and she was able to continue her successful career as a privately owned blockade runner out of Charleston, South Carolina. With the occupation of Charleston in 1865 by Federal forces, *Lady Davis* was captured and turned over to the Light House Board by Admiral John A. Dahlgren.

When the *Cornubia* had left Wilmington on the 16th, ten other blockade runners were in the port, two of which left with her; eight steamers were still in port waiting for cotton, all the supplies there having been destroyed by fire.[24] Just like St George's, Wilmington was undergoing its own phase of "incendiarism" (see below). So efficiently was the *Cornubia* running the blockade that the *Bermuda Royal Gazette* stated that "This vessel now runs with the regularity of a packet, between these islands and Wilmington, notwithstanding the very efficient blockade which is set to be kept at that place".[25] However, all was not as easy as it seemed and the following day a US cruiser sighted and pursued the *Cornubia*, faster than her and running her down. *Cornubia* was not only carrying contraband but also several Confederate officers and agents; another passenger was Clement Laird Vallandigham. Vallandigham was an Ohio politician and leader of the Copperhead faction of anti-war Democrats during the Civil War. He served two terms in the United States House of Representatives.[26]

Clement Laird Vallandigham

Being concerned that the cruiser was rapidly bearing down on his ship, Captain Burroughs asked Vallandigham if he had any British uniforms onboard. On receiving an assent, Burroughs dressed up as many of his men as possible, to make *Cornubia* look like a British transport. Seeing so many scarlet jackets, the cruiser then went off on her original course, leaving Burroughs, his relieved crew and passengers, to carry on to Bermuda. There seems no reason for Vallandigham to have these uniforms and no reason seems to have been given and one wonders if this is a tale which has "grown with the telling". Another point against this story is that the likelihood of a Federal cruiser running down on the *Cornubia*, still one of the fastest steamers afloat, seems vanishingly small.

Vallandigham had been causing problems in the United States. While in the Ohio state legislature, he voted against the repeal of the "Black Laws" (laws against the civil rights of African-Americans), but wanted the question put to a referendum by the voters. He was also a vigorous supporter of constitutional states' rights. He believed the federal government had no power to regulate a legal institution, which slavery then was. He also believed the states had a right to secede and that the Confederacy could not constitutionally be conquered militarily.

Vallandigham supported the Crittenden Compromise.[27] He blamed sectionalism and anti-slavery sentiment for the secession crisis. He proposed a series of amendments to the US Constitution. The United States would be divided into four sections: North, South, West and Pacific. The four sections would each have the power in the Senate to veto legislation. The Electoral College would be modified. The term of President and Vice-President would be increased to six years and limited to one term unless two thirds of the electors agreed. Secession by a state could only be agreed to if the legislatures of the sections approved it. Migration between the sections was a guaranteed right.

After General Ambrose E. Burnside issued General Order Number 38, warning that the "habit of declaring sympathies for the enemy" would not be tolerated in the Military District of Ohio, Vallandigham gave a major speech on May 1, 1863, charging that the war was being fought, not to save the Union, but to free the slaves by sacrificing the liberty of all Americans to "King Lincoln". Burnside also suppressed circulation of the *Chicago Times*. On 5th May 1863, Vallandigham was arrested as a violator of the General Order, following which his enraged supporters burned the offices of the *Dayton Journal*, the Republican rival to the *Empire*. Vallandigham was tried by a military court on 6th and 7th May. His speech at Mount Vernon, Ohio (after which the ship was named) was cited as the source of the arrest.

On 19th May 1863 President Lincoln ordered that Vallandigham be deported and sent to the Confederacy. When he was within Confederate lines, Vallandigham said: "I am a citizen of Ohio, and of the United States. I am here within your lines by force, and against my will. I therefore surrender myself to you as a prisoner of war". To add insult to injury, on 2nd June, having been banished to the South,

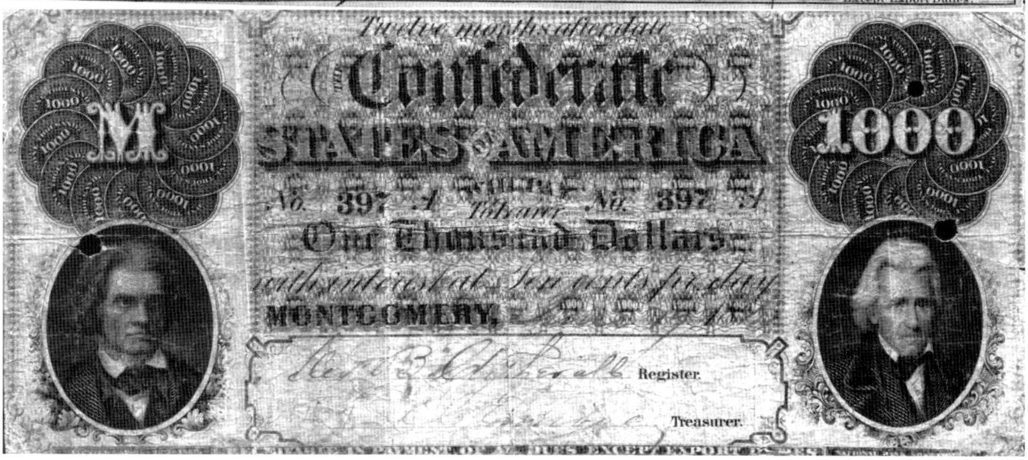

Confederate currency was backed by cheap cotton, not by hard assets, and simply by a promise to pay the bearer after the war, on the prospect of Southern victory and independence. Early in the war the currency was high, but rapidly fell in value as the war progressed.

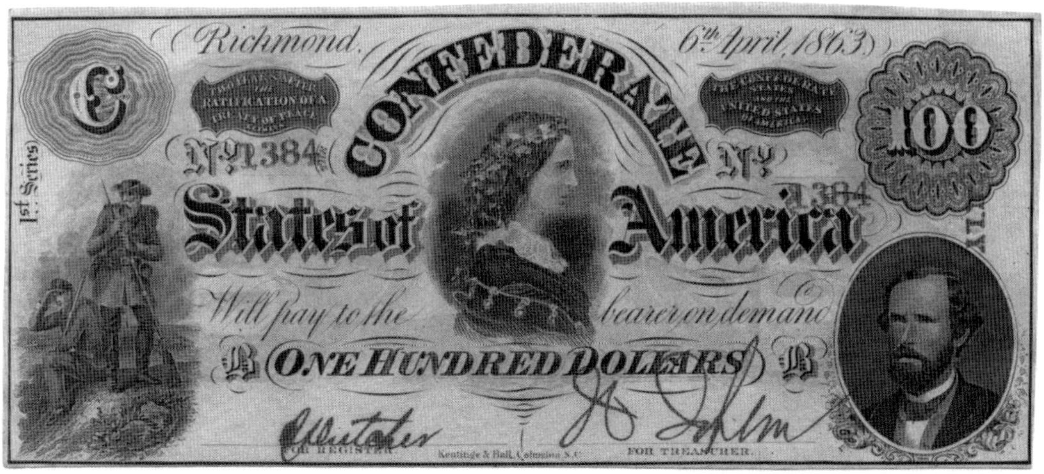

Vallandigham was sent to Wilmington by President Davis and put under guard as an "alien enemy".

Vallandigham travelled to Richmond, Virginia, where he told Robert Ould (Lawyer, Officer, Assistant Secretary of War (briefly) and Chief of the Bureau of Exchange for the Confederate States of America) not to invade Pennsylvania because it would unite the North against the Copperheads in the 1864 presidential election. However, a letter to the Editor of *The New York Times* gave a different version, saying that Vallandigham had encouraged the invasion.

On 30th June Major Walker was at his wit's end regarding the coal problem. Desperately writing again to Caleb Huse he said:

> Send us coal, coal, coal! Each steamer takes one hundred and eighty tons – so that six hundred tons will quickly be consumed.[28]

By the end of June yet another new vessel arrived on the scene, the USS *James Adger*.[29] The *Adger* had been launched in 1851 in New York, built by William H. Webb; she was purchased by the US Navy for $85,000 and commissioned on 20th September 1861, commander John B. Merchand. On 19th December she was sent to help blockade Georgetown and in April ordered to Port Royal for repairs. On 14th May 1862 she was sent to Charleston. The following year she was recalled to Port Royal to embark prisoners (the crew of the CSS *Atlanta*) for passage to Fort Monroe, following which she steamed to Philadelphia for new boilers.[30] Arriving there on the 25th June (she was involved in a collision with an unknown steamer off Cape Henry, Virginia, on the night of the 24th) she was coaled and immediately sent off in pursuit of the Confederate commerce raider CSS *Tacony*, then operating against Union merchantmen far up the East Coast. She arrived New York on 3rd July but four days later, despite her repairs not having been carried out she received orders for Wilmington for duty with the North Atlantic Blockading Squadron.[31]

On 30th June the *Harriet Pinckney* cleared St George's for Halifax, Nova Scotia. Apart from 440 bales of cotton she carried an interesting collection of passengers, including Clement Vallandigham and Captains Halpin, Burroughs and Stiles.[32] Other passengers were John Martin, a Royal Navy storekeeper, Dr Rein, Major Pirson, William Tucker and two members of the 39th Regiment, Dr Abbott and Sergeant-Major Kearney, the latter with his family. After reaching Canada, Vallandigham declared himself a candidate for Governor of Ohio, subsequently winning the Democratic nomination *in absentia*.[33] (Outraged at his treatment by Lincoln, the Ohio Democrats, by a vote of 411-11, nominated Vallandigham for governor at their 11th June convention.) He managed his

Where it all began in 1858: the quaysides at Hayle. The original shipyard slipways are buried behind the wall in the centre of the image. The channel on the right is from the Carnsew Pool, used to provide water to clear out the channel. One of the few original foundry buildings can be seen at right rear.

St George's Harbour, Bermuda, during the Civil War: many blockade runners can be seen in this image, including one on the right which is very similar to the *Cornubia.*

John Staples
The Hayle & Bristol S
"COR
(OFF

Bristol. 1859.

...acket Co.s Iron Steam Ship

...BIA."

...EAD.)

Raphael Semmes aboard the CSS *Alabama*. NHHC image NH 44519-KN.

The USS *Kearsarge* meets the CSS *Alabama*, already sinking. NHHC image K 29827.

campaign from a hotel in Windsor, Ontario, where he received a steady stream of visitors and supporters.

On Saturday 4th July a "grand pic-nic" was held at Walsingham Caves, organised by the officers of the *Cornubia*, *Eugenie* and *Emma*, to celebrate Independence Day.[34] "Champagne, dancing and good cheer in general" took place, with the three steamers "gay enough dressed," though in the case of the *Eugenie* with the new Confederate flag alone. Up to 100 people, ships' crews and various invited guests, were ferried to the stalactite-filled grotto from about 10am. An exploration expedition into the caves was one of the first steps on arrival, "and a number of ladies, escorted by gentlemen of the party, threaded their way through the mazy, slippery and, we are sorry to add, grimy windings of the subterranean galleries, regardless alike of the dangers of sprained ankles and soiled dresses". Once the exploring party reappeared, a luncheon was served under the Calabash Tree which overhung the mouth of one of the caves. The tables were served three times in succession. Captain Gordon presided in the place of Captain Gayle, who was too ill to attend. 'Captain' (purser) J. T. Gordon (who was probably on one of the other two vessels at this time) made an introductory address which was followed by several toasts, the most interesting of which was

> "The Sovereign who reigns in the hearts of her Subjects with the Sceptre of Love – Queen Victoria". This was received with demonstrations worthy of the esteem and affection entertained for Her Majesty – Capt. Leslie, of the Str. Emma, was called out, and responded very feelingly.

Recovered or not, Gayle with the *Cornubia* left Bermuda on 9th July with cargoes from the *Harriet Pinckney*, *Merrimac* and the *Alpha*, the latter from Halifax.[35] Once again most of this appears to be munitions, though 190 barrels of beef and pork were included. On her arrival at Wilmington she was found to have carried "47 cases art. carbines" and "12 cases cav. carbines": of these, 940 artillery carbines were sent to the Selma Arsenal in the CSS *Alabama* under the command of Captain White, while the 240 cavalry carbines were sent to Major Downer at Richmond.

It was at about this time that there were reported to be seventeen blockade runners at Wilmington, five of which were owned by the Confederate government.[36] One was reported to have landed a hundred pieces of field artillery, while cargoes of bacon had arrived "from Cincinnati via New York, Liverpool, Nassau and Bermuda". It was rumoured that this could supply an army of one hundred thousand men for a year. Two gunboats were also reported at Wilmington, one ready for sea and the other nearly. The *Cornubia* was due to leave the port on the 22nd for a cargo for the latter.

The desperate Major Walker wrote again to Huse on 9th July regarding his impoverished coal stocks; the following day he ran out.[37] On 22nd July, Gayle was informed that he had been appointed lieutenant for the war by the Confederate President. He was required to sign an oath of office before a magistrate should he accept.[38]

The next day Major Smith Stansbury wrote to Huse stating that the *Florida* and the *Robert E. Lee* were unable to leave because they had no coal and that he had had to send to Halifax, Nova Scotia, for supplies.[39] What he needed was 700 tons of "Cardiff coals" (*i.e.* anthracite, which was more fuel efficient and produced a much less cloudy smoke; the export of this smokeless coal had been banned by the United States early on in the war) per month and a stockpile of 2,000 tons.

The blockade runner *Advance*, sometimes (incorrectly) called the *A. D. Vance*.

Gayle was in Wilmington when he received his appointment, having arrived on 14th July, and he, with the *Cornubia*, was back in St George's on the 27th, her cargo comprising 236 bales cotton, 32 barrels of turpentine and 104½ tierces (a barrel equal to 1-6th of a tun) of tobacco.[40] This was her 8th round trip. She arrived at St George's with the *Eugenie*, *Banshee* and *Lord Clyde* (*Advance*), while the *Merrimac* and *Emma* were also expected; none of these could leave because of the lack of coal. Tactfully, Major Walker wrote to Huse:

> Fearful that in your pressing engagements you might overlook this important subject, I wrote to Messrs. Fraser, Trenholm & Co., soliciting

shipments. Their letter of May 12 informs me that they had called your attention to the subject, and that in the mean time they would make shipments themselves.[41]

On the same day Major Walker, in a letter to Caleb Huse, reported an unusual event:

> The *Florida* has been in port for nine days. After undergoing pretty thorough repairs, she went to sea last evening. The day after her arrival she saluted Her Majesty's ensign, which was handsomely returned with twenty-one guns. This is the first salute which the flag of the Confederate States has ever received in a foreign port, and consequently we dwellers in the little island of Bermuda think very proudly of it.[42]

The *Harriet Pinckney*, which had been despatched to Halifax for coal, had recently returned, just in time to supply the *Florida* and the *Robert E. Lee*. Unfortunately, she only carried 300 tons, which was quickly disbursed.[43]

On 31st July Rear-Admiral Lee wrote to Gideon Welles regarding his concerns over the state of the blockade and the condition of his vessels. After meeting the *State of Georgia* at Hampton Roads he had sent her on to Philadelphia for repairs; the *Penobscot* was also waiting for work to be carried out.[44] Neither the *Cambridge* nor the *Shenandoah* had rejoined the blockade "which is now at this trying time very weak". The *Mount Vernon* had been condemned and the *James Adger* was suffering from "low speed and weak boilers". It had been suggested that the *Merrimac* be taken into service and sent to his part of the blockade. The *Merrimac* had been captured by the *Iroquois* off the coast of the Cape Fear River on 24th July; however she would not be purchased by the Navy from the New York Prize Court until 10th March 1864. She was lost in a storm on 17th February 1865 although her crew, under Acting Master William Earle, was saved.[45]

Yet another order regarding certain blockade runners was distributed by Gideon Welles on 4th August:

> Order of the Secretary of the Navy to Commander Navy, U. S. Navy, commanding U. S. S. Connecticut, to cruise for the interception of blockade runners
>
> Navy Department, August 4, 1863.
>
> Sir: Proceed on the *Connecticut* with all possible dispatch to cruise offshore in the tracks of vessels bound to Wilmington from Bermuda and Nassau. I transmit herewith some printed extracts containing information relative

to vessels that are engaged in running the blockade. The most noted that ply between Bermuda and Wilmington are the *Robert E. Lee* and the *Cornubia*, the latter now called the *Jeff Davis*.

The Department desires to call your special attention to the *Sumter*, now called *Gibraltar*, which sailed from Liverpool on the 3d of July last. She has on board, it is said, a number of guns in cases, also two very large Blakeley guns and munitions of war.

When out of coal proceed to Hampton Roads and replenish. Should you capture any steamers, send them to Boston for adjudication. Very respectfully, etc.

Gideon Welles,

Secretary of the Navy

Commander John J. Almy,

Commander of U. S. S. Connecticut, New York[46]

The reference to sending captured 'prize' steamers for adjudication was an old practice whereby captured vessels and their cargoes could be sold on, the ships often transferring into the opposing navy. The proceeds of the sale would go towards the crew, though the crews of other vessels in sight were usually eligible for a share, as were the local commanding officers. Many British naval captains and their admirals made fortunes this way fighting the French and Spanish.

At the beginning of August, on the 5th, two fires broke out in St George's.[47] The first broke out about midday among the cotton bales on one of the wharves. Fortunately, both the *Cornubia* and *Eugenie* were in port close enough to render assistance with their fire engines and crews. Once the main fire was being damped down the process of moving and heaving the ruined cotton bales into the harbour started and more than 200 bales were disposed of; by 7 o'clock in the evening only the bottom tier of bales remained. By this time the men from the two steamers alongside were "pretty well fagged" and the *Cornubia* hauled off into the harbour, being replaced by the *Ella and Annie*, which continued to play water hoses on the remaining bales throughout the rest of the night.

The *Bermuda Royal Gazette* said that "serious troubles" were occurring from Negro labourers, who were demanding higher wages for their work discharging blockade runners. Possibly with regard to the fire, the report finished "Several assassinations have occurred, and incendiarism is frequent". Following the fire a meeting of citizens was held, and a reward of £200 offered for the arrest of the culprit. Another reward, of £500, was being offered for the person behind an unsuccessful assassination attempt. In addition, John T. Bourne had summarily

Acting Master Frank Bonneau.

dismissed all of his manual labourers, then earning 8s per day, and offered to take them back at 6s.[48] This did not go down well with these men, many of whom were wandering the streets late into the nights.

On 13th August 1863 the *Cornubia*, with *Gibraltar*, *Venus*, *Eugenie* and *Advance* all sailed for Wilmington. The *Cornubia*, *Gibraltar* and the *Advance* all arrived in Wilmington safely; however the *Gibraltar* had broken down before arrival "and sailed through the blockade, the enemy taking her for one of their own ships". The *Gibraltar* had sailed from Liverpool at the beginning of July with guns in cases as well as "two very large Blakeley guns and munitions of war".[49] The *Eugenie* arrived on 25th August, as did the *Cornubia*, where she had unloaded 226 cases of rifles and 2 cases gun fittings, which included 4,824 Austrian rifle-muskets.[50] This shipment was to have included 12,000 Austrian rifle-muskets from the *Ella and Annie*. Loading of these arms commenced at St. George's on 1 September 1863, however their departure aboard the *Ella and Annie* was delayed, ostensibly for coaling, but later it was reported

> My faithful and efficient clerk Mr Gibson and I toiled to get the "Ella and Annie" off with her precious cargo. If Captain Bonneau had taken the same interest, I am satisfied that his steamer could have left a week earlier than she did . . . In the meantime Captain B. beguiled his time in Hamilton, 12 miles distant. He says that he was sick, but if common report is to be credited, a woman who came over with him was the magnet, which detracted him from his duty.[51]

At this time, Colonel Lamarr, an agent for the Confederate States in Paris, was negotiating Confederate cotton bonds.[52] Confederate currency was all but worthless in Europe by this time and in January 1863 the Confederate Congress had secretly authorised bankers at the noted Paris-based financial house of Erlanger et Cie to underwrite $15 million of Confederate bonds, to be denominated in British pounds or French francs. Unlike ordinary bonds these were backed only by the faith and credit of the issuing country, at the option of the holder an Erlanger certificate could be converted into a receipt for a pre-specified quantity of cotton. The conversion rate for the cotton bonds was fixed at 12 cents a pound, regardless of the commodity's market price, at the time about 48 cents. In addition, the bonds paid a 7 percent annual interest rate.

During July and August the South had received a supply of 50,000 muskets, as well as cannon, "some of the largest description".[53] In seven months 43 steamers had carried cargoes into Charleston and 49 into Wilmington. The difficulty of getting a ship into either harbour was described as "only nominal". So far none of the ships actually owned by the Confederate government had been captured. The problems of running the blockade were apparently so slight that *The Times* reported "the blockade of the Confederate ports is the veriest farce. On this very facility the Confederate Government found a demand that the blockade shall be declared illegal and non-existent by the nations of Europe". The latter was a reference to the 4th Article of the Declaration of Paris, which declared that "Blockades, in order to be binding, must be effective - that is to say, maintained by a force really sufficient to prevent access to the coast of the enemy". Because of this issue the Confederate government intended to formally dispute the legality of the blockade.

The *Times* also provided some very positive information regarding how the South was surviving the blockade. It claimed that the South was stronger "and better in heart than ever".[54] After two years of hostilities larger supplies of food were available, more military stores had arrived and the armies consequently better provided for. The Confederate States which had formerly imported flour from the North, allegedly had enough flour to supply the entire population for three years. However, the following winter potatoes, meat and flour for the army would be rationed. Even so, "Articles of every kind have been run through the blockade in enormous quantities".

It was on 4th September that J. T. Gordon was attached to the *Cornubia*, then in Wilmington, as Purser. Gordon kept a small notebook, a "diary of current events" between this date and 7th November.[55] On 5th September, at 11:25 pm, *Cornubia* left her anchorage off Fort Fisher and crossed The Bar at 00:25. Despite the bright moon, and the fact that "the furnaces were so hot that the flame flashed out over the tops of the funnels or smokestacks" the Union cruiser spotted at 3am did not see the *Cornubia*. Despite the pleasant weather on the 6th, some of the passengers were sea sick, though Professor Bledsoe, "the most agreeable sea sick companion I ever met with" was only slightly so and able to joke about it.

Albert T. Bledsoe, an Episcopal priest, attorney and professor of mathematics, entered Confederate service in 1861 as a colonel and later became assistant Secretary of War.[56] He was then sent to London in order to research various historical problems relating to the North-South conflict, as well as guiding British public opinion in favour of the Confederate cause. After the war he became an apologist for the South.

Francis (Frank) Nathaniel Bonneau, Acting Master of the steamer *Ella and Annie*, wrote to Major Walker on 7th September regarding the finances required for his vessel to make a return trip to Texas.[57] Bonneau had been informed that Walker would disburse the required funds.

> Dear Sir: It will require the following amount of money to disburse the *Ella and Annie* upon the trip she is about to make to Texas and return, which amount I was informed by the agent of the War Department would be furnished by you, viz:[58]
>
> Pilotage, harbor fees, light dues, water, etc., at Kingston, Jamaica. $400
> 250 tons of coal at Kingston and Havana, including expense of taking same on board at $20.. $5,000
>
> Pilot engaged for Sabine Pass, $1,000; if he proves himself a good pilot, $250 to be paid for the balance upon arrival there. Recommended by Captain Stiles, of the Confederate Navy, as a good pilot............ $1,000
>
> Port expense in Havana:
> Tonnage fee, $2.50 per ton, 800 tons.. $2,000
> Light fee, harbor dues, etc., which in Havana are unusually large and numerous.. $2,000
>
> Total $10,400

On Tuesday 8th September 1863 the *Cornubia* was back at the Bermuda light, having completed another round trip; the journey from Wilmington had taken 64½ hours; she was back in St George's harbour by 6am.[59] *Cornubia's* cargo was 384 bales of cotton with some turpentine and specie. Whilst in Wilmington, the editor of the *Wilmington Daily Journal* received, through Richard Gayle, from Joseph Long, *Cornubia's* chief mate, one hundred dollars, with the request that it should be applied to the relief of the sick and wounded soldiers.[60] However, it was decided later that the money was needed more at Charleston, to where it was sent. "In order to prevent miscarriage, we will hand it to a North Carolina officer of high standing now here, but about to return to his command at Charleston".

It was not until 9th September that the *Ella and Annie* finally set off for the Texas coast. Bonneau's voyage was not a good one; initially he turned back when a Union blockader spotted his ship. Two days later he ran into a major storm that tore away her paddle boxes, wheel-house and hatches and caused other damage; it was not until the 14th that she managed to creep back into St. George's harbour.[61] According to Bonneau, the ship hove-to at 7am on the Friday morning (about a hundred miles from Bermuda) in gale-force winds; at noon the wind reached hurricane force, the sea breaking completely over the vessel. Back at St George's the most water damaged of the weapons onboard were transferred to the *Cornubia* so that they could be refurbished in the Confederacy, since St. George's had no facilities for repair or examination of muskets and rifles.

> St. George's Ba.
>
> September 14th, 1863
>
> Capt. Gayle, Steamer "Cornubia"
>
> Captain - Please receive on board: 150 coils rope, 27 bales hammocks, 4 casks, 6 bales (cotton shirts), 8 bales white flannel shirts, 4 bales blue cloth great coats, 5 bales duck trousers, 33 bales duck frocks, 2 boxes combs, 2 casks tin pots.
>
> Per Geo. G. Gibson
>
> Major Smith Stansbury[62]

A number of passengers had journeyed out with the *Cornubia* from Wilmington. These included Gordon's companion Professor Bledsoe, Commodore James Barron, a Mr Volk and Lieutenant William Conway Whittle II, "all of whom are very pleasant company".[63] Commodore Barron was yet another former US Navy officer; former commander of the USS *John Adams* (as Commander) and the USS *Wabash* (as Captain) he had resigned his commission in April 1861, though this was denied by the US Navy and he was subsequently listed as having been dismissed.[64]

Barron then accepted a commission as Captain in the Virginia Navy and, as chief of the Office of Naval Detail and Equipment, later assisting in organising the coastal defence of the Virginia and North Carolina coastlines. After holding several other positions, Barron was captured during the Battle of Hatteras Inlet and later released during a prisoner exchanged in 1862. His appearance on the *Cornubia* came about because he had been assigned to go to Liverpool to take command of the two Laird's Rams, the CSS *North Carolina* and the CSS *Mississippi* (later renamed, after intervention by the British government, the *El Toussoun* and *El Monastir*). After this he travelled to France, remaining in Paris as "Flag Officer" commanding the Confederate States Naval Forces in Europe and acting as a contact for Confederate naval officers as well as blockade runners and privateers until 25th February 1865.

The journey from Wilmington was later described by Lieutenant Conway Whittle:

> Every light on our vessel was out except one in the binnacle, and the strictest silence was observed except an occasional "starboard" or "port" from the pilot. Just at 12 the moon rose increasing the danger of our being seen and chased. At 12:30 the lead colored, low sidewheel steamer *Cornubia* crossed the bar and stood boldly out with every eye on board cast ahead of the vessel, which was going at a rate of thirteen miles per hour, and straining every nerve to catch a glimpse of some Yankee blockader awaiting to catch rebels who attempt to run out. The moon was up now and as far as that was concerned the chances against us — another tell-tale which calculated to lead to our discovery was this — not withstanding all

CSS *Mississippi* foreground being watched by the HMS *Majestic* while the CSS *North Carolina* is at anchor to the rear

precautions to prevent some of the bad Wilmington bituminous soft coal got mixed with our good anthracite and just as we got into the dangerous neighborhood a black column of smoke came from our smokestack and I expected any moment to see ahead of us a signal rocket which always proceeds the boom of a Yankee gun — but I was agreeably disappointed. The black smoke had all passed out when an order was carefully passed to put the helm to starboard, that there was a Yankee right ahead. We discovered him not too soon and it was not long before we lost sight of his low black hull on our starboard quarter. The danger was now half over. We had passed through the inner line — about 10 mile further out we ran right close to another Yankee steamer underway — we were so near that we could distinguish that he was a walking beam side wheel steamer. He must have seen us and mistaken our vessel for one of theirs.[65]

Cornubia left St George's on 18th September, the start of her ninth round trip. However, there were rumours that all was not well; in a letter from Major Stansbury to Colonel Gorgas, the former wrote:

Colonel: The Steamer "Cornubia" left this Port on the 18th, Instant for Wilmington. It is commonly reported, and believed, that she was captured shortly after her departure by one of the enemy's cruisers, and seen in company with her. I however discredit this report, but will send by the next Steamer a copy of all papers forwarded by the "Cornubia".[66]

A somewhat amusing chance meeting was described by Purser Gordon in his diary:

Tuesday 22d Sept 22 1863

Pleasant clear weather. At day light, sighted an Hermaphrodite Brig on the starboard bow, in distance [a hermaphrodite brig is a two-masted sailing ship which has square sails on the foremast combined with a schooner rig on the mainmast (a triangular topsail over a gaff mainsail). As such it has a mix of the two main types of sail plan, hence the term hermaphrodite]. She hoisted the Yankee flag, with the Union down, as a signal of distress - Her Fore & maintopmasts were carried away, shorn off at the cap. She was under Fore Staysail, Foresail, main staysail & new storm topsail. We went down to her to see what was the matter & if we could aid her. She proved to be the "Caroline" of East Machias, bound to New York. When we hailed her & asked what was the matter, she answered "can't you see what is the matter" - where upon we kept on our course, rejoicing.

The Cape Lookout lighthouses were made in the afternoon and *Cornubia* made land at sunset; by 2.30am she was off Fort Fisher and safe, though not completely so; passing over the New Inlet Bar at 6am she grounded on The Rip, and was stuck there until the afternoon's high tide; it was not until the quarantine station below Wilmington was reached that *Cornubia* could anchor for the night.[67]

Of the 201 cases (4,824 pieces) of Austrian rifles brought into Wilmington and unloaded on 25th September, 193 cases were sent to Major Cuyler at Macon, Georgia, where they presumably could be refurbished, while four cases were sent to Captain J. C. Little at Fort Fisher for its garrison.[68]

On 25th September a letter was sent out from Josiah Gorgas to Richard Gayle giving guidance on keeping the ownership of the *Cornubia* as discreet as possible:

> Sir: For special reasons it is deemed advisable that our steamers engaged in running the blockade should not carry pennants or other insignia of vessels of war. You are requested when in foreign ports to carefully guard against all acts tending in any manner to cause issuance of orders by the authorities curtailing the facilities and privileges our vessels now enjoy. Your conduct should be such as to leave the impression that your steamer does not belong to the Government, but is simply used by it as a carrier.[69]

In October the Confederate agents were still making enquiries regarding the acquisition of new ships from England. On the 2nd the London Engineering & Iron Shipbuilding Company Ltd. of Cubitt Town, London, wrote stating that its previous contract would remain in place for three months after 25th October.[70] The company was prepared to build three steamers of specified dimensions and price, to be delivered ready for furnishing for sea at the end of four months from the date of their having received a deposit instalment. A model had been made, to be given to the boatyard at Richmond.

In another letter, this from 3rd October, the Blackwall Iron Works gave an undertaking to

> ... supply you with marine screw engines for line of battle ships or rams from 200-horsepower to 400-horsepower for the sum of £48 10s. per horsepower, to be made of the best material and workmanship, all the pipes to be copper, engine bearings moving in the best gun metal, or white metal, if approved, to be finished to the entire satisfaction of any person the mercantile marine company or yourselves may appoint; and I also agree to make the engines from plans and specifications to be sent home from

the Confederate Government's engineer, and to be finished in six to eight months from date of order.[71]

The company was also prepared to send men out to put the engines in their respective ships, though at the expense of the Confederate government.

Gordon's diary entry for the 3rd, though it starts with "nothing of interest" it concludes with "Late in the evening went up to Fair Bluff with an interesting young lady - at 2 o'clock at night started back supply arrived in Wilmington at 6 a.m". Unfortunately, the name of the interesting young lady is not given, nor the reasons that she was regarded as such.

On 5th October, Colonel Lamarr, now in Paris, received a letter from John Burroughs; this is almost certainly not the same man who first captained the *Cornubia* for the South. He wrote:

No. 4 Madison-place, London, E. C.,

Oct. 5, 1863. Col. Lamar, Paris:

Dear Sir:

Mr. Bigbee has not yet returned to London, but in reply to mine he says he would be willing to sell the ships he is building. The first to be ready in November and the other in December; they will draw 10 feet loaded, carry 1,200 to 1,300 bales and four days coal, full steaming. There are one or two particular advantages connected with these boats over any I have yet beard of, and to that I wish to call your attention. The engines are so constructed as to be driven at a very much higher pressure in tropical waters than any engines can be unless so constructed. The consequence is they can maintain very great speed when required. Again, they are built so as to be valuable in case of peace at a moderate cost for alterations; also, considerable attention has been paid to these maintaining a larger speed in proportion when loaded than when light, and then being so soon ready greatly increases their value over the [missing], ready in January next.

PRIVATE. -- Mr. Bigbee would, I know, like to enter into arrangement with some one like yourself, of good standing, to manage things on the other side. I can assure you, from my own knowledge, that no one in this country possesses the practical knowledge that he does, which is necessary for steamship making, and if you will make a point of letting me know when you will be in England, I shall have great pleasure in arranging for you with him. I have no doubt it will lead to business. Mr. Bigbee asks £33,000 for the first boat; the half therefore would be £17,500; this he would be disposed to take, say £10,000 either in cash or bills three to four

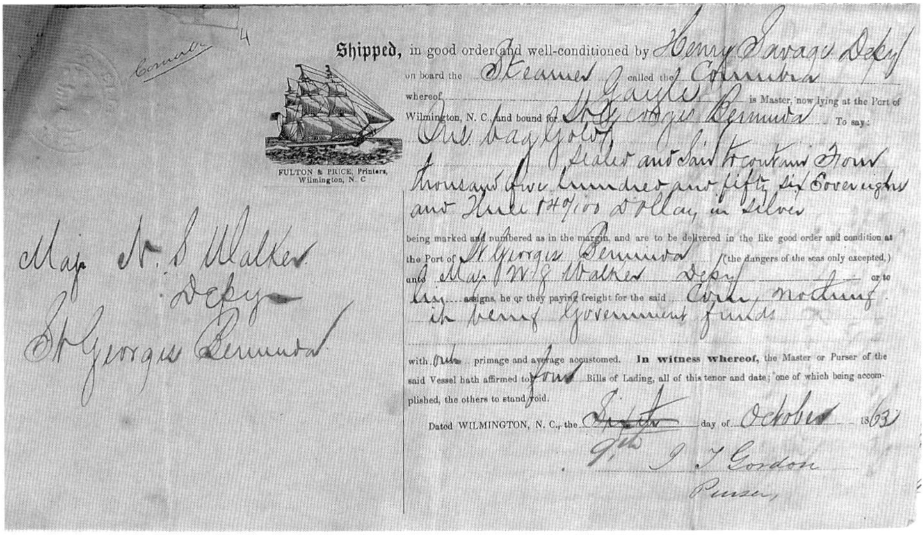

Cornubia 4

FULTON & PRICE, Printers, Wilmington, N. C.

Maj N. S. Walker Depy St Georges Bermuda

Shipped, in good order and well-conditioned by Henry Savage Depy on board the Steamer called the Cornubia whereof Gayle is Master, now lying at the Port of Wilmington, N. C. and bound for St Georges Bermuda To say: One bag gold sealed and said to contain Four thousand five hundred and fifty six Sovereigns and Three 140/100 Dollars in Silver being marked and numbered as in the margin, and are to be delivered in the like good order and condition at the Port of St Georges Bermuda (the dangers of the seas only excepted,) unto Maj. N. S. Walker Depy or to his assigns, he or they paying freight for the said Coin nothing it being Government funds with out primage and average accustomed. **In witness whereof,** the Master or Purser of the said Vessel hath affirmed to four Bills of Lading, all of this tenor and date; one of which being accomplished, the others to stand void.

Dated WILMINGTON, N. C., the ~~Sixth~~ 9th day of October 1863

J. T. Gordon
Purser

Manifests issued for the *Cornubia's* departure from Wilmington, 6th October 1863.

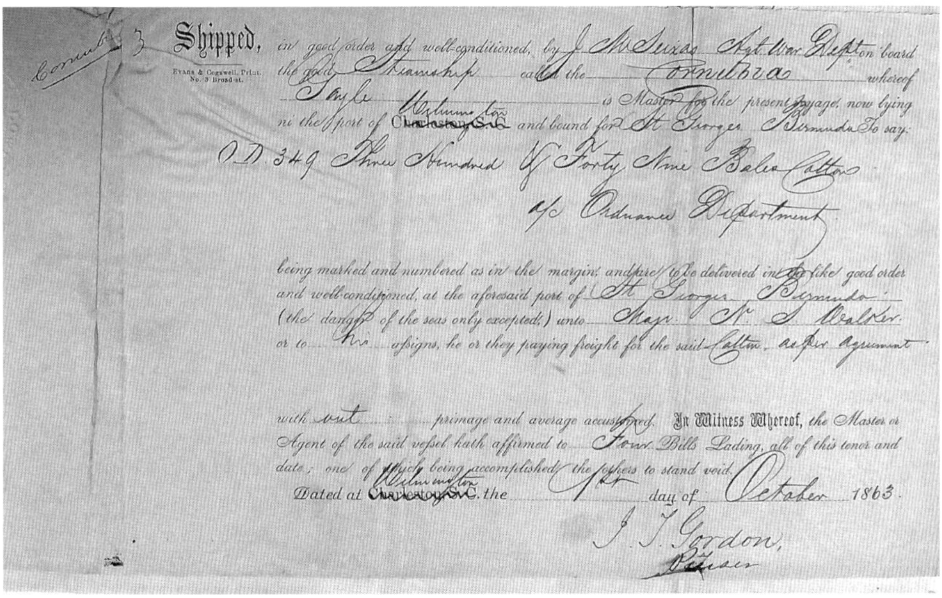

Cornubia 3

Shipped,

Evans & Cogswell, Print. No. 3 Broad st.

in good order and well-conditioned, by J. M. Seixas Agt. War Dept on board the good Steamship called the Cornubia whereof Gayle is Master for the present voyage, now lying in the port of Wilmington ~~Charleston S.C.~~ and bound for St Georges Bermuda To say:

O.D. 349 Three Hundred & Forty Nine Bales Cotton a/c Ordnance Department

being marked and numbered as in the margin, and are to be delivered in the like good order and well-conditioned, at the aforesaid port of St George Bermuda (the danger of the seas only excepted,) unto Maj. N. S. Walker or to his assigns, he or they paying freight for the said Cotton as per agreement

with out primage and average accustomed. **In Witness Whereof,** the Master or Agent of the said vessel hath affirmed to Four Bills Lading, all of this tenor and date; one of which being accomplished, the others to stand void.

Dated at Wilmington ~~Charleston S.C.~~ the 1st day of October 1863.

J. T. Gordon,
Purser

months English, and balance on ship's leaving. Awaiting the pleasure of your reply,

I am, dear Sir, yours respectfully,

John Burroughs.[72]

On October 7th another new vessel arrived to join the blockade. This was *Cornubia's* old stalker, the USS *Tuscarora*. She had returned to the Philadelphia Navy Yard late in March from her station on the eastern side of the Atlantic. In June she was sent to look for the barquentine CSS *Tacony*. Following this she headed north and cruised between Cape Henry and the coast of Nova Scotia before arriving at Boston 12 days later. During her time at sea, she failed to locate the *Tacony*. During August, *Tuscarora* searched for Confederate raiders off the Grand Banks, Newfoundland, but encountered none before she returned to Boston on 3rd September.[73] Commander Craven was not with the vessel (her captain is not recorded) however; he had been transferred to the USS *Tecumseh*, launched 12th September at Jersey City and commissioned at the New York Navy Yard on 19th April 1864.*

Colonel Lamarr was himself writing on 10th October 1863 to various parties regarding his cotton bonds. It seems that he had various deals lined up, though it is clear that some of the parties did not know who some of the others were. One of his "friends" was very uneasy that his contract was to be executed in England, though he thought it would be profitable.[74] An interesting point to note was that, with the combination of Lamarr and his friend, they would have the protection of Lord Russell, which was not extended to English merchants, "and which makes the whole business a safe one - just as much so as though we were in time of peace".

I repeat it here again, it is agreed and understood between myself and my friend, that should we get the contract transferred to him upon these gentlemen allowing him, on account of his risks, advances, or rather disbursements and influence, we would be entitled, first, to five per cent.

***On 5th August 1864 the ironclad USS *Tecumseh* was at the Battle of Mobile Bay.[75] Just after 7.30 am the *Tecumseh* struck a 'torpedo' (a mine) and sank in less than 30 seconds. Craven and 94 of his crew died; ten men were rescued by a boat from the USS *Metacomet*, "under one of the most galling fires I have ever saw"; seven men reached one of the *Tecumseh's* own boats and four were able to swim to shore, where they were captured. Of the eight Congressional Medals of Honor awarded during the battle, six were awarded to the crew of the *Metacomet* for their gallantry. On 3rd August 1873 the salvage rights to the wreck, which is upside-down in 9m of water, were sold to James E. Slaughter for $50. Three years later relatives of the dead crew petitioned Congress**

commission upon the whole value of the orders to be filled; second, thirty per cent. upon the difference between the invoice bill and the net proceeds of the cotton sold here.

These gentlemen allowing us even five per cent. upon their interest, and the money advanced by you, would make it a glorious thing.[76]

In another letter he wrote:

We have from the Confederate Government raised, or to raise in a few days, an amount of £40,000 to £45,000, in cotton bonds. We shall wish to have an advance of fifty per cent. on their value, and run the blockade on joint account with the party who will advance the money. Since the cotton in these bonds is reckoned at five pence per pound, the party who will advance that money in running the blockade will have cotton purchased at two and a half pence, since we require only £20,000 for a value of more than £40,000 in cotton bonds at five pence, to be delivered at any port of the Confederate States at thirty days' notice, at five pence. If you can't manage the thing, or if you prefer [to] buy the bonds, we shall be very glad to sell them at a fair price.[77]

On 9th October the *Cornubia* had coaled and was anchored off Fort Fisher; she was waiting to leave port the following day, along with the *Gibraltar*.[78] The latter had not been bought by the Confederates and was waiting for a crew to take her back to England, probably to have her boilers repaired, most likely the reason she had not been bought. Other vessels were the *Margaret and Jessie*, *Fannie*, *Flora* (propeller), *Flora* (side-wheel), *Antonica* and the *General Beauregard*. The *Eugenie* had been run on shore by the USS *Nansemond* on the evening of the 8th September and had been so damaged that her repairs were still not finished.[79] The *Flora* was a ship which had crossed trails with the *Cornubia* in the Bristol Channel as she was also a regular there, running from Bristol to Cork and back.

On the 10th the *Advance* ran into the Cape Fear River under heavy fire from

to stop the salvage, which was to include breaking-up the wreck with explosives. More recent projects to raise her have come to nothing though some artefacts have been recovered. She is now a war grave and under US Coast Guard surveillance. It was at this battle that Acting Rear-Admiral David Farragut is alleged to have given what has become one of the most famous naval orders of all time: "Damn the torpedoes. Four bells, Captain Drayton". Then to the commander of *Metacomet*, which was lashed to his ship's (the USS *Hartford*) side, "Go ahead, Jouett, full speed". Over the years this has become simplified to "Damn the torpedoes, full speed ahead."

the blockaders, which was replied to by the guns of Fort Fisher.[80] She managed to ground on The Rip and was still there the following day when the *Cornubia* left at 6 am. On crossing The Bar at 7am another blockader was spotted but, once again, *Cornubia* was not. In wet and squally weather the *Cornubia* stood off the land at 1 am and again at 3 am, sighting the Bermuda light at 5 am, the crossing having taken 82 hours.

Passengers on this trip included "Mrs Tyler & her little son" (Julia Gardiner Tyler, widow of United States President John Tyler), John Tyler junior (later to join the Confederate Navy, then the Army), his daughter Pearl and son Walter, their coloured nurse, a Mr G. Alexander, Mr Black and CS Navy Paymasters Moses and Harwood.[81]

During October, US Navy Lieutenant Lamson reported on prisoners which he had taken from the runner *Douro* by an interesting subterfuge.[82] In this action he was aided by D. W. Morris, also known as Norris. The latter had arrived in Wilmington via Boston and Nassau and had shipped on the *Douro* as second officer. The *Douro's* cargo consisted of 550 bales of cotton, 279 boxes tobacco, 21 tierces leaf tobacco and a quantity of turpentine and rosin, owned by the Confederate Government. Morris stated that he had entered this service purely for the purpose of obtaining information regarding blockade runners, to be given to the United States Government, and that it was his intention to betray any vessel in which he might be into the hands of any blockaders. On coming

The USS *Mount Vernon*, pencil sketch, date unknown

on board Morris gave Lieutenant Lamson two ounces of chloroform and eight ounces of laudanum, which Morris had bought to put into the whisky and water given the men in the fire room. Unfortunately there are no more details regarding the actual capture of the crew, though doubtless many of them were too weary to put up much resistance.

On 19th October Captain John Maffit wrote to Colonel Lamarr bemoaning the problems at Wilmington, at odds with the opinion printed in *The Times*.[83] "The news from the blockade runners is decidedly bad," he wrote, "Six of the last boats have recently been caught, among them the *Advance* (also known incorrectly as the *A. D. Vance*) and *Eugenia*. NOTHING HAS ENTERED WILMINGTON FOR ONE MONTH," which statement appears to be incorrect. He considered it useless to consider any steamer that could not run 17 miles (per hour). He ends "The sooner the "fastest boat in the world" is started, the better. She will become the "floating California". Which ship he was describing is not known. Despite his assertion that the *Advance* had been captured, she arrived in St George's on 26th October.

At the end of October eight steamships, including the *Cornubia*, were at St George's, with twenty-five sailing ships which carried cargoes for "the confederates". The *Boston* had arrived "leaky" from Halifax and had not yet been repaired.[84]

On 2nd November Gayle gave a party onboard; according to Gordon's diary it was "for a Bride". Georgiana Walker described *Cornubia* as

> covered in with canvas & hung with a hundred Flags; numberless lights were hung in all directions; - the band of the 39th was playing its best; the bright English redcoats enlivened the scene; the ladies were all in fine spirits; then the strains of music on the water, all conduced to making it charming.[85]

Despite this, Julia Tyler remarked that "it seems as if we had danced upon her very grave". On 4th November, starting her twelfth round trip, *Cornubia* carried a mixed cargo comprising items from several other ships:

> From W. L. Penno's warehouse, imported per *Harriet Pinckney*: 58 cases bacon, 3 casks bacon, 19 hogsheads bacon, 3 cases cartridge paper, 1 case blankets.
>
> From same warehouse, imported per *Rover's Bride*: 12 bales, 1 case
>
> From Hunter's warehouse, imported per *Glendower*, London: 15 cases caps, 36 pigs lead, 360 sacks saltpeter

A warm welcome for blockade runners: a 32-pounder smooth-bore gun mounted at the stern of the USS *Mount Vernon.*
NHHC image NH 45740

From A. J. Musson's warehouse, imported per *Miriam*, London: 64 cases rifles

From Higgs and Hyland's warehouse, imported per *Harkaway*: 4 quarter casks brandy[86]

For the blockade runners and the Confederates, this would not be a very good day, though Gordon's diary entry only includes "Pleasant weather - number of sails in sight". Just after midnight on the 7th-8th, the *Cornubia* was eleven miles north of New Inlet as Gayle prepared for his 23rd run.

Commander Thomas H. Patterson took his ship to within half a mile of the beach, and three miles to the south of Masonboro Inlet, a lookout aboard the USS *James Adger* sighted the *Cornubia* over on his port bow, just east of Masonboro Inlet. The *James Adger's* position was well fixed by the 'brilliant lights' of the salt works to the south of the Inlet.[87] The salt works, and the lights, extended for four miles south of the Inlet, an extraordinary fact in that it must have made the job of the runners much more difficult. The salt works was destroyed on 21st April 1864 by boats' crews from the USS *Niphon*, *Howquah* and *Fort Jackson*.[88]

Commander Patterson later reported:

> At midnight of the 7th instant, while lying 3½ fathoms water, about 3 miles south of Masonboro Inlet, we discovered a vessel on our port bow heading to the eastward; started in chase, but in half an hour lost sight of her. I continued chasing in the direction I had last seen her until 1am, when I concluded that if the chase was a vessel attempting to run the blockade, and seeing us stand to eastward, she would steer in for the land, hug it close, and run for New Inlet.[89]

On the fore topsail yard was the 38-year-old Acting Master Robert C. Patterson, doubtless a relative of his captain. Signals challenged the stranger but were ignored, so the *Adger* made chase. After 15 or 20 minutes a lookout on the foreyard, presumably Robert Patterson, hailed his captain and reported the strange vessel ashore and blowing off steam. On coming abreast of the grounded ship, Patterson ordered a shot to be fired over her. At this point a hail from the stranger requested a boat to be sent; Thomas Patterson then ordered the younger Patterson to take an armed crew to take possession. He also ordered his Executive Officer Lieutenant C. L. Franklin to take charge of the vessel and to determine if she could be hauled off; if not she was to be destroyed.[90]

During the chase, Patterson had driven the stranger towards another blockader, her old antagonist the USS *Niphon*. Her captain, Acting Master J. B. Breck, reported

The USS *James Adger*, pencil sketch, date unknown

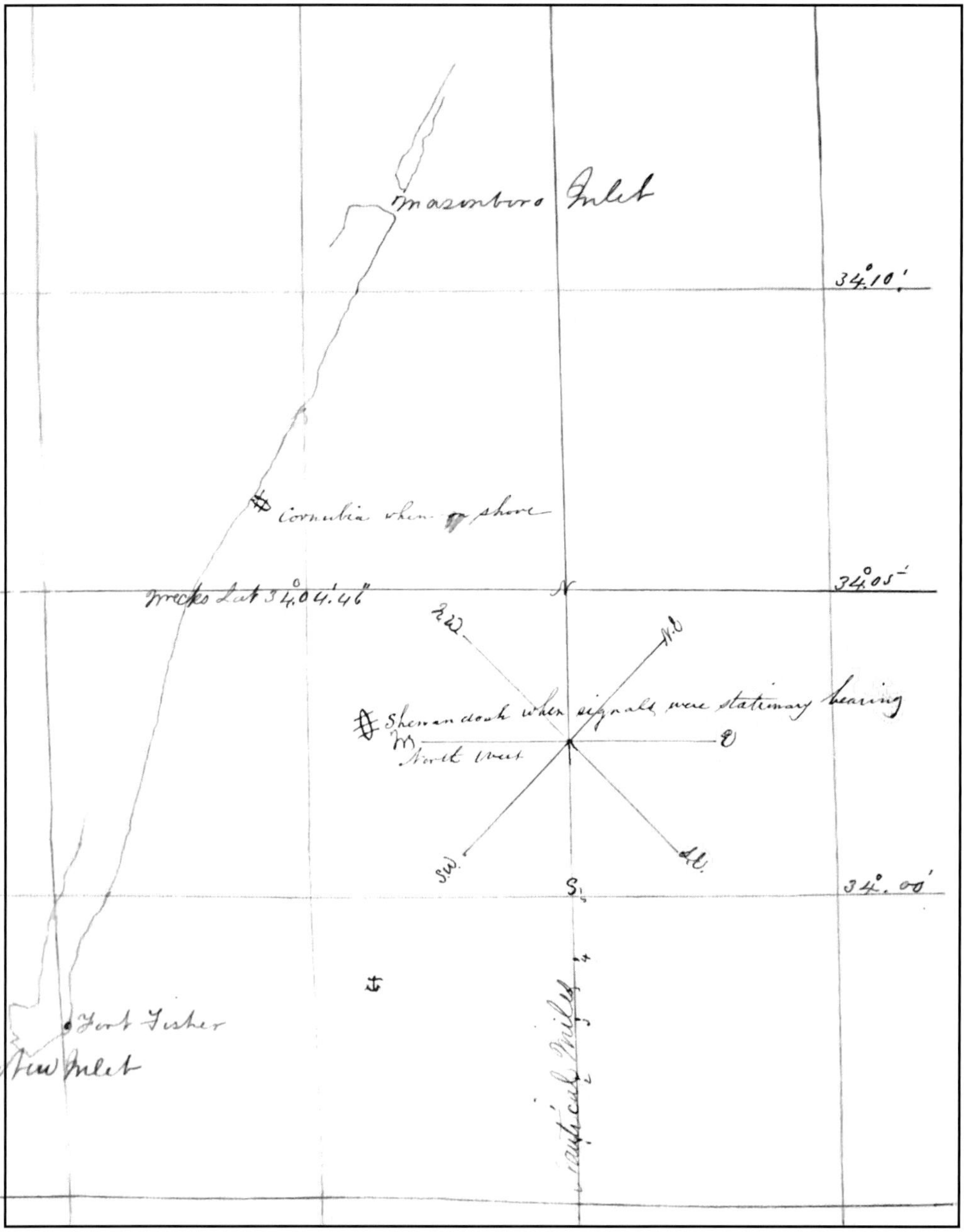

Original map drawn by Captain Daniel B. Ridgeley of the USS *Shenandoah* depicting the directions of the signals sent during the chase to capture the *Cornubia*. This was prepared for his ship's claim towards a share in the *Cornubia*.

On the morning ... about 2 o'clock, while lying inshore near the beach in 3 fathoms water, saw a rocket thrown up from the northward; went to quarters; stood inshore to 2 fathoms of water. In a few moments saw a steamer running fast towards me along the beach, the *James Adger* in chase. Stood in to cut him off, and when near him the steamer ran ashore, which proved to be the *Cornubia*.[91]

At the same time that the *Adger's* crews were boarding the *Cornubia*, a boat from the *Niphon* appeared alongside and asked Thomas Patterson if he required any assistance. Patterson required in the negative and ordered Breck to take position to the south of the *Cornubia*.[92]

Acting Ensign Joseph B. Breck, USN. NHHC image NH 56238.

The blockading fleet was supposed to use Coston's night signals, a system of flares. It was a type of semaphore and apparently simple to use. Three lights of different colours, white, red, and green, were flashed or burned in combinations representing the numerals 1, 2, 3, 4, 5, 6, 7, 8, 9, 0, and also two letters, A and P, in all twelve combinations. The light was produced by the combustion of a peculiar pyrotechnic composition for each of the desired colours. Interestingly the inventor of this system, which only came into use in 1861, was a woman, Martha J. Coston.[93] An almost chance remark by Acting Master Patterson, that the signals were only really effective at quite close range, caused an inquiry to be held at the end of 1863.[94]

Thomas Patterson concludes the story

[A] few moments after came up with the strange steamer, which had run ashore about 11 miles north of New Inlet, having been headed off by the

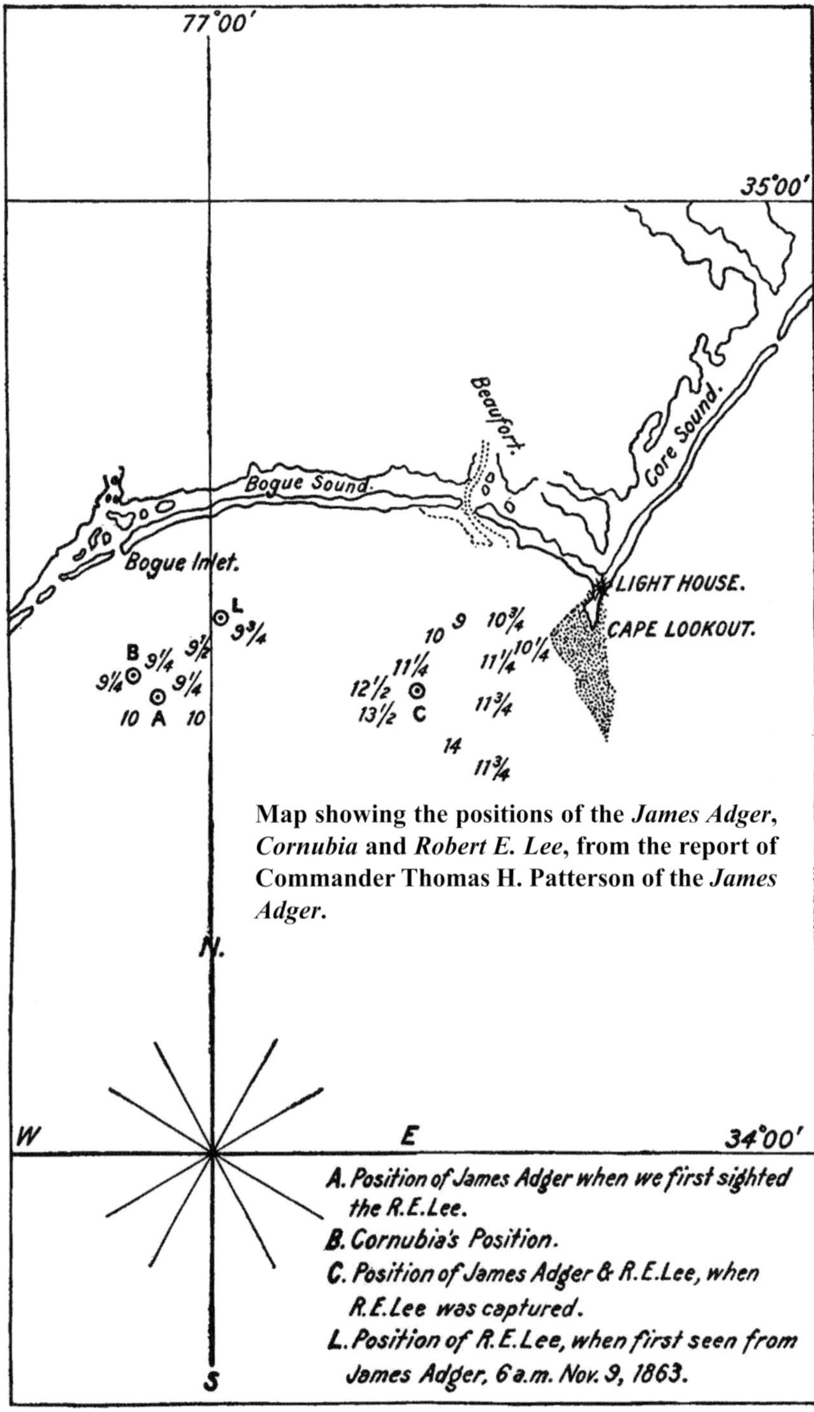

Map showing the positions of the *James Adger*, *Cornubia* and *Robert E. Lee*, from the report of Commander Thomas H. Patterson of the *James Adger*.

USS *Niphon*, and was blowing off steam.

I sent Lieutenant Franklin, my executive officer, and Acting Master R. O. Patterson to take possession of the prize, with an engineer and two firemen to examine into the condition of her engines.

The officers, crew, and passengers were escaping, and all succeeded in reaching the shore except the captain, carpenter, and one seaman who remained aboard.

As the tide was running flood, I made fast a hawser to the prize and commenced trying to haul her off, directing Acting Master Breck, commanding the *Niphon*, to keep to the southward, close inshore, and enfilade the beach with grape [shot] and about 3 am succeeded in hauling the *Cornubia* off.

Lieutenant Franklin notified me that her engines were in good order, but the steam being down, I towed her offshore and at daylight stood for the anchorage of the senior officer present.

I have ordered her to Boston, in charge of Acting Master R. O. Patterson.[95]

Among the passengers on the *Cornubia* who escaped after she was beached were Colonel L. R. Smoot, Quartermaster General of Virginia, Colonel C. E. Thorburn and Paymaster James N. Harwood, CSN. According to purser J. T. Gordon, the *Cornubia* had been completely hemmed-in, leaving only two options, either to run the gauntlet or beach her.[96] Beaching was a common tactic near Confederate ports; often the beached ship could be protected to some extent by mobile artillery and the cargo recovered later. Captain Gayle, "with promptness and great coolness," decided to run through the blockading vessels and take their fire. He ordered pilot Thomas Grissom not to beach her but in trying to pass by in very shallow water just off the beach the *Cornubia* ran aground. Immediately following this she fell over on to one side.

In a very few moments the blockaders were alongside, with the *Cornubia's* crew shoving off from one side while she was being boarded from the other. Gayle seems to have been unable to abandon his ship because of his recent illness and he was captured along with William Gilbert, *Cornubia's* carpenter, and John Morfitt, a seaman,[97] both British subjects; it is not known if these men volunteered to remain with Gayle. The boarders fired on the escaping boats with muskets and pistols but caused no injuries. The boats were pursued vigorously, though no more crew were captured.

The *Wilmington Journal* of 12th November states that Gayle was accompanied by the 1st and 2nd cooks, but this is the only mention of this version of events.

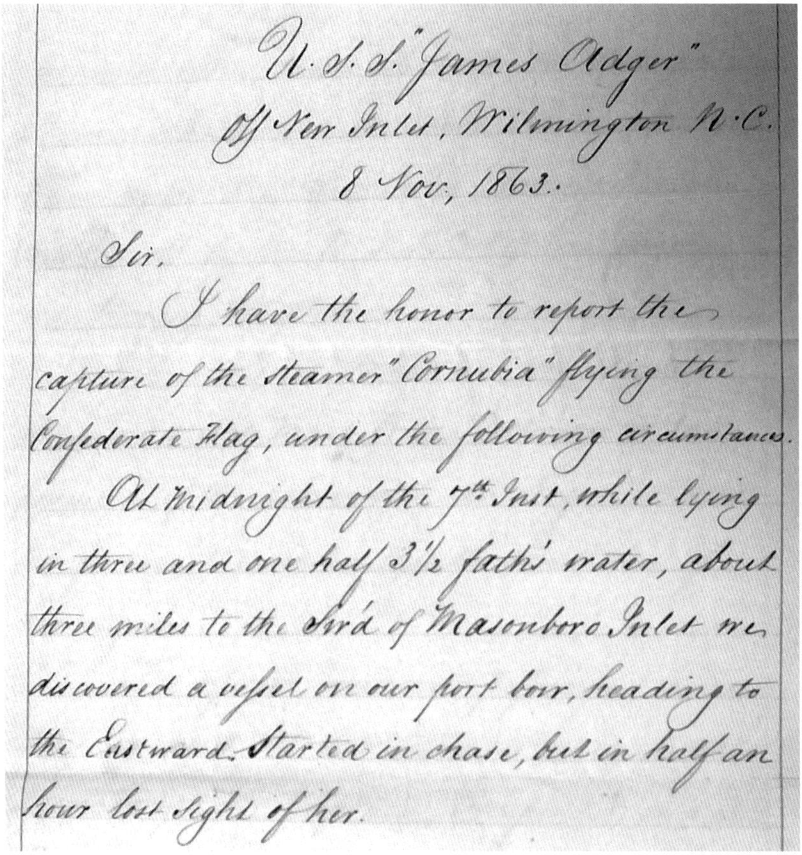
U. S. S. "James Adger"
Off New Inlet, Wilmington N.C.
8 Nov, 1863.

Sir,

I have the honor to report the capture of the steamer "Cornubia" flying the Confederate Flag, under the following circumstances.

At midnight of the 7th Inst, while lying in three and one half 3½ faths water, about three miles to the Sw'd of Masonboro Inlet we discovered a vessel on our port bow, heading to the Eastward. Started in chase, but in half an hour lost sight of her.

Part of Commander Thomas Patterson's report on the capture of the *Cornubia*.

It appears that as a contingency each crew member on the *Cornubia* was assigned to one of three boats, "so as to prevent confusion and undue crowding of any one boat".[98] Richard Gayle had charge of the starboard-quarter boat, the First Officer the port-quarter boat and the Second Officer the forward lifeboat. When lowering Gayle's boat, the man who had charge of the bow tackle let it "go by the run," which caused it to fill with water. Captain Gayle, seeing it could not carry its complement without endangering the lives of his men by swamping of the boat, "in the nobleness of his nature determined to sacrifice himself and let as many of his men escape as possible". However, this does not tie in with the description of him being too ill to leave the ship. It does seem clear though that Gayle only decided to beach the *Cornubia* as a last resort.

Following *Cornubia's* beaching, Robert Patterson also claimed to have heard someone on her cry "don't fire," followed by "send a boat". While the first is eminently reasonable, the second is not and he may have heard an order from the *Niphon*.[99]

With the tide running flood, Thomas Patterson made the decision to make fast a hawser to *Cornubia's* stern; she was eventually pulled off the beach at about 3am and taken well outside the reach of Fort Fisher's guns, to the USS *Shenandoah*, some seven miles offshore.[100] Robert Patterson later stated that the place of *Cornubia's* capture was near Big Hill, ten or eleven miles from Fort Fisher.

For the Confederate government, the loss of the *Cornubia* was a disaster beyond the mere loss of a blockade runner. When she was sent to Boston as a prize, she was accompanied by a bag of water-soaked mail, which one of her officers had tried to dispose of in the surf, and the three captured crewmen. The mail became known as the '*Cornubia* papers', and quickly became a Rosetta stone to unlock the management secrets of the Confederate blockade-running fleet on the eve of a putative major new ship building programme in Britain.

The most immediate result was a new, tough policy toward British seamen caught challenging the blockade. U.S. District Attorney Richard Henry Dana, Jr., at Boston, was designated to receive a sealed packet of all papers taken in the prize. Transmitting them to Secretary Welles, 26th December 1864, after study, Dana wrote:

> We have found in the prize steamer *Cornubia* letters which prove that the steamers, the *R. E. Lee*, and *Ella & Annie* and others of their class are the property of the Confederate Government and that their commanders are in the service of the Confederate Navy Department. This raises the question whether, in like cases, the Government will detain foreign seamen found on board as prisoners of war. The letters also show that they are under orders to conceal these facts while in neutral ports, in order to escape the rules applicable to public vessels of belligerents.[101]

Welles endorsed the letter: "The persons captured on the boats mentioned and others in like cases to be detained as prisoners".

Commander Patterson noted,

> Her captain remarked to my executive officer that "though the *Cornubia* is a small vessel the Confederate Government could better have afforded to lose almost any other vessel".[102]

The end of the *Cornubia* was described by Frederick W. Gregory, the signalling officer, who had been onboard at the end:

...we left Bermuda with a cargo for Wilmington in charge of Captain Gale [sic], with Mr. Robert [sic] Grissom as pilot and myself as signal officer. We made land some miles above Wilmington, apparently through bad navigation, almost as far north as Cape Lookout, and when opposite Masonboro in coasting down we observed rockets going up directly ahead of us. We were running at full speed, when to our consternation rockets appeared quite near abreast of us; in fact we were apparently surrounded by cruisers. There was a hurried consultation on the bridge. I was at my post with my lights, waiting to be called, when the order was given to head for the beach and drive the ship high and dry. The blockaders were then cannonading us very heavily. When our good ship struck the beach she ploughed up the sand for a considerable distance, and keeled over on her side. The boats were lowered, and every man told to look out for himself, which I assure you we lost no time in doing, as we had scarcely left the ship before the enemy were boarding her on the opposite side and firing briskly with small arms. They followed us to the beach, and kept up a heavy fire from cannon and small arms for an hour. We dodged about in the bulrushes as best we could, and made our way toward the fort. Captain Thomas, acting chief officer, took ashore with him two fine chronometers, and selected me to carry one for him, but after beating around with them in the rushes for a mile or so, we became exhausted and had to throw them away. I have no doubt they are still lying in the rushes on the beach. We at last met a company of soldiers who protected and escorted us to the sound. We forded the sound and remained all night and were sent to Wilmington the next day, overland, by mule teams. I always thought it was a shame that the *Lady Davis* was lost, having no doubt we could have put to sea and escaped on the occasion referred to, although I was not informed as to the supply of coal on board.

Richard Gale had been very sick the day before, and was too feeble to leave the ship, so remained on board and was captured and taken to Fort Warren. The U. S. S. *James Adger*, commanded by Capt. James Foster of Bloomington, Ind., had the good fortune to capture our ship, and hauled her off as a prize.

After reaching Wilmington and supplying myself with clothing and a hat, I immediately went on board the steamer *Flora* with Captain Horner and made a successful run to Bermuda. The *Flora* was considered too slow and sent back to England. I then joined the *Index*, commanded by Captain Marshall, and made several successful voyages on her, but she too was condemned as too slow and was returned to Glasgow.[103]

CSS *Cornubia* allegedly shortly after capture, place unknown.

***James Adger's* commander, Commander Thomas H. Patterson, circa 1862. He was commissioned Captain 25th July 1866, Commodore on 2nd November 1871 and Rear-Admiral in 1877.**

The mention of Captain James Foster is incorrect, as shown above. The battle around the area continued after sunrise. Commander Patterson ordered Acting Master Breck to keep to southward of the *Niphon* and *Cornubia,* to close into the shore and enfilade the beach; possibly he was concerned that troops from Fort Fisher might try to recover his prize. Breck later reported that he had remained off the beach until daylight, when he saw several men (presumably Union) on shore making signals to be taken off. While sending a boat for them some thirty or more soldiers charged down upon them and took them prisoners. "I sent a round of grape and canister among them which killed and wounded several; also killed some cattle that were near. We shelled them in their retreat as long as we could see them" (the actual artillery expenditure was two 32-pounder 5-second shell, six grape, two canister and six 20-pounder time shells).[104] Breck seems fairly indifferent to the possibility that he may have killed or wounded some soldiers on his own side. Shortly after he saw some more men making signals to the north; he sent in boats and took the eight men off, after which the *Niphon* stood offshore to her anchorage.

Later that morning at early daylight, another steamer was discovered to the northeast, to which the *James Adger* turned to check. When Patterson was about 20 miles from Beaufort Bar he started in chase.[105] The steamer was now standing to the southward and eastward, but, with the Cape Lookout Shoal to the eastward of her she could not keep off and make the chase a stern one. Eventually she was obliged to change course across the *James Adger's* bows, which enabled the ship to overhaul the stranger. About 7:30 Patterson took possession of the *Robert E. Lee*, which had left Bermuda only five hours after the *Cornubia.* She had a number of passengers and a large crew, but no registry papers were found on board, most likely they had been disposed of. Shortly after she stopped, the Confederate flag was hoisted for a few moments, but when Patterson's executive officer demanded it the Lee's captain informed him that he had burned it.[106]

The *Robert E. Lee* was "said to be loaded with arms, saltpeter, blankets, and shoes, and to have treasure in her keelson".[107] The officers, crew, and passengers numbered 76, all of whom, except some to be retained as witnesses, were sent to Hampton Roads the following day in the USS *New Berne*, to be delivered to Acting Rear-Admiral Lee. Among the passengers were the Belgian Consul at Charleston, two British artillery lieutenants and a captain of the Confederate artillery. Patterson had ordered her to Boston under the command of his executive officer, Lieutenant C. L. Franklin.[108] Once again Thomas Patterson declared that the *James Adger* was on her own at the time of the capture. After 21 voyages in 10 months the *Lee* had transported over 7,000 bales of cotton to Bermuda (worth an estimated $2,000,000) and brought back munitions valuable to the Confederacy.[109] The two runners were conceded to be "easily the most noted that ply between Bermuda and Wilmington".[110]

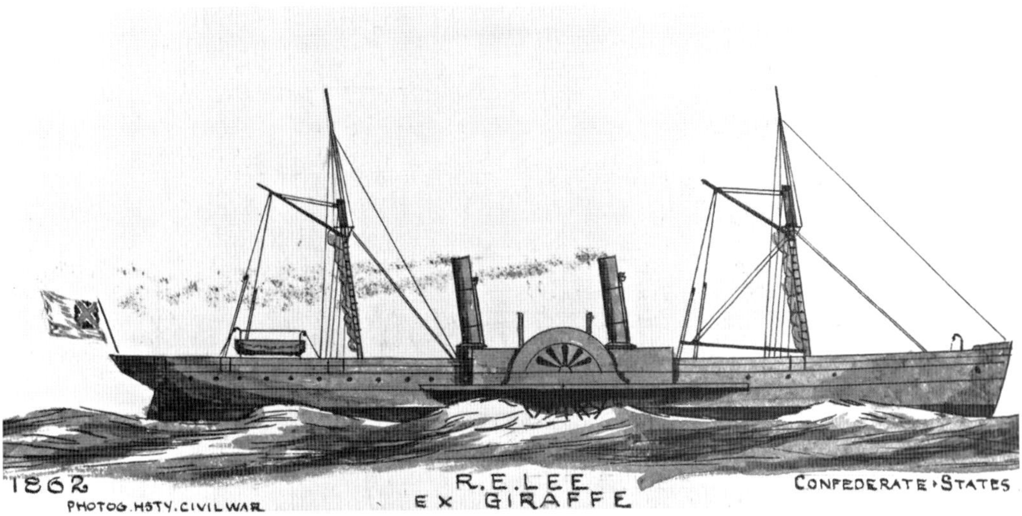

CSS *Robert E. Lee*, the former *Giraffe*. NHHC image NH 63888.

With Robert Patterson in command of the *Cornubia* and the officer first placed in command of the *Robert E. Lee* ill, Thomas Patterson stated that he was "compelled to order the only other reliable officer, my executive, Lieutenant Franklin, to take charge of the *R. E. Lee* as he considered her too valuable a prize "to run any risk".[111]

Patterson was then ordered to proceed to Boston to replenish his coal (following the action with the *Robert E. Lee* he only had nine tons left in his bunkers); he was also to take the *Cornubia* with him. Once the latter was in a more sea-worthy condition he was to dispatch her with a prize crew. In addition, all of the secret papers and other correspondence captured with the *Cornubia* were to be sealed and sent to the US District Judge in Boston. Patterson had previously implied that no other ships were in the vicinity when the *Cornubia* was run down. If this were the case, only he and his crew would be eligible for the bounty when she was eventually sold on. Captain (later Commodore) Daniel

Boone Ridgely of the USS *Shenandoah*, and Patterson's superior officer, was of a different mind and finished his orders with "I would respectfully suggest to you that the *Shenandoah*, *Tuscarora*, and *Howquah* were in signal distance and saw the signals made by you of the approach of a blockade runner".[112]

It seems however that the *Cornubia* was not removed from the area straight away. Georgiana Walker later claimed to have met a man who had been in Wilmington that day. He had

> ...watched the vessel which captured her sail up & down in site of Fort Fisher, but without the range of her guns, with the Yankee Flag flying, & the Confederate Flag beneath it, upside down.[113]

Patterson did take the *Cornubia* out to sea, but if he actually paraded her in such a way sounds unlikely. Certainly she was towed out by the *James Adger* at a speed of 3½ knots; at 5.30 am, about seven miles from where the *Cornubia* was captured, Patterson received news from the *Cornubia* that her own engines could be used and the tow line was cast off. The two then sailed to the day anchorage of the senior officer, another two miles away.

The importance of *Cornubia's* paper cargo soon became known, initially in great secret, though many letters were later published in newspapers such as the *New York Times*. Most of the correspondence had been in the care of Lieutenant Colonel Charles E. Thorburn, CSA, who was on a leave of absence. One letter was an official dispatch from Edwin De Leon, dated Paris, September 30th, 1863, to Hon. J. P. Benjamin, Secretary of State, Richmond, CSA. This paper was of great interest and value, relating "to the intrigues and disappointments of the rebel emissaries abroad" and the subsidising of the press on behalf of the Confederate Government.[114] It also indicated that the Confederates had lost all confidence in intervention from either France or England. Another letter contained a certified copy of an agreement between Colonel Gorgas, on behalf of the Confederate States, and C. E. Thorburn, Esq., on behalf of himself, Charles H. Reid & Co., and others, of London, "to run five steamers on joint account from the port of St. George, Bermuda, or Nassau, New Providence, to the Confederate port of Charleston, S. C, or Wilmington, N. C".[115]

Other correspondence related to an arrangement made or proposed to be made by Major Caleb Huse with the Mercantile Trading Company, on behalf of the Confederate States, to obtain goods in exchange for cotton, and a proposal to Colonel Thorburn for the building of a rebel gunboat in England. This also included certificates of stocks in the Mercantile Trading Company, Limited, in favour of Charles E. Thorburn, worth £10,000. Other letters were

The USS *Daylight*, one of *Cornubia's* captor's.

from various private parties abroad to correspondents in the Southern States. One of these referred to the building and equipment of war vessels at Mobile and its neighbourhood, and the number and quality of vessels, both ironclad and wooden, being built for the Confederate Navy in France and England, especially to "four or six small ironclads (bulldogs); very formidable". One of the most interesting, though probably not important, documents was No. 8, J. T. Gordon's "diary of current events". The transcription of this is reproduced in full in Appendix II.

Another blockade runner had more luck that night. At about 1 am the *Niphon*, stationed at the north end of the line of blockaders, north of the Big Hill (the Mound battery of Fort Fisher), saw another runner coming to The Bar. Running along the beach at full speed and sending up rockets the *Niphon* gave chase. Acting Master Breck ordered his guns to open up and several shots hit the stranger.[116]

The latter was very fast however and was soon lost sight of. As the *Niphon* came within range of the Half Moon Battery it opened fire and she turned out of range, nothing then being visible of either blockaders or runners. The *Shenandoah* and *Tuscarora* stood in to intercept her, however she passed so close to the beach that they could not make her out. The picket boat *Howquah* was also in her way and gave her "a warm reception," a broadside from her battery, but the runner still managed to squeeze past.[117] A second runner approached the bar without being observed until the *Howquah* saw her; despite this the runner managed to get into Wilmington. The guns of Fort Fisher then opened up on the *Niphon*, which then stood to the northward again and beat a retreat. At 3 am yet another steamer was sighted, chase given and a gun fired, but this too slipped away.

At 5:25 am off Masonboro Inlet, another steamer was seen to the northward, coming down the coast. Chase was immediately given and at 5:30 the *Niphon* opened fire upon her. The runner now turned towards the *Niphon* at full speed, intent on running her down. *Niphon's* helm was put hard astarboard and all of the starboard guns were fired directly into the oncoming steamer; the vessels were brought nearly side by side, colliding with a great crash at the bows and carrying away *Niphon's* bowsprit and stem and causing other damage; it was later found that her decks leaked badly. The vessel turned out to be the *Ella and Annie*, of Charleston.[118] The *Ella and Annie* had departed St George's on 5th November in company with the *Robert E. Lee*. The two ships had separated

Frank Bonneau's ship; built in 1860 as the *William G. Hewes*, she was renamed the *Ella and Annie* after being seized from the Union Navy. After her recapture she was renamed the USS *Malvern*. She is depicted here wearing Confederate colours.

The *Margaret and Jessie* was built in Glasgow in 1858 for the Isle of Man Steamship Company and called the *Douglas*. After her capture she was taken into the US Navy as the USS *Gettysburg*, being recommissioned twice, in 1866 and 1875. She was sold out of service in 1879.

off Carolina and the *Ella and Annie* steamed for Wilmington. Unfortunately she was delayed by a storm and arrived just in time to be intercepted by the *Niphon.*

While the two vessels were momentarily together the enemy steamer was boarded, a hawser hove on board and made fast and she was taken, the whole affair lasting only five minutes from the firing of the first gun. A keg of powder and slow match were found ready to blow her up, but these were quickly removed and made safe. At 5:55 am another of the blockading vessels was seen, and at 6:50 am the vessel proved to be the USS *Shenandoah.* For his actions, Frank Bonneau was later convicted of piracy by a Boston court, but the presiding officer, who had been a flag officer himself, suspended the sentence on the grounds that he would have done exactly the same thing had he been in similar circumstances.[119] Nevertheless, once captured, he was destined to be imprisoned for either the duration of the war or unless swapped for another prisoner.

Captain Frank Bonneau in prison in Fort Warren, Boston, date unknown.

The *Ella and Annie* was 905 tons burden, and apart from "some small damages from shell and grape" was found to be in good order.[120] Her cargo was mostly composed of 480 sacks of salt, 500 sacks saltpeter, 281 cases Austrian rifles, 500 barrels of beef and 42 cases paper. In the collision three men on board the *Niphon* and four on board the *Ella and Annie* were slightly injured. Acting Master Breck's work towards her capture and that of the *Cornubia* did not go un-noticed, and Captain Ridgely, senior officer, commended "his spirit and promptness". Acting Rear-Admiral Lee hoped "that the Department, in view of this especial and other good service on the part of Acting Master Breck, will favorably consider my application for his promotion".[121]

The *Ella and Annie* had been built in Wilmington and was light and fast and would "be very convenient for general purposes in this squadron, being available either for inside or outside service. I would suggest that she be purchased by Government and sent to this squadron, if, after examination, she be found suitable".[122] This news may have pleased Breck even more than his possible promotion. Following all of this action a report was made on the condition of the *Niphon*, and she was ordered back to Norfolk, Virginia, for repairs and to take the crew of the prize *Ella and Annie*. She was also later taken into the US Navy and saw service as the USS *Malvern*.[123]

Following all of this, Captain Ridgely of the USS *Shenandoah* was pleased to write:

> During this dark of the moon four rebel blockade runners have been captured—the *Margaret and Jessie*, *Cornubia*, *Ella and Annie*, and the famous *R. E. Lee*, all belonging to the rebels and carrying contraband of war.[124]

It is interesting to note that it was the *Robert E. Lee* that was 'famous' and not the *Cornubia*, the more proficient blockade runner. Doubtless her name was the cause of her fame.

Ironically, some of *Cornubia's* last cargo of blockade cotton did get through as the ship *President Hooper* passed the Isles of Scilly on 18th November 1863, "twenty days out from Bermuda, loaded with a full cargo of cotton, taken out of the celebrated blockade runner *Cornubia* (late of Hayle)".[125]

> The cargoes of the *Robert E. Lee*, the *Ella and Anna*, and the *Cornubia* are very valuable, and will be a great loss to the Confederate States. Four hundred and thirty-one Austrian rifles, with ammunition, saltpeter, paper, shoes by thousands, and other merchandize, besides mail matter including private and public dispatches. There were few natives of this country on board, of the vessels, which had no ships' papers. – The *Cornubia* was owned entirely by James A. Seddon, of Richmond.
>
> *Cadiz Democratic Sentinel*, 18th November 1863

The *Boston Post* of 20th November 1863 stated that the *Cornubia* had been stopped after two shots had been fired into her. It also stated that not only Gayle, but "other officers" had been captured. The paper also noted that "she is said to be the fleetest blockade runner with one exception", though the latter was not named.

On 24th November the *Bermuda Royal Gazette* printed an article on the capture of one of its nation's favourites. It seems that it was necessary to show that the ship had not been given up lightly.

> The *Cornubia*. – We are glad to learn from an officer who made his escape from on board the *Cornubia*, that it was from no wont of "resolute determination" on the part of the commander of the *Cornubia*, or any other

officer, or the crew, that the *Cornubia* was not run safely into port. All that was possible was accomplished—every effort having been made to save the ship. She was not run on shore by any order, but she grounded in consequence of being hotly and closely pursued by three blockaders; and those who escaped had a narrow chance. Commander Gayle is spoken of as having acted with great coolness and determination, and the loss of his ship is more mortifying to him than it can possibly be to any outsiders. We have made this statement in order that the public mind may be disabused of any allusion we have made in regard to the loss of the *Cornubia*.

P. S. Since the above was in type, we have received the following explanation from the officer alluded to, and we have implicit confidence in his statement. He was the last man who left the ship. He says:-

"Captain Gayle, when hemmed in by the blockaders, resolved to run the gauntlet, and so ordered. In endeavouring to execute this determination, and pass between one of the blockade[r]s and the beech [sic], the *Cornubia* grounded, and they were alongside instantly, while the crew were escaping from one side, the enemy were boarding the *Cornubia* on the other". Wilmington Journal, Nov. 12.[126]

By the end of November the *Cornubia*, *Robert E. Lee*, *Ella and Anna* and the *Ella* were at Lewis Wharf, Boston; the *Ella and Anna* had nearly been emptied. All four had similar cargoes, cases of rifles, saltpeter, salt, beef and pork. The *Lee* was in a poor state, engines "out of order" and her bottom foul, so she was running slowly. Despite this she was value at about $150,000; the *Cornubia* $125,000 and the *Ella $60,000.*[127] In his diary Gorgas wrote:

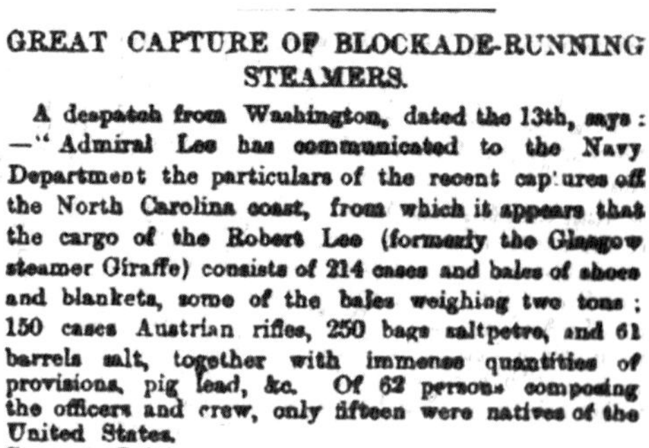

GREAT CAPTURE OF BLOCKADE-RUNNING STEAMERS.

A despatch from Washington, dated the 13th, says:—"Admiral Lee has communicated to the Navy Department the particulars of the recent captures off the North Carolina coast, from which it appears that the cargo of the Robert Lee (formerly the Glasgow steamer Giraffe) consists of 214 cases and bales of shoes and blankets, some of the bales weighing two tons; 150 cases Austrian rifles, 250 bags saltpetre, and 61 barrels salt, together with immense quantities of provisions, pig lead, &c. Of 62 persons composing the officers and crew, only fifteen were natives of the United States.

News of 'Black Sunday' begins to appear in the UK press. *Dundee Courier,* 30th November 1863.

November 11th. . . On Sunday we heard also of the capture of the "Cornubia," and on Monday learned that Dick had been captured with her. This is a heavy blow, in all respects. . .

However the loss of these three ships must have shaken him badly, and he later wrote, quite bitterly, and possibly unfairly:

. . . it is a great reflection on our commanders that they allow their vessels

> to fall unhurt into the hands of our enemy . . . People abroad will distrust a nation that conducts its affairs with so little skill.[128]

The last comment on the loss of the *Cornubia* is from Georgiana Walker, in Bermuda:

> The sad news of their capture soon reached us! I mourn for the *Cornubia* as for an old & well tried friend. She brought me & mine safely across the waters, & then she had so often been the bearer of bonny tidings from home. I grieve over the capture of her gallant Captain. Poor Gayle![129]

In 1877, when four Cape Fear pilot boats, including two of the *Cornubia's* former pilots, were at sea on Friday 13th April, "a terrible storm of wind and rain raged all day long".[130] At the end of the day two boats were missing, the *Uriah Timmins*, under Kit Morse, and the *Mary K. Sprunt*, under Thomas Grissom. Both pilot boats had stood offshore in truly dreadful conditions and no sign was seen of them for days. The *Timmins* eventually arrived in Wilmington on the 17th, having survived an incredible adventure in mountainous seas; this gave hope that the *Sprunt* would also turn up, if battered, later. Around 24th April, Kit Morse, still searching for his missing friends, found the wreck of the *Sprunt*; on the 29th, the body of Thomas Grissom was found by the crewmen of the *Henry Westerman*, nine miles off the coast. From the bruises on his body it was determined that he had been at the *Sprunt's* helm, lashed to the cockpit; no sign of his fellow pilots (Charles Dosher (the boat's owner), Lawrence Gillespie, Robert S. Walker (Dosher's brothers-in-law) and Christopher Pinner) was ever found; an un-named steward was also in the crew. A sixth pilot, Jim Williams, had been onboard but had joined the British brig *Baltic* in order to bring her into harbour.[131] In May 1879 a memorial was erected in the Old Smithville Burying Ground, a few miles north of Fort Caswell, to the pilots of the *Mary K. Sprunt* with the words

Memorial to the pilots lost on the Mary K. Sprunt at the Old Smithville Burying ground.

The Wind and the Sea
Sing Their Requiem
And shall
For ever more

As a blockade runner, the war was over for the *Cornubia*; however, it had been a successful one. Using information given by Stephen R. Wise, some 173 vessels ran the Atlantic blockade during the war, from either Bermuda or Nassau, mostly to Wilmington.[132] These vessels made a total of 825 trips, of which 672 were successful, an average of 4 successful trips out of 5, which demonstrates that the majority of runs, if not runners, were successful; however, many were captured or destroyed on their maiden run. The odds against getting captured were 1 in 10 in 1861, 1 in 8 in 1862, 1 in 4 in 1863, 1 in 3 in 1863 and 1 in 2 in 1865.[133] The Union blockaders managed to capture 136 runners and destroy another 85. Altogether the runners smuggled around 350,000 bales of cotton from Southern ports during the war; while this was less than 20% of the annual pre-war exports it nevertheless represented a significant income for the Confederate government. Unfortunately, it was not enough: too many runners brought in luxury goods rather than war supplies.

The five most successful runners on the Atlantic run were:

> *Syren*, 33 successful attempts from 33 runs; *Herald I*, 24 from 25; *Alice*, 24 from 24; *Cornubia*, 22 from 23 and *Lucy*, 21 from 23. The much better-known *Robert E. Lee* was much farther down the list, with 14 successful runs from 15 attempts.[134]

Further analysis of the information shows that 49 vessels were prevented from making any successful runs at all, in fact 133 vessels made five successful runs or fewer and only 9 vessels made more 20 runs or more. Looking at the runners more generally, Wise gives information on where 259 vessels (out of 453) were built. Of these, about 72% were built in the UK:

> 44% were built in Scotland, mostly on the Clyde; 15% the Liverpool area; 9% London; 5% Tyne-Tees area

Of the remainder, some 27% were built in America with a very small number in Canada and Cuba (4 vessels in all).

Following the capture of the *Cornubia* in December 1863 Dick Gayle was taken to a hotel in Boston because of his illness; once his health improved he was then taken to prison in Fort Warren.[135] While there, he corresponded regularly with Julia Gardiner Tyler, then residing at Staten Island, New York. While here her sympathy for the Confederates strained relations with her family and her home there was almost burned down by enraged Union veterans when it was discovered that she was flying a Confederate flag on the property. His expectations of exchange or parole came and went but he was eventually sent to Virginia, with a hundred other prisoners, to be exchanged. He was finally released on 1st October 1864 and sent south on the steamer *Circassion*; he then joined the Gorgas family in Richmond. As noted by Gorgas:

> Dick reached here on Tuesday evening looking a good deal the worse for his years' imprisonment at Fort Warren. About 120 Naval officers returned with him.[136]

Richard Gayle's last command, the *Stag*. She was built in 1853 by William Denny & Brothers of Dumbarton; at 548 grt she was of similar size to the *Cornubia*. She was sunk in the Cape Fear River in January 1865, apparently without loss of life.

Gayle was promoted to First Lieutenant on 18th October 1864 and ordered to report to Wilmington Station on 6th December to take charge of the steamer Stag; ironically the *Stag* had been brought into Wilmington by Gayle's mentor John Burroughs, from whom he received the ship.[137] Gayle received special instructions from the Secretary of the Navy prior to sailing. One of these was regarding the possibility of capture:

> Before leaving port you will station your crews for the different boats of the steamer, having placed in them water and provisions, and also nautical instruments. When capture in your judgement becomes inevitable, fire the vessel in several places and embark in the boats, making for the nearest land.
>
> The Department leaves to your discretion the time when and the

circumstances that must govern you in the destruction of the *Stag* in order to prevent her falling into the hands of the enemy.[138]

On 9th January 1865, while attempting to reach Wilmington via the Cape Fear River, unfortunately after the town had fallen to Union forces, he was captured again, having been lured into New Inlet by false lights from the Federals.[139] He was sent for detention at Fort Monroe and then back to Fort Warren, where he moved into his old quarters on 7th February 1865, being released again early in June 1865; in the meantime he had resumed his correspondence with Julia Tyler.

During the capture the *Stag* received three shots into her from the blockading cruisers.[140] She was ordered to New York under a prize master, Acting Master E. S. Goodwin, and sold that year to F. Nickerson of Boston where she became part of his coastwise service to New York and New Orleans as the *Zenobia*. In 1867 George Savary & Co. bought her; resold 17th November in Buenos Aires for $82,000, she disappeared from the North American scene, although she is believed to have been in service until at least 1885.[141]

The Gayle family grave at Mobile.

After release Dick Gayle went to Richmond, Virginia. Unsure of his future, he considered trying to obtain command of a steamer, possibly from South America to Europe or New York to New Orleans. However this never came about and he operated a small sawmill in Mobile for a short time before moving to New Orleans, where he married Flora Levy on 17th November 1866. The couple had no children. Gayle's health seems never to have been good and was exacerbated by his wartime incarcerations and he died on 9th April 1873, aged 41. He was buried at the Magnolia Cemetery, Mobile.[142]

Chapter 10

Poacher turned Gamekeeper

Cornubia was sold, apparently very quickly, at the Boston Prize Court in November for $65,000, a bargain, bearing in mind that her Prize Court valuation was nearly twice this.[1] One of the letters found onboard her tells an interesting tale: written by Frank Smith, of Memphis, Tennessee, who wrote to Henry Hart in Wilmington with regard to a cargo he had, which he was eager to dispose of.[2] One of the reasons he was so anxious to sell this cargo was that he was equally eager to buy either the *Margaret and Jessie* or the *Cornubia* when they were sold. It seems likely that whichever vessel was bought would have returned to run the blockade.

While still not officially part of the US Navy, she was caught up in what became known as the *Chesapeake* Affair, the principal events of which took place between the 7th and 16th December. The *Chesapeake* Affair was an international diplomatic incident; on 7th December 1863 Confederate sympathisers from Canada's Maritime Provinces captured the American steamer *Chesapeake* off the coast of Cape Cod. The expedition was planned and led by Vernon Guyon Locke of Nova Scotia and John Clibbon Braine, acting in the name of the Confederacy. However this was carried under the alleged authority of a second-hand letter of marque issued on the 27th October to the former captain of a privateer sold as unseaworthy in Nassau some months earlier. Locke was in fact a British subject who, under the assumed name of Parker, had been put in command of the privateer *Retribution* by the man actually named as her commander at that time. George Wade of New Brunswick shot and killed one of the American crew, the second engineer.[3]

The crew was faced with the problem that neutrality regulations forbade the bringing of prizes into British waters. Despite this, Locke took the *Chesapeake* to St John, New Brunswick, as planned but was unable to load coal for a voyage south to Wilmington. As a result, the steamer made her way to Nova Scotia; they eventually reached the LaHave River on 14th December, where they spent two days, loading some coal and selling some of the stolen cargo for supplies.

This was an act of aggression which the US government could not ignore;

the US Navy was determined to catch the *Chesapeake*; on 10th December J. B. Montgomery, Commandant of the Charleston shipyard, wrote "At request of U. S. Marshal Keyes and the collector of Portland, I have armed, manned, and dispatched the prize *Ella and Annie* in pursuit of the *Chesapeake*. The prize steamer *Cornubia* has also been offered, and unless otherwise directed by the Department will be prepared upon arrival at this yard".[4] On December 15th Montgomery wrote to Welles stating "The prize steamer *Cornubia* has been in readiness for three days to go in pursuit of *Chesapeake*; detained by thick weather. Is it desirable to send her at so late an hour, or shall she be kept in readiness?"[5] To which the answer, telegraphed on the same day, was curt: "Send the *Cornubia* as early as possible. The *Chesapeake* was off Margaret's Bay yesterday".[6] The *Cornubia* was summarily despatched north under the command of Acting Volunteer Lieutenant Breck, the same Breck from the *Niphon* who helped capture her. Joseph Berry Breckborn was invalided out of the Navy in November 1864 and moved to California for a more conducive climate. He died the following year aged 35.

The *Chesapeake* at night, shortly after capture.

The *Chesapeake* was nearly caught by the *Ella and Annie* on the LaHave River. Under the cover of night, the *Chesapeake's* lights were all extinguished and she slipped behind Spectacle Island and out on the LaHave River without being detected. The *Chesapeake* was again able to avoid capture at Lunenburg and made her way to Halifax. The vessel moved through Mahone Bay. At St Margaret's Bay Inlet some of the crew left the ship. By 16th December, the ship arrived at Mud Cove harbour at Sambro. Once there Locke went to Halifax overland and arranged to have a schooner come to Sambro to load coal. While the *Chesapeake* was being loaded the *Ella and Annie* and the *Dacotah* arrived.

Upon the arrival of the Federal warships, most of the crew of the *Chesapeake* fled. Lieutenant Nickels of the *Ella and Annie* violated British sovereignty and international laws and proceeded to arrest the three men that remained – one New Brunswicker and two Nova Scotians. George Wade, who had killed the ship's second engineer, was among the prisoners. US Secretary of State William H. Seward told the British that he wanted the *Chesapeake* returned immediately and the captured crew put in jail to be extradited to the United States.

William Johnston Almon was generally regarded as the unofficial Confederate Consul in Halifax and worked with Alexander Keith, Jr. to free the Confederate sympathisers. The *Chesapeake* was to await adjudication in the colonial Admiralty court, while Wade was to be given to the United States authorities for extradition. Almond and Keith arranged for Wade's escape in a rowboat to Ketch Harbour and then on to Hantsport. The United States Government was understandably outraged and, in response, the British put a warrant out for the rest of the crew. Eventually a few of them were tried but found not guilty on a technicality.[7]

On 15th February 1864 the Court of Vice-Admiralty at Halifax, Nova Scotia, found that the capture "was undoubtedly a piratical taking. But in its origin, in the mode of the recapture, in short, all the concomitant circumstances, the case is very peculiar". The captors were then dismissed as "This court has no prize jurisdiction, no authority to adjudicate between the United States and the Confederate States, or the citizens of either of those States. The prisoners were not surrendered to the United States under the Ashburton treaty for trial on charges of murder and piracy."[8] In fact Commander A. G. Clary of the USS *Dacotah* had prevented the *Ella and Annie* from taking the recaptured prize and prisoners into Boston; instead the *Chesapeake* was taken to Halifax, where she was turned over to local authorities, conceding that her recovery in the (allegedly at least) neutral waters of Canada had been extra-legal.

In November 1863 *The Times* printed an article on the capture of the *Robert E. Lee* and the *Cornubia*.[9] The article stated that the latter had been built by Messrs. Denny of Dumbarton, the information originating from *The Scotsman*. A week later a rather terse letter of correction was printed in *The Times*, straight from Harvey and Co. in Hayle.[10] It seems most likely that the confusion arose because

TO THE EDITOR OF THE TIMES.

Sir,—In the quotation from the *Scotsman* which appeared in *The Times* of the 28th inst. it is stated that the celebrated blockade runner Lady Davis, formerly named the Cornubia, was built by Messrs. Denny, of Dumbarton. The Cornubia and her engines were built by Messrs. Harvey and Co., of Hayle, in 1857, to run between that port and Bristol, and were sold to a London firm in 1861.

I am, Sir, your obedient servant,
W. J. RAWLINGS.

Foundry, Hayle, Cornwall, Nov. 30.

the earlier *Cornubia* was built in Glasgow. *Cornubia* arrived at New York on her return from Halifax on about 24th December under the command of Lieutenant Breck.[11]

At the end of January some of the less war-like parts of the cargoes of the *Cornubia*, *Robert E. Lee* and the *Ella & Annie* were sold in Boston. This included clothing, fancy goods and tableware.

UNITED STATES MARSHAL'S SALE

UNITED STATES OF AMERICA

Massachusetts District, 88

Boston Jan. 16, 1864

Pursuant to three warrants of sale from the US District Court, I shall sell at public auction, on FRIDAY, the 29th day of January, at 11 o'clock, AM, at store No.147 Congress-street, Boston.

The balance of the cargo and sundries from the prize steamers R. E. Lee, Ella & Anna, and Cornubia, consisting of:

Cases BOOTS AND SHOES

Cases DRY GOODS

Cases FANCY GOODS

Cases STATIONERY

Trunks CLOTHING

BEDDING, CARPETS, LINEN,

CUTLERY, TABLEWARE, JEWELRY

And numerous other articles.

Libelled in said Court in causes of prize, and ordered to be sold as aforesaid.

Catalogues ready on the morning of sale.

JOHN S. KEYES[12]

Chapter 11

Captain Charles Behm

In January 1864 the *Cornubia* received her new commander, Acting Volunteer Lieutenant C. F. W. Behm. Behm had been ordered to take command of the *Cornubia* "by the 4th Jany 1864" by Gideon Welles.[1]

Charles F. W. Behm was a German-born merchant sea captain who joined the US Navy. He was appointed Volunteer Lieutenant in August 1861 and commanded the barquentine USS *Brazilliera* and the steamer USS *Southfield* in the North Atlantic Blockading Squadron prior to taking command of the *Cornubia*.[2] The USS *Southfield* took part in the Battle of Roanoke Island.

The website NavSource Online states that Behm died in Andersonville Prison, Georgia, however this probably refers to a Charles Behm who was part of an infantry company raised in Niagara County, part of the 8th Heavy Artillery Regiment.

Volunteer Acting Lieutenant C. F. W. Behm, the first commander of the USS *Cornubia*.

Captain Charles Behm was involved in a rather disturbing incident in May 1867 while in command of the paddle steamer *Santiago de Cuba*, another former US Navy vessel, now part of the North American Steamship Company.[3] The vessel was travelling from Nicaragua to New York; on 20th May the vessel was believed by the passengers to have grounded briefly off Cape Hatteras. On the evening of the 21st the *Santiago de Cuba* was off the New Jersey coast in heavy fog, which then cleared to a clear night. Two of the passengers were Captain Kelly, of the steamer *Montana*, and Captain Patton, of the steamer *Idaho*. At one o'clock on Wednesday morning Captain Kelly told Behm of his concerns that the ship was too close to the shore. Behm replied that there was no danger, and even ordered the man at the wheel to steer still closer.

Shortly before the ship struck the shore, a steerage passenger was said to have rushed on deck and shouted to Captain Behm "You son --- port your helm, there is light on land on the port bow". Behm then, far too late, ordered a hard turn to port.

About half-past three in the morning the vessel was near the point known as Dry Inlet, and five or six miles to the south of Atlantic City (a place now known as Absecon Beach). At this time, according to some of the passengers who were on deck, the *Santiago de Cuba* was steering directly for the light-house at the latter place, while others assert that her course lay between the light-house and the adjacent shore. At about 3:45 am the ship's bottom struck the sand again. The keel struck five or six times before it stuck, and it was not until the vessel was unable to move that the wheels were reversed. Captain Kelly then took charge of evacuating the vessel, using three "surf-boats" and an Indian rubber raft. Unfortunately one of the boats overturned and two women and two girls were drowned.

Behm was later accused by the passengers of the *Santiago de Cuba* of gross negligence and intoxication during the incident and apathy afterwards, though he was later defended by a small number of passengers. Another accusation was that the running aground was a deliberate act, the result of bribery from another shipping line. It was later alleged that, according to the register of the Shipmaster's Association, Behm was not regarded as being a duly qualified sea-captain, having failed to comply with the specified rules of the Association.[4] After the incident a number of crewmen, some of whom were described as army deserters, plundered passengers' luggage that had reached the shore. Others refused to help the passengers and ran away when threatened by the mate, who had a revolver.[5]

Charles Behm died in 1882, aged 69; it has not been possible to discover if any action was taken against him for the *Santiago* affair.

Chapter 12

Under the Stars and Stripes

On 9th March 1864, refitted and armed with a 20 pounder rifled gun and two 24 pounder smooth bore cannon, the *Cornubia* left Boston on her maiden voyage as a Federal vessel.[1] The CSS *Cornubia* had been re-commissioned as the USS *Cornubia*; her other officers comprised:

> George Ferris, Acting Master, Executive Officer; Frank P. Bibbles, Acting Ensign, Sailing Master; George A. Harriman, Frank Millet, Acting Ensigns; John G. Dearborn, Acting Assistant Surgeon; A. P. Eastlake, Acting Assistant Paymaster; Samuel R. Brummage, Acting 1st Assistant Engineer; Robert Fleming, Thomas I. Savery, Orin T. Hill, Acting 2nd Assistant Engineers, James A. Boynton, George Altham, Acting 3rd Assistant Engineers; William Warren, W. H. Wood, Acting Master's Mates.[2]

The *Cornubia* was given her own class name; naturally she was the only *Cornubia*-class vessel in the US Navy.

It is clear that Behm was disappointed with his new command as he had written to a friend a month before taking charge of the *Cornubia* regarding her short comings. His friend replied "And so the "Cornubia" turned out after all your fond anticipations to be quite a failure. Well, it is another lesson to us that beauty & goodness are not always inseparable...".[3] He had apparently also mentioned *Cornubia's* high usage of coal. In all fairness the ship had had a difficult life over the previous year as a runner, her engines often used at high speed and her furnaces burning fuel such as turpentine, rosin and meat fat to achieve improbable bursts of speed. It seems likely that her boilers would have been in a poor condition too, following this abuse, and it is also possible that her hull was in poor condition

Consul Allen had reported again from St George's on 31st March.[4] The *North Heath* and *Caledonia* had left the previous day, with Captain John Burroughs still master of the former. Captain Wiley "a southern man" was in charge of the latter. The steamer *Index* was also due to leave the same day for Wilmington, with the *Greyhound* under Captain Beers, late of the *Dee*, to leave the following day. Regarding Beers, Allen said "Captain Beers was formerly in our Navy. He is called the Admiral here and is considered the King of blockade runners. If captured he will claim to be an Englishman and will, I am informed, disguise himself at Nassau".

Since Allen's last report no runner had arrived in port. Captain John Maffit was "still here waiting for a steamer. He is drunk the greater part of the time".[5] Maffit, inaccurately known as the Prince of the Privateers for his capture of Federal ships while evading a large Federal squadron which had chased him from Mobile, Alabama, had been forced to give up command of the CSS *Florida* because of the lingering effects of yellow fever, as well as a severe heart attack he suffered while in Brest.[6] Maffit had never been a privateer but always an officer of the Confederate Navy. On 7th May Allen recorded the departure of the steamer *Pevensey* "for Wilmington or Charleston," another mount for the apparently unstoppable Captain John Burroughs.[7]

Cornubia was ordered to New Orleans to join the Gulf Blockading Squadron and sailed from New Orleans on 4th April 1864 arriving on her new station on the 8th May.[8] She patrolled off Mobile and Pensacola but her appetite for coal, which mattered little when she was a runner, was a disadvantage for ordinary navy work.

On 13th May *Cornubia* was required to transfer some heavy guns from New Orleans to Pensacola, Florida. Acting Rear-Admiral Farragut did not "feel satisfied" leaving them at the former port and doubtless had other uses for them.[9] Shortly after this it appears that *Cornubia* was laid up for repairs and was ordered, together with the USS *Pocahontas*, to Texas.[10]

On 28th May she was ordered to Pensacola Bay, to Commander Alexander Gibson, senior officer afloat. Lieutenant Behm was further ordered to report to Commander William Smith, commandant of Pensacola Navy Yard, for repairs and for coal for the *Cornubia*.[11] Following this she was stationed off Mobile.

On 2nd June 1864 Farragut asked the commandant of the Pensacola Navy Yard to cooperate with her Chief Engineer Mr. Williamson "for the purpose of superintending some alterations I desire made to the boilers of the *Cornubia* to reduce her consumption of fuel.....please allow the machine shop to assist him in the work".[12] Despite this work, or, most likely, instead of it, *Cornubia* was at Galveston two days later. The port of Galveston, Texas, had initially been held by Union forces but captured by the Confederates under General John B. Magruder. However, their occupation of the city was difficult, not least because of a yellow fever epidemic in 1864 which "left it forsaken".[13]

Like many other naval officers, Farragut had ships named after him. To date the US Navy has given his name to five ships, all destroyers, the most recent in 2006. Not only that but four USS *Farraguts* have featured in Star Trek, the most recent in the 2009 J. J. Abrams remake.

On 24th July 1864 *Cornubia's* 20 pounder Parrott gun was replaced by a 30-pounder[14] and she was ordered to join the blockade of the Texas coast, viz. to stay where she was, and where she would remain for the rest of the war.[15] Her task here was to disrupt the flow of arms and contraband from Havana into the Texas ports, though the shallow sandy waters of the Gulf were not ideal for the fast runners from the Carolina coast.

Charles Behm left the *Cornubia* late in December 1864. It seems that Behm had had medical problems while in command of the USS *Southfield.* In October 1863 Lieutenant Commander Flusser wrote to Commander Davenport, stating "If Behm should be sent home by the board of survey I should be much pleased to see French put in command of the *Southfield*".[16] No information has so far been found of Behm in the US Navy after this time and it may be that he retired.

Chapter 13

Captain John Alexander Johnstone

On 27th November Acting Lieutenant Behm, who had "gone North under medical survey",[1] was replaced by Acting Lieutenant John Alexander Johnstone, who would command her for the remainder of the war. Johnstone was probably born in Annan (but possibly Gretna), Scotland, on 15th June 1836 into a seafaring family.[2] His journey to the United States is currently not known. However, he became a naturalised citizen on 31st May 1860. On 10th September 1861 he joined the US Navy and was appointed Master's Mate at the Navy Yard, Washington DC; he may have been a merchant captain prior to this. This was the lowest officers' rank at the time. He was then sent to gunnery school.

On 4th December 1861, he was promoted to Acting Master, sent to the Brooklyn shipyard and given a place under Captain Collins on board the USS *Octorara*, a gunboat which had just been launched. The ship then went into sea trials. The *Octorara* was commissioned on February 28 and was sent south to blockade and was also part of the "Flying Squadrons". On March 17, 1863, Johnstone took a prize crew of four sailors to take charge of the captured blockade runner *Rosalie* of Charleston. The *Rosalie* was taken into Federal service and given to Johnstone with a crew of five men; on a cruise on 19th March 1863 they boarded and captured the schooner *John Williams*, of Nassau, laden with iron plates for the Confederate rams. This feat won him much distinction, and he was especially complimented by Acting Rear-Admiral Farragut, who corresponded with him for the rest of his life.[3]

For this he was promoted to Acting Volunteer Lieutenant on November 12, 1863. By 1st January 1864 he was described as the commanding officer of the USS *W. G. Anderson* (of the West Gulf Squadron) and took part in the battle of Mobile Bay. From April he served on the USS *Seminola*, which he commanded from 28th 1864. On 19th May 1865. He became one of only 13 foreign born Union officers to achieve the rank of Acting Volunteer Lieutenant Commander, though the date of his commission is not known. The *New York Times* of 7th August 1865 states that Johnstone had achieved the rank by the time he was ordered to take the *Cornubia* to Pensacola. At some point after his arrival in the United States Johnstone met Saadi M. DeClifford, a Southern Belle and abolitionist from Virginia; they married in Philadelphia in September 1865.[4] At the close of the war he had declined service as an officer in the US Navy, was honourably discharged, and went back to the mercantile marine.

From 1875-6 Johnstone was captain of the barquentine, sometimes called a schooner, *Elvina*. The *Elvina* had been built at Bath, Maine, in 1874 and was owned by Reynold & Co. and registered in New York. She was 127.2 feet long and 30.7 feet wide and weighed 353 tons; her pennant JQKS.[5] The *Elvina* sailed regularly between Mexico, the Caribbean and New York, carrying cargoes such as sugar, mahogany and hemp.[6]

In December 1880 Johnstone was to discover that some of the worst dangers he was to face were on land, rather than on the sea. On 18th December, as the *Elvina* was ready to sail from St Thomas, US Virgin Islands, to St Croix, Johnstone had to visit the US Consulate to get his ship's papers, without which he could not leave.[7] After meeting with the Consul's clerk, and seeing his bill, words were exchanged. A $5 charge had been made for a "survey of the hatches", at which Johnstone stated that he had no occasion for official services of that nature and had not asked for them. Furthermore, so far as Johnstone knew, "this service had not been rendered to his knowledge, and the Captain thought it hard that he should be obliged to pay for it". He then told the clerk that if Colonel Thompson (Victor Thompson was a former Confederate officer from Oxford, Mississippi) continued to make such demands "he would run the risk of not remaining American Consul much longer".

At this point Thompson appeared and the clerk repeated to him what Johnstone had said. Johnstone then declared that it would be useless to continue the discussion as he would get no satisfaction and would pay the charge, under protest, and report the matter to the State Department when he got back to New York. Thompson was evidently unhappy, or at least in a state of high dudgeon, and said "You have used certain expressions in this office, and I intend to make you personally responsible for them". Johnstone replied that it would be useless to continue the controversy, and tendered a $20 American gold piece in payment of the bill, which totalled $19.53, and asked for the change.

Extending the argument, Thompson then said "I have no right to make you any change; you bring me the exact amount in American gold, or pay me 4 per cent, premium in addition". "Sir, I think I can get you in American gold; for the fractional part I may be able to get you American silver, and I really think that for that sum American silver is a legal tender," replied Johnstone.

Thompson then became "very angry and profane" and then raised a heavily loaded cane (one weighted with lead at one end) in a threatening manner. This was a mistake: "Capt. Johnstone, who during the war was an officer in the Federal Navy, is quite expert at fencing". After a brief struggle he took the cane from the Thompson who, after trying to attack Johnstone again, was struck on the shoulders with the cane by the latter. When the clerk went to assist his principal, he was given the same treatment.

At which point things escalated when Thompson placed his hand on his hip-pocket; Johnstone, anticipating the drawing of some deadly weapon, closed with Thompson and "twisted out of the hand of the latter a loaded Derringer revolver". At this point Johnstone also had unintentional hold of the chain to Thompson's spectacles; he then left the Consulate holding the loaded cane, revolver and spectacles. It was while passing through the outer gateway of the Consulate that a shot was fired and a bullet hit the archway over Johnstone's head, showering him with plaster.

Realising that he had no other recourse than the authorities, Johnstone first went to the office of his consignees, then, with one of their representatives, went to the "Police magistrate", where he made a statement "and delivered up the articles which he had taken from the enraged Consul". The USS *Kearsarge* was in port by that time, and Johnstone wrote to her captain, Commander H. F. Pickering, who Johnstone may have known from previous service. Thompson told Pickering that Johnstone had to apologise before having his papers returned. A representative of the consignees then went to the Consulate to pay the fees and collect the papers, but this was refused; Johnstone then duly visited the Consulate again, possibly with a guard, and was seen by the clerk. The business was finished quickly and the *Elvina* weighed anchor and left for New York.

Shortly after departing Progreso, Mexico, on 21st January 1881, the *Elvina* was caught up in severe weather and was nearly driven ashore.[8] On 26th January, when just off Cape Catoche (the northernmost point of the Yucatan Peninsula) a heavy north-easterly gale set in, and continued for five days. With the very real risk of the *Elvina* being wrecked, "...sail was crowded on till the spars bent and threatened to give way. For six hours she carried a dangerous quantity of canvas, but, fortunately, her spars stood the strain". By this means she was able to clear the land, but was driven down through the Yucatan Channel into the Caribbean Sea. Following that the *Elvina* met with other severe gales from the same direction before being able to return to New York.

On 9th May 1881 the *Elvina* arrived at New York from Guantanamo, Cuba; it was while near this spot that Saadi gave birth to a son, Guy Rene.[9]

John Alexander Johnstone was killed in an accident on 7th March 1883 in a dry dock in New York. While attempting to lower an anchor with his eldest son in order to repair a fluke, a chain cable slipped and a cleat caught in his legs and he was thrown from the foc'stle of the barquentine *Elvina* into the side of a dry dock; he was 46 years old.[10] Johnstone was part owner of the vessel, along with E. Debereau & Co. and had recently arrived from Laguayre, Mexico, loaded with mahogany. Johnstone's wife and seven children were onboard.

John Alexander is buried at Mt. Olivet Cemetery, Maspeth, New York, with his wife and several of their children.

Following Johnstone's death the *Elvina* was taken over by a man whose name gave problems for the newspapers; he was variously called Hulse, House or Hows.[11]

Chapter 14

Service to the end of the War

In December *Cornubia* was ordered to New Orleans for yet more repairs, which took several months. *Cornubia's* officers, as of 1st January 1865, are listed in The Naval History of the Civil War, however the ship herself is misidentified:

> "CORNELIA" – FOURTH-RATE
>
> Acting Volunteer Lieutenant, John A. Johnstone; Acting Assistant Surgeon, J. G. Dearborne; Acting Assistant Paymaster, A. Eastlake; Acting Master, George Ferris; Acting Ensigns, G. A. Harriman, Frank Millett and G. F. Brailey; Acting Master's Mates, W. H. Wood and G. H. Russell; Acting 1st Assistant Engineer, S. R. Brummage; Acting 2nd Assistant Engineer, T. J. Lavery; Acting 3rd Assistant Engineerss, J. A. Boynton and George Altham.

Fort Fisher, the bastion of safety on the Cape Fear River that had protected the runners since the beginning of the war, finally fell to Federal troops on Sunday 15th January 1865 after a two-day bombardment by a huge naval force.[1] The bombardment commenced from five monitors, led by the USS *New Ironsides*, just half a mile southeast of the fort. The counter-battery bombardment from the fort had no effect on these ships, following which it was switched to the timber-hulled ships; these being farther out they also suffered little damage. The fort was out-gunned though, the *New Ironsides* and the *Minnesota* between them having nearly as many guns between them as were arranged against them. The bombardment carried on through the night; however it was shown later that it had little effect on the thick walls of the fort. Ironically the Federal supply vessels included several former blockade runners; these included the *Advance*, *Fort Donelson* (the former *Robert E. Lee*), *Emma*, *Lilian*, and the *Little Ada*.

Colonel William Lamb and Major-General Whiting had previously requested help from General Braxton Bragg in Wilmington, but only a few hundred troops were sent, giving the two men about 1,500 troops to defend the fort. Federal troops had been repulsed from their attack on the fort the previous December,

The bombardment of Fort Fisher. This lithograph depicts just some of the ships firing on the fort. This was undoubtedly the heaviest naval bombardment up to this date.

and Bragg had thought it therefore impregnable; this seems to have affected his impressions of defending the place. Unfortunately he was in error as the weather had been the deciding factor during that attack.

During the frantic attack, Major-General Whiting, an engineer and commander

The battle for Fort Fisher, a dramatic engraving from *Harper's Weekly Magazine.*

of the Wilmington district, travelled to Confederate Point and offered his services to Colonel Lamb, the fort's commander. He declined Lamb's offer to take command however.[2] Whiting was seen charging around the parapets and shouting encouragement to the men. He was hit twice by gunshots and fell bloody and wounded to the ground. A short time later Lamb was trying to lead a counterattack against an enemy-occupied bunker when he was hit in the hip by a lead ball. Whiting and Lamb were carried to a temporary shelter, where they lay side by side, unable to help their men in the final minutes of battle.

Major-General Whiting died of dysentery, while recovering from his wounds, at Governor's Island, New York, on 10th March and was buried nearby; his wife had his body exhumed in 1900 and moved to Oakdale Cemetery in Wilmington, North Carolina. Colonel William Lamb, though grievously wounded, eventually recovered and became mayor of Norfolk, Virginia from 1880 to 1886. He died in Norfolk on 23 March 1909. In 1864 he had a paddle steamer named for him, running the blockade briefly between November 1864 and January 1865.

Once Fort Fisher fell the Confederates were obliged to evacuate Wilmington, thus closing a major chapter of the Civil War. It also removed the whole *raison d'etre* of the North Atlantic Blockading Squadron, the largest force in the US Navy.

Wilmington had been ill-used during the war. The city had been an important centre for trade at the beginning of the war. Late in August, or early September, 1862, the *Kate* (ex-*Caroline*) arrived there with a large cargo. Her arrival was met by a large crowd as this was one of the early runners to visit. Unfortunately many members of the *Kate's* crew were infected with yellow fever, then endemic in the Caribbean.[3] The first death from yellow fever occurred on 9th September. Nearly 1,000 people soon contracted the disease, of which more than 300 died. The city became more important through the war as the resources of the Confederacy contracted. With the increased importance came a lessening of supplies for the local population; prices increased dramatically (for example $50 for a ham, $100 per pound of coffee or tea and $500 for a pair of boots)[4] and those who could leave, did, leaving a more and more desperate group behind.

The Battle of Wilmington took place between 11th and 22nd February 1865. The defending troops, under General Bragg, burned supplies and equipment and stores of tobacco and cotton before leaving the city. The battle closed what was the last major port of the Confederate States, and with this act finally completed the blockade of the South. While the city was in a very poor condition, it gave the Union army a port to supply its forces, although initially some of this material had also to feed paroled soldiers and the remaining civilian population.

In March 1865 *Cornubia* was ordered to the West Coast Blockading Squadron.

Named for Fort Fisher's commander, the 1788-ton *Colonel Lamb* was registered on 16th September 1864 and ran the blockade twice in November, into and out of Wilmington. After being reputedly sold to Greek interests after the war and renamed *Boulabina* she was destroyed by an explosion while loading munitions in Liverpool in 1866 or 1867.

On the 24th she was involved in the capture of the steamer *Corn*, while on the night of the 19th a steamer was seen grounded on a bar off Galveston from which *Cornubia* recovered 89 bales of abandoned cotton, with another 50 recovered by the *Gertrude*.[5] The steamer, which escaped, was identified as the *Denbigh*. At about 10pm on the evening of the 21st, the *Cornubia* ran down the schooner *Chaos*, attempting to run from Galveston; her cargo of 170 bales was also captured.[6] On 1st April her armament was increased by the addition of two 12-pounder rifles.[7]

While Galveston was not officially retaken by Union forces, under Major General Gordon Granger, until 19th June (now known as Juneteenth) Confederate forces had not been there since the previous month; the city having been essentially abandoned on May 24th. Three days prior to this 300 paroled Confederate officers (including General Wilcox) and men had been brought to the city to convince the military authorities to give up; evidently this had worked.[8]

On the morning of the 24th a blockade runner was seen aground in the Bolivar Channel, separating Galveston Island and Goat Island; this turned out to be one of the remaining big prizes of the war, the *Denbigh*, one of the very few runners to complete more trips from Bermuda than the *Cornubia*.[9] She had run so regularly into Mobile and Galveston she was popularly known as *The Packet*. Trying to slip out in thick hazy weather she ran aground on Bird Key Spit. The

Cornubia, *New London*, *Princess Royal* (yet another former regular visitor with the *Cornubia* to Bristol) and *Albatross*, under orders from Captain Benjamin F. Sands (officer commanding the West Gulf Blockading Squadron) got under way from their night stations and stood in towards the land.[10] The water was too shallow for them to get very close but after getting as near as possible they opened fire (40 shots were fired) but inflicted little damage. Boats then put out from the nearby USS *Kennebec* and USS *Seminole* and the runner was set on fire and "effectively destroyed" by 7am. Unfortunately Seaman Luke Robins of the *Seminole* was killed by the accidental discharge of his own gun while leaving the wreck.[11]

Following the destruction of the *Denbigh*, Captain Sands wrote to his superiors that:

> I have the satisfaction to report the destruction of the famous blockade runner *Denbigh*.....she was discovered from this vessel at daylight this morning aground on Bird Key Spit, near Bolivar Point. I sent the *Cornubia* and *Princess Royal* to open fire upon her, and boats were sent from the *Kennebec* and *Seminole* to board and destroy her, which effectively done by 7am .... She is now a complete wreck and has made her last voyage.[12]

Johnstone and the *Cornubia* were ordered to stand by the *Denbigh* in order to prevent any Confederate boats from boarding the burning wreck until she was completely destroyed. While anchored in shallow water a schooner (acting as a guard boat) was seen half a mile off, which got under way when the *Cornubia* was discovered approaching. After two shots were fired at her, the schooner hauled down her sails and part of her crew escaped in a boat. An armed boat from the *Cornubia*, under Acting Ensign Frank Millett, was sent to board the schooner

The blockade runner *Denbigh*, painted in 1864.

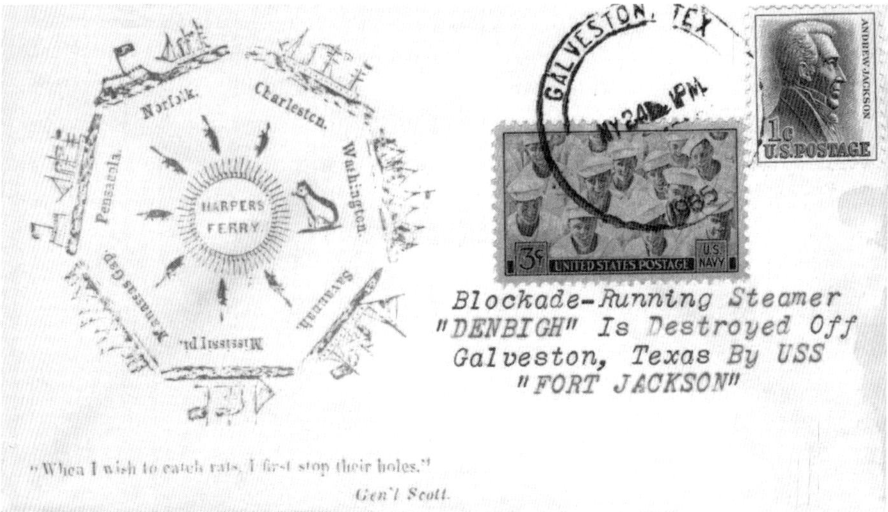

This cover was issued in 1964 to commemorate the destruction of the *Denbigh*. Unfortunately it gives credit to the USS *Fort Jackson*, a vessel which was not actually in the area at the time.

and bring her out if possible.[13] Unfortunately she was stuck fast; Millett had a 24-pounder howitzer thrown overboard and brought off the four remaining crew members, five carbines, five new Enfield rifles, a steering compass and a rebel flag. She proved to be the *Le Compt*, a guard boat from Galveston. This turned out to be the *Cornubia's* last ship to ship action, as Galveston was then being evacuated by the Confederates.

The flag taken from the *Le Compt* is considered to be the last Confederate flag captured in a naval action during the Civil War. It was passed on to Captain Sands who in turn gave it to Acting Rear Admiral H. K. Thatcher.[14] On June 29th he in turn passed it on to Secretary Gideon Welles along with a letter of explanation; its current whereabouts are unknown.

The crew of the *Le Compt* gave the information that the only reason no one had opened fire on the various vessels at Galveston was that there were insufficient gun crews for the task.[15]

The crew of the *Denbigh* managed to escape capture and find refuge, or as much of it as there was, in Galveston.[16] Later that day the blockade runner *Lark* managed to reach the harbour where she was mobbed by desperate citizens who removed everything they could from the vessel, almost completely stripping it. After the crowd finally dispersed, *Lark's* captain took aboard the *Denbigh's* crew and dashed out to sea again, the last blockade runner to clear a Confederate port.

Captain Sands reported the following month:

> On the morning of June 5th I hoisted my divisional pennant on the U. S. S. "Cornubia". I crossed the bar at the entrance to Galveston Harbor, and in company with Commanders Stevens and Downes and Lieutenant-Commander Wilson, with my orderly and Chief Quartermaster Knight, I landed in Galveston, and was met upon the wharf by the Mayor of the city, Van Horten, who conducted us to his office, followed by a large number of the citizens.
>
> Arriving at his office the Mayor made an address to the assembled citizens, informing them that I had come ashore to hoist the flag of the Union over the public property, and expressing the hope that good order would be preserved and continued.[17]

However, it was not until the arrival of Major General Granger that President Lincoln's Emancipation Proclamation was read to the general population, two and a half years after it became official on 1st January 1863. Granger's proclamation read:

> The people of Texas are informed that in accordance with a Proclamation from the Executive of the United States, all slaves are free. This involves an absolute equality of rights and rights of property between former masters and slaves, and the connection heretofore existing between them becomes that between employer and free laborer.[18]

Chapter 15

End of Service

On 13th July 1865 the *Cornubia*, along with the *Preston*, *Gertrude*, *Penquin*, *Antona* and *Albatross*, were ordered to proceed to Philadelphia, leaving only the sloop *Oneida* and the gunboat *Port Royal* to patrol Galveston;[1] from this time the US Navy was to be reduced from 626 vessels to about 90 and then to an "ineffectual hodgepodge of obsolete vessels" (fewer than twenty) by the late 1870s.[2]

The blockade officially ended on 23rd June. On 21st July 1865 *Cornubia* sailed for Philadelphia; she hauled down the Stars and Stripes on 9th August and was sold out of the US Navy on 25th October 1865 at New York, by Burdett, Jones &. Co. to Merrick & Sons for $19,000 at public auction; the gross proceeds of her sale were $104,332.03; costs were $5,139.82, leaving $99,192.21 to go to the US Navy.[3] Merrick & Sons was a Philadelphia shipbuilder better known for building the engines for the *New Ironsides*, which took a major part in the final bombardment of Fort Fisher, the hull being built by the nearby Cramp Shipyard.[4] Merrick & Sons, Iron Founders, constructed almost all of the machinery for the US Navy steamers during the war and it seems natural that the company would buy up good-looking steamers after the war. Ironically they had also built the USS *Tuscarora*.

In the military, time often runs slowly. While *Cornubia* was sold quickly, the proceeds of her capture would not be sent to the Fourth Auditor of the US Treasury for distribution until 22nd January 1866.[5] This was distributed amongst the crews of the *Niphon*, *Daylight* and *James Adger*; there is no mention of the *Shenandoah*, *Tuscarora* or *Howquah*, despite the request of Captain Ridgely to Thomas Patterson of the *James Adger* to include them. Lieutenant Francis Swells' appeal, on behalf of the *Daylight* to be included in the claim, was successful (it was countersigned by Acting Rear Admiral Lee) although she played no active part in *Cornubia's* capture.

The Boston Prize Court's deliberations were somewhat tedious, not least because several witnesses from each claiming vessel were required to be interrogated. Adding the three remaining crew of the *Cornubia* gave twenty-two depositions for the court to ponder. Fortunately for the maritime experts drafted as judges, all of the witnesses were given the same seventeen questions to answer.[6]

The *Niphon* and *James Adger* were comparatively successful ships with regard to prize money; the former was involved in the capture of the steamers *Annie*, *Ella and Annie*, *Kate* and *Cornubia* and her crew had a share of $638,807.29 while the latter was credited with the steamers *Elizabeth*, *Kate*, *Cornubia* and the *Robert E. Lee* and the schooner *Sarah* and a share of $330,547.50.[7] The smallest prize during the war was $1.11 (!) between twelve ships for the capture of the sloop *Last Trial*; it will be no surprise to learn that the amount was too small to divide. The single largest prize of the war was $510,914.07 to the crew of the USS *Magnolia* for the capture of the steamer *Memphis*. James Sprunt[8] estimated that the US government made $21,759,595.05 from the public sales of prizes as recorded in *The Naval History of the Civil War* plus $10,000,000 for sales not recorded in that publication, plus another $10,000,00 for ships and cargoes "stranded or destroyed by accident".

During the war the US Navy had bought 497 vessels; of these, 363 were disposed of by sale, 97 had been lost, destroyed, sunk as obstructions or transferred to the army, and 37 were still in service.[9] Sixty three of these vessels were sold along with *Cornubia* in New York in October; she was said to have been sold on October 10th. A report in the *New York Times* stated that both the *Cornubia* and the *Lord Clyde* were brought into New York on the 24th of October, towed in by the USS *South Carolina*.[10] At a prize court adjudicated on 1st May 1868, *Cornubia's* crew was credited with 89 bales of cotton, captured from the schooner *Chaos*.

Cornubia is listed in Lloyd's Register for July 1865-June 1866 as a steamship under the command of W. Gill, though as this is the same master as given in the Register for 1859-62; this is incorrect. In 1866 the USS *Cornubia* was re-registered as a merchant steamer with the new name *New England*, though if she ever sailed as a steamer under this name is not known; certainly there appear to be no records.

Chapter 16

New England: The *Cornubia* Reborn

The next reference to the *Cornubia* is in the *Register of American Shipping* for 1871-1872 where she is now the "New England, ex-Cornubia"; there is no further mention of her under her new name in the Lloyd's Register. Her master was Obediah Baxter and she was owned by N. Gibson of Boston. The register also noted that her engines had been removed in March 1871 and that she was now rigged as a barque (or barquentine). While the work to do this may have ended in that month, it most certainly did not start then, possibly not even in that year.

The term "barquentine" is 17th century in origin, formed from "barque" in imitation of "brigantine", a two-masted vessel square-rigged only on the forward mast, and apparently formed from the word brig.[1] A barquentine or schooner barque ("barkentine" or "schooner bark" on the west side of the Atlantic) is a sailing vessel with three or more masts; it has a square rigged foremast and fore-and-aft rigged main, mizzen and any other masts. This type of rig has the advantages of requiring a smaller crew, a good performance before the wind and the ability to sail relatively close to the wind while carrying a heavy cargo. It was a particularly popular rig at the end of the 19th century.

At the close of the American Civil War a number of surplus men-of-war were offered for sale by the United States Navy. Many of these were wooden gunboats built for blockade duty; these hulls were in good condition and represented good bargains for thrifty ship owners. However, there were many steamships, all of which were iron-hulled. Those which were to be converted to sailing vessels were somewhat longer than the usual contemporary sailer (usually around about 200 feet in length) and presented a rigging problem; the answer, in at least four cases in the late 1860s, was to give them four masts instead of the then customary three.

The appearance of these vessels was something of a surprise to later historians; while the barquentine rig seems to have evolved in Canada in about 1838 (on a three-masted vessel), the first Canadian four-master was not built untill 1884 while the first US four-masted barquentines were not built on the Pacific coast until 1890.[2]

In October 1867, three such war-built gunboats were sold. *Osceola*, built at East Boston in 1863, became the four-masted schooner *Eliza*, an early example of this rig in the Atlantic. *Genesee*, as *Hallie C. Besse*, was rigged as a 'schooner chasing a brig'. The *Agaivam*, built at Portland, Maine, in 1863, was converted in 1868 to *Mora*, very probably the world's first four-masted barquentine. *Mora's* conversion was carried out at Baltimore, and upon completion she was sailed to the River Plate with a cargo of naval stores. One of *Mora's* owners was a Captain Gibson of Boston, and this provides a possible link with the later *New England*. A report in a number of newspapers in May 1875 confirmed that the *New England* was purchased in 1870 by Captain Gibson of East Boston and that it was he who was responsible for the conversion.[3] Whether he bought the hull with or without the engines is not known.

N. Gibson is likely to be Nehemiah Gibson of East Boston; the title 'Captain' was probably added as an honorific for a ship owner. Gibson was born in Ashby, Suffolk, Massachusetts on 16th April 1816 and died in Boston, Suffolk, Massachusetts on 25th April 1882.[4] Following his arrival in Boston in 1837 he became heavily involved in the wood and coal business through his business, N. Gibson & Company, which was located on Lewis Street. Working through this business he became associated with Alonzo Crosby, when they acquired a large number of government transports, several of which were altered to sailing vessels and used in the merchant service. One of Gibson's ships was the barquentine

The four-masted barquentine *Mozart*; *New England* would have looked very similar to this.

Nehemiah Gibson, although this was built as a barquentine and not a conversion. Gibson bought the USS *Penobscot* in October 1869.[5]

The work, most likely carried out by Merrick & Sons, possibly even using the nearby Cramp Shipyard, would essentially have required gutting the *Cornubia*. The paddle wheels may well have required cutting off as they would surely have been badly corroded. Deck superstructures, as well as the fore and aft masts, would have been removed to allow access to the engines and boilers, and then new decks and bulkheads fitted below following their removal. Following this four taller masts and a new, lengthened, bowsprit were fitted and all new rigging attached. New deck superstructures would have been fitted; possibly some of the original passenger space at the stern was kept for crew accommodation. Finally the whole ship would have been re-ballasted to ensure that she was stable; in all a great deal of work, particularly re-ballasting. While the *New England* was technically the *Cornubia* reborn, little beyond the original hull would have remained.

In a parallel, *Cornubia's* would-be adversary, the USS *Vanderbilt*, was also converted after the war, in 1873, having been laid up in ordinary (laid up under the direction of the officers of a navy-yard or dockyard) since 1867. She was given a graceful clipper bow and renamed *The Three Brothers*.[6]

It is remarkable that *Cornubia* had kept her name for so long. Many of the ships acquired for blockade running had their names changed while many of the runners captured and taken into Union service had their names changed. The *Robert E. Lee* is a case in point, starting life as the *Giraffe*, running the blockade as the *Lee* and trying to stop the blockade as the USS *Fort Donaldson*. It seems that not even an apparently official name change, to the *Lady Davis*, could change *Cornubia's* name. However, as a four-masted sailing ship the name change was obviously justified, though it has caused problems for modern historians as the name *New England* is not as unusual as it might be.

Of course there may be more obvious reasons for changing and not changing names. Regarding the *Lee*, it seems unlikely that the US Navy would not tolerate the name of the enemy in its service, while not changing the name of the *Cornubia* could be a way of flaunting the name of one of the South's darlings.

It is possible that the *Cornubia's* disappearance between 1865 and 1871 was down to the time required for the conversion, although she may just have lain derelict at the shipyard after the removal of her engines. Neither the *American Lloyd's Register of Shipping* nor the (British) *Lloyd's Register* gives much information on the vessel, though the *New York Maritime Register* fortunately does. In fact, although *Cornubia's* wind-powered career did not last for very long in terms of years, it certainly did in terms of miles.

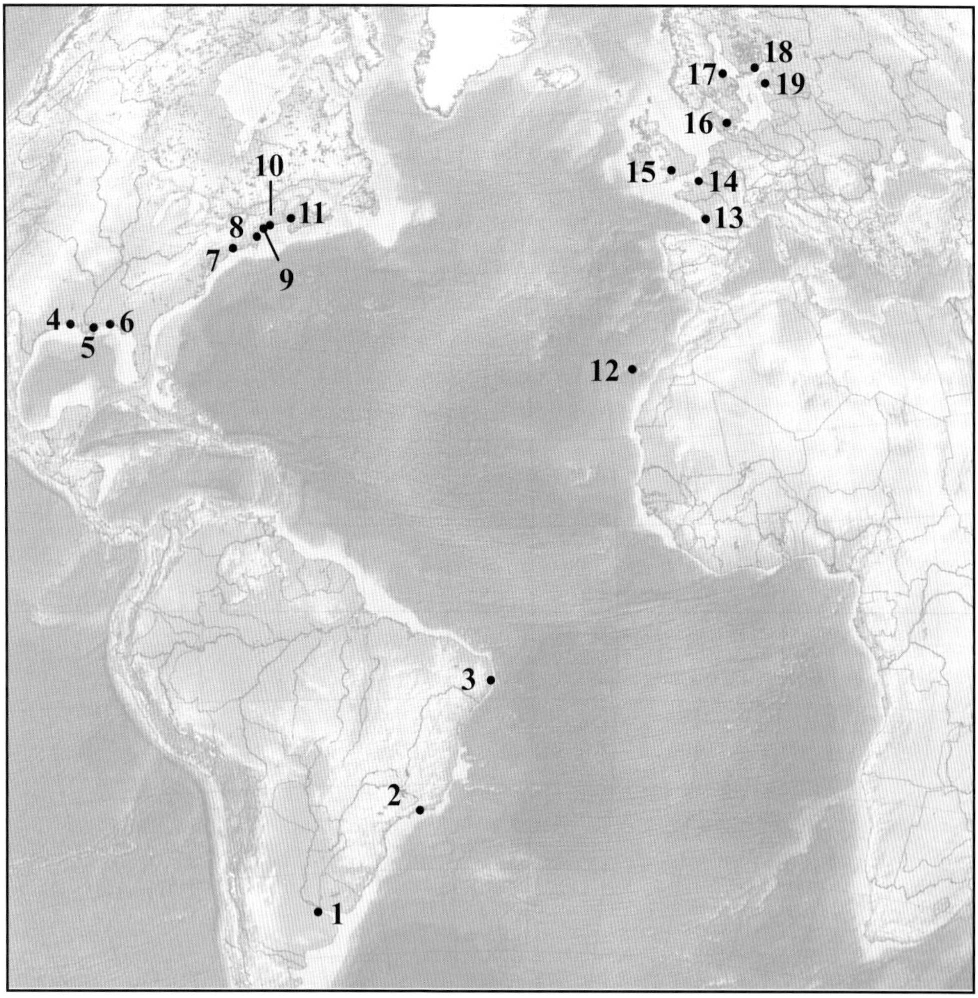

Ports of call of the barquentine New England.

1. Buenos Aires, Argentina
2. Rio de Janeiro, Brazil
3. Pernambuco (state), Brazil
4. Galveston, Texas
5. New Orleans, Louisiana
6. Pensecola, Florida
7. New York
8. Boston, Massachusetts
9. Portland, Maine
10. Bath, Maine
11. St John, New Brunswick, Canada
12. Santa Cruz de Tenerife
13. Bordeaux, France
14. Le Havre, France
15. Bristol, UK
16. Elsinore, Denmark
17. Helsingfors, Sweden
18. Hudickswall, Sweden
19. Pernau, Estonia

Each of her voyages was different and she must be considered a 'tramp,' that is, a vessel which operates without a fixed schedule or published port of call, going wherever required to deliver her cargoes.

Between March and September 1871 the *New England* operated between Boston and Mobile, her old Union Navy hunting ground.[7] On 8th September she arrived in St John, New Brunswick, while on 27th October she arrived at Santa Cruz de Tenerife on her first Atlantic crossing. Arriving at New York on 4th January 1872, she was in New Orleans by about 21st February with goods for Geo. A. Fosdick & Co.[8] She left that port on the 9th April with 1,385 bales of cotton and on 23rd May she arrived in Elsinore, Denmark, travelling between there and Pernau, Estonia,[9] during June and July; she left Pernau for home on 5th July. Following her fourth Atlantic crossing she arrived back in Boston on 28th August. Barely drawing breath she left Boston on 26th September,[10] arriving in Galveston on 14th October.[11] Leaving that port on 11th November,[12] she arrived in Le Havre on 29th December 1872.[13]

It was during the visit to Le Havre, ironically after discharging 1,175 bales of Texas cotton, that the *New England* was painted by the French artist Eugene Grandin (c.1833-c.1919), who produced a miniature of her.[14] In 1965 this was in the possession of Mrs Albert B. Lewis, of Weymouth, Massachusetts, a neighbour of Commander Francis E. Clark, USN (retired). Clark carried out research into the vessel which resulted in an article entitled *An Early Four-Masted Barquentine.*[15] The current location of the miniature is not known but presumably it is with one of Mrs Lewis' relatives. Also missing is a carved-wood relief of a sailing vessel, presumed to be the *New England,* and signed by Augustus Hallet (see below), formerly in the museum of the Historical Society of Old Yarmouth, at Cape Cod.[16]

After leaving Le Havre, *New England* arrived in Bordeaux on 3rd February 1873;[17] following a delay, presumably waiting for a cargo, she departed on 20th March[18] and arrived in Buenos Aires on 24 May.[19] Arriving at Rio de Janeiro on 10th August,[20] she departed on 4th Septembe[21] and arrived in New Orleans on 24rd October (delivering 5000 bags of coffee to Johnston, Gordon & Co.).[22] Departing on the 26th she was back in Boston on 16th December.[23] The *New Orleans Republican* of 24th October names her master as Davis, rather than Baxter, however the same paper for November 27th names Baxter. After spending all of February in Mobile, Alabama, leaving on 6th March, *New England* arrived at Helsingfors, Finland, on 12th April,[24] her seventh Atlantic crossing. Between April and June she sailed around Estonia, finally departing Hudickswall, Sweden, around June 20th.[25]

The *Bristol Mercury* for the 4th July 1874 noted

SHIPPING INTELLIGENCE

ARRIVED....*New England*, Baxter, Hudickswall

Did anyone recognise the tired, shabby-looking sailing ship as the elite paddle steamer which had arrived in that same port with such great celebration just sixteen years before? Would her master have thought to have mentioned it at the dockside? Doubtless it would have brought him a few drinks from listeners eager to learn about *Cornubia's* Civil War exploits (if he knew about them – see below). Following a brief stop-over in Newport, Gwent, in July, *New England* made her eighth, and final, Atlantic crossing, arriving off Pernambuco, Brazil, on 31st August[26] 1874 and leaving on 1st October.[27]

Arriving at New Orleans on 11th November,[28] and departing on the 27th, *New England* visited Galveston, Boston and New York, arriving at the latter port on 9th April 1875.[29] The *New England's* arrival at New York was printed in the *New York Sun* and the report repeated in a number of other publications, including the *York Herald* of 14th May 1875. The piece starts: "The fastest sailing vessel in the world is at Pier 3, East River. She is known as the *New England*". Unfortunately after this the account swerves away from historical accuracy rather quickly, stating that the vessel had been built in Hull as the *Canubria*

A VESSEL'S HISTORY.

FIRST A BRITISH MAIL STEAM PACKET—THEN A BLOCKADE-RUNNER, AND LAST A BARKENTINE—THE FASTEST SAILING VESSEL IN THE WORLD.

The iron clipper-built barkentine New-England, now lying at Pier No. 3 East River, may safely be regarded as having had one of the most eventful histories of any vessel at present engaged in the Atlantic merchant marine service. She was built in Hull, England, in 1858, for the British mail service, and was employed in carrying her Majesty's mails across the Channel. She was at that time a side-wheel steamer, and was built entirely with a view to speed and strength, and is said to have been one of the fastest steamers that ever crossed the Channel. Shortly after the breaking out of the war of the rebellion she was employed as a blockade runner, in which capacity she is said to have been very successful, having made noless than six trips from Wilmington, N.C., to Liverpool, with as many cargoes of cotton. At that time she was known as the Canubria. She was finally captured in 1863, by the United States gun-boats, while leaving Wilmington with her seventh cargo. She was afterward used by the United States Government as a dispatch-boat for a short time, and in 1870 was purchased by her present owners, Mr. Gibson, of East Boston, and Mr. Baxter, of Dennis, Cape Cod. She was then changed from a steamer to a barkentine, and her name changed to the New-England. The New-England is a remarkably beautiful, stanch-looking vessel, and is said to have retained her fast-sailing qualities. It is claimed for her that she is the fastest sailing vessel in the world, having actually made sixty knots in four hours. Her length is 210 feet, depth of hold 15 feet, breadth of beam 25 feet, 462 tons burden, and 800 tons measurement capacity. She has made the trip under sail from Mobile, Ala., to Elsinore, Denmark, in twenty-eight days, and from Boston to Mobile in ten days and eighteen hours. Her career since she came into the hands of her present owners has been as pecuniarily successful as it had been remarkable. She has never met with an accident or lost a spar, and has earned for her owners an aggregate of about $100,000 in four years, or a net income of $60,000. Her present value is about $35,000. Her crew consists of eight men, including officers and sailors. She has been chartered by Messrs. R. W. Cameron & Co., No. 23 South William street, and is loading for Sydney, New South Wales. She is commanded by Capt. Obia Baxter. During her career as a British mail-boat she is said to have run down and sunk some six or seven vessels in her passages across the Channel. The plates of which she is constructed are said to be an inch thick, and those on her bottom are of the best English steel.

A description of the fastest sailing ship in the world, from the *New York Times* of 4th April 1875. Some facts are plainly wrong while others are close enough to the truth. The clipper *Soveriegn of the Seas*, capable of 22 knots was the alleged fastest sailing ship in the world.

for the “British mail service across the Channel”. She was then alleged to have made six trips from Wilmington to Liverpool, being captured on her seventh trip and then used as a government despatch boat. It is sad that her real history seems to have been lost so quickly.

She had made the voyage under sail from Mobile to Elsinore in 28 days and from Boston to Mobile in 10 days and 18 hours. She had frequently made 60 knots in four hours, *i.e.* her sailing speed was 15 knots. This was a remarkably fast speed for a vessel of this type; while probably not the actual fastest ship in the world, she was probably in the top 5% for sailing vessels. This report also confirmed that the *New England* was purchased in 1870 by Captain Gibson of East Boston and that it was he who was responsible for the conversion.

By this time, unfortunately, she was beginning to show her age. While being loaded at New York for Sydney a few days later, for what would have been her longest journey to date, she was found to be leaking badly, possibly a result of her hard wartime uses or even the major work to convert her to a barquentine.[30] The cargo had to be discharged and was eventually forwarded via a British brig; *New England* was dry-docked and then returned to Boston, abandoning the Australian voyage and arriving in port on 22nd June.

It was while she was in Boston that she acquired a new master, Captain Augustus Hallet, who must have been the first mate for at least one voyage under Captain Baxter in order to familiarise himself with the vessel. Under Baxter, and possibly because of her delicate condition, *New England* was kept to familiar territory, travelling the coastal routes from Boston to Galveston (7th September 1875)[31] to New Orleans (9th October),[32] Galveston (30th October), Provincetown (Maine: 1st January 1876),[33] Bath (Maine: 4th January),[34] Portland (mid-January), New Orleans (1st March),[35] Boston (12th May),[36] Galveston (21st July),[37] Pensecola (22nd August) and Boston (30th September 1876).[38] *New England* was still in port on 17th October but there is no record after that date; it seems she was laid up at this point. In September 1877 she was resurveyed and the results must have been unfavourable.[39] On 8th August she ran aground west of the channel into New Orleans at 1pm; she was refloated during the night though the incident could not have done her any good.[40] *New England* was still listed in the 1879 edition of *Merchant Vessels of the United States*, but not in the 1880 volume; it is presumed that sometime about then she was sent to the scrap yard; however there is an as yet unproven reference that she foundered at sea in 1878.[41]

Summary

Coastal packet steamer, blockade runner, man-of-war and tramp sailer, the *Cornubia* lived a varied and adventurous life. Launched as one of the fastest ships of her generation she ran the packet route between Hayle and Bristol for nearly three years, her career cut short by the encroachment of the railway line into Cornwall. Her brief appearance for the South Western Steam Packet Company appears to be entirely down to trials on behalf of Thomas Begbie, who might politely be described as an entrepreneur. During her three-year steam packet career the *Cornubia* travelled some 6,888 miles between Hayle and Bristol and 6,145 miles between London and Lisbon in about three months.

After arriving in St George's, Bermuda, she ran the blockade successfully twenty-two times, bringing large quantities of much-needed war materials to the beleaguered South. While other runners made great fortunes for their crews by carrying what might be described as expensive 'fripperies', the *Cornubia* was owned by the Confederate government and carried very little that was not essential to the war effort; muskets, pistols, lead bars, saltpeter and others, returning with bales of cotton to pay for those supplies. Including travelling to Glasgow for repairs and Bermuda for starting her career as a blockade runner, she clocked up another 18,400 miles to her total.

Cornubia's career as a blockade runner should not be under-estimated. Approximately 100 ships ran the Atlantic blockade from Bermuda or Nassau to the Carolina coast. Statistically, these runners made four successful attempts out of five; *Cornubia* ran 22 out of 23, making her the fourth most successful runner. The most successful ship was the *Syren*, with 33 out of 33. Including all other blockade runner routes, *Cornubia* was the fifth most successful of the war.

Even capture by the Union navy could not stop *Cornubia*, and for the remainder of the war she sailed under the Stars and Stripes, ironically capturing the last Stars and Bars of the war from a Confederate ship. *Cornubia's* travels as part of the US Navy cannot be easily estimated but it should exceed 10,000 miles.

Perhaps, ironically, it was after her engines were removed and her conversion to a barquentine, that the *Cornubia*, as the *New England*, really travelled. Her eight trans-Atlantic trips and various other trips along the East Coast of the USA added another 88,300 miles to her theoretical odometer. There are implications of trips around the Baltic which have not been taken into account. An estimate of the total distance travelled by the *Cornubia* and *New England* is 130,000 miles, enough to circumnavigate the earth five and a quarter times. The distances used here however, are taken from a website which gives distances between ports for modern merchant ships; the *New England* would have taken different routes between the ports and also had the weather to take into account; the 130,000 miles is therefore likely to be something of an underestimate.

It seems unlikely that the shipwrights of Harvey & Co. of Hayle ever knew the full story of their creation, her subsequent career, or her travels; they would undoubtedly have been proud that their ship had survived so many situations that they had not even considered when she was being planned and built.

Appendix I

Details of the *Cornubia's* Blockade Runs and Cargoes

* estimated date

1a As *Cornubia*
From: St George's Date left: 12.12.1862 (CBR/BRG)
Date left: 13.12.1862 (DFB)
To: Wilmington Date arrived: 17.12.1862* (LLC)
Cargo: 525 bales containing general merchandise from Justitia, London, 1 trunk, 1 case (CBR)
Cargo: government stores, shoes, blankets, iron plates (WJ)

1b As *Cornubia*
From: Wilmington Date left: 14.1.1863 (DFB)
To: St George's Date arrived: 19.1.1863 (DFB/BRG)
Cargo: 300 bales cotton, 80 barrels rosin, tobacco, turpentine (DFB)

2a As *Cornubia*
From: St George's Date left: 26.1.1863 (CBR/DFB/BRG)
To: Wilmington Date arrived: 30.1.1863* (LLC)
Date arrived: 31.1.1863 (WD/WJ)
Cargo: Imported per Justitia, London: general merchandise, 157 bales, 260 cases, 1 cask, 100 pigs lead, 50 bundles steel rod (CBR)
Imported per Merrimac: 35 cases brandy (CBR)
Imported per Harriet Pinckney: 1 case merchandise, 1 cask brushes (CBR)
Cargo: "Blankets, Boots and Shoes, clothing," etc. (DFB)
Cargo: 260 cases = 5,200 Enfield rifle muskets (SAD)

2b As *Cornubia*
From: Wilmington Date left: 15.2.1863* (LLC)
To: St George's Date arrived: 17.2.1863 (YE)
Date arrived: 19.2.1863 (DFB)
Cargo: 324 bales cotton, 23 boxes tobacco, 2 barrels turpentine (BRG)

3a As *Cornubia*

From: St George's — Date left: 25.2.1863 (CBR/DFB/BRG)
To: Wilmington — Date arrived: 1.3.1863 (LLC/LM/MDA)
Date arrived: 2.3.1863 (ORN)

Cargo: Imported per Justitia, London, value £10,000: 130 bales and 25 cases manufactured merchandise, 50 barrels saltpeter, 100 boxes tin, 100 pigs lead, 100 ingots tin (CBR)
Imported per Gladiator, value £4,500: 111 cases hardware, 72 boxes combustible merchandise, 178 boxes combustible merchandise (CBR)
Imported per Delta: 1 package wearing apparel (CBR)
Imported per Miriam: 1 case wearing apparel (CBR)
Imported per Merrimac: 600 barrels gunpowder; 4 cases stationery, £50.0.0, 45 cases brandy from John T. Bourne's warehouse (CBR).
Cargo: 111 cases hardware = 2,200 Enfield rifle muskets (SAD)

3b As *Cornubia*

From: Wilmington — Date left: 18.3.1863 (DFB)
To: St George's — Date arrived: 22.3.1863 (DFB/NYT/BRC)

Cargo: 314 bales of cotton, 29 casks of tobacco, 2 casks turpentine (DFB)
Passengers: Mrs N. S. Walker and family and Colonel Robinson

4a As *Cornubia*

From: St George's — Date left: 27.3.1863 (CBR/BRG)
To: Wilmington — Date left: 28.3.1863 (DFB)
Date arrived: 1.4.1863 (LLC/LM/MDA)

Cargo: Imported per Justitia, London: 122 cases manufactured merchandise, 42 casks hardware, 150 barrels saltpeter, 100 pigs lead, 100 ingots tin, 350 boxes cartridges, 5 bales merchandise (CBR)
From W. L. Penno's store, imported from London per Gladiator: 50 bales general merchandise (CBR) Imported per Dashing Wave: 8 cases general merchandise, 250 cases hardware (CBR)
From Hunter's and Penno's warehouse, imported per Phebe: 200 cases brandy (CBR)
From John T. Bourne's warehouse, imported per Merrimac, London: 80 cases brandy. 6 packages merchandise, value £50-0-0 (CBR)
Cargo: 122 cases = 2,440 Enfield rifle muskets (SAD)

4b As *Cornubia*

From: Wilmington	Date left: 15.4.1863* (LLC)
To: St George's	Date arrived: 22.4.1863 (DFB)
Date arrived: 24.4.1863 (NYT)
Cargo: 370 bales cotton (NYT)

5a As *Cornubia*

From: St George's	Date left: 8.5.1863 (CBR/BRG)
To: Wilmington	Date arrived: 13.5.1863* (LLC/LM/MDA)
Date arrived: 19.5.1863 (DFB)
Cargo: From W. L. Penno's warehouse, imported per Gladiator, Liverpool: 200 cases hardware, 250 boxes combustible ammunition (CBR)
From same warehouse, imported per Justitia, London: 25 bundles hardware, 151 barrels saltpeter, 50 pigs lead, 44 cases merchandise (CBR)
From same warehouse, imported per Merrimac, London: 133 packages hardware (CBR)
From same warehouse, imported per Dashing Wave, London: 15 cases hardware, 56 cases general merchandise (CBR)
From same warehouse, imported per Phebe, London: 200 cases brandy. From John T. Bourne's warehouse, imported per Merrimac, London: 63 cases brandy (CBR)
From warehouse, imported per Princess Royal: 21 bundles telegraph wire (CBR)
Group of cargo, valued at £169.0.0: 37 barrels beef and pork, 34 boxes cheese, 5 barrels molasses, 16 sacks salt, 56 boxes harness(CBR)
Cargo: 200 cases = 4,000 Enfield rifle muskets (SAD).

5b As *Cornubia*

From: Wilmington	Date left: 25.5.1863* (LLC)
To: St George's	Date arrived: 28.5.1863 (DFB)
Date arrived: 29.5.1863 (BRG)
Cargo: cotton, turpentine and tobacco

6a As *Lady Davis*

From: St George's	Date left: 5.6.1863 (CBR/DFB/BRG)
To: Wilmington	Date arrived: 9.6.1863* (LLC)
Date arrived: 10.6.1863 (MDA)
Cargo: From A. J. Musson's warehouse, imported per Miriam: 100 boxes combustible merchandise, 99 cases hardware, 101 boxes combustible ammunition (CBR)
From W. L. Penno's warehouse, imported per Justitia, London: 50 pigs lead,

41 bales general merchandise, 63 cases general merchandise, 25 bales general merchandise, 5 carboys acid (CBR)
From John T. Bourne's warehouse, imported per Miriam, London: 5 cases brandy. 3% barrels borax, 30 coils telegraph wire, 100 barrels beef and pork, 40 boxes bacon, 76 barrels onions (9880 lbs.), 1 barrel potatoes (CBR)
Cargo: 41 packages and 72 boxes dry goods, 201 boxes cartridges, 100 boxes Minié rifles, 100 barrels salt provisions, 50 boxes tin, 50 pigs lead and six carboys acid (DFB)
Cargo: 99 cases hardware = 2,376 Austrian rifle muskets (SAD)

6b As *Lady Davis*
From: Wilmington	Date left: 16.6.1863* (LLC)
To: St George's	Date arrived: 20.6.1863 (DFB)
Date arrived: 22.6.1863 (NYDT/BRG)
Cargo: 17 bales of cotton, 20bls turpentine
Passengers: C. L. Vallandigham, (DFB)

7a As *Lady Davis*
From: St George's	Date left: 9.7.1863 (CBR/BRG)
To: Wilmington	Date arrived: 13.7.1863* (LLC)
Date arrived: 14.7.1863 (LM/MDA)
Cargo: From Penno's warehouse, imported per Harriet Pinckney, London: 500 cases, 22 bales, 6 boxes, 4 barrels, 4 rolls general merchandise. 208 pigs lead (CBR)
From John T. Bourne's warehouse, imported per Merrimac: 43 cases brandy (CBR)
From same warehouse, imported per Alpha, Halifax: 2 cases merchandise, 190 barrels beef and pork, 5 rills matting, 2 bales and 1 box bunting, 2 coils telegraph wire, 4 coils manila rope (CBR)
Cargo: 500 cases = 47 cases art. carbines, 12 cases cav. carbines = 940 artillery carbines and 240 cavalry carbines (SAD)

7b As *Lady Davis*
From: Wilmington	Date left: 22.7.1863* (LLC)
To: St George's	Date arrived: 26.7.1863 (CCC)
Date arrived: 27.7.1863 (BRG)
Cargo: 236 bales cotton, 32 bls turpentine and 104½ tierces of tobacco (BRG)

8a As *Cornubia*

From: St George's		Date left: 13.8.1863 (BRG/CBR)
To: Wilmington		Date arrived: 18.8.1863* (LLC)
Cargo: From W. L. Penno's warehouse, imported per Harriet Pinckney, Halifax: 50 coils rope. (CBR)
From C. Hunter's warehouse, imported per Harriet Pinckney, London: 190 boxes cartridges, 50 boxes cartridges, 50 bales merchandise (CBR)
From W. L. Penno's warehouse, imported per Harriet Pinckney, London: 225 pigs lead, 218 boxes ammunition (CBR)
From C. Hunter's warehouse, imported per Harriet Pinckney: 226 cases rifles, 2 cases gun fittings (CBR)
From John T. Bourne's warehouse, imported per James, London: 1 case merchandise (CBR)
Cargo: 228 cases rifles, 2 cases gun fittings = 5,472 arms (SAD)

8b As *Cornubia*

From: Wilmington		Date left: 18.8.1863* (LLC)
To: St George's		Date arrived: not recorded
Cargo: not recorded

9a As *Cornubia*

From: St George's		Date left: not recorded
To: Wilmington		Date arrived: not recorded

9b As *Cornubia*

From: Wilmington		Date left: 4.9.1863* (LLC)
To: St George's		Date arrived: 10.9.1863 (DFB)
Cargo: not recorded, plus passengers

10a As *Cornubia*

From: St George's		Date left: 18.9.1863 (CBR)
To: Wilmington		Date arrived: 22.9.1863* (LLC)
Cargo: From Ella & Annie: 200 cases rifles. (CBR)
From Higgs and Hyland's warehouse, imported per Harriet, Nassau: 50 barrels alcohol (CBR)
From C. Hunter's warehouse, imported per Liz Barnard: 150 barrels pork; from Florida, Nassau: 4 barrels white lead, 1 hogshead linseed oil. 545 coils rope, 6 casks general merchandise, 94 bales general merchandise, 2 boxes general merchandise (CBR)
From Musson's warehouse, imported per Henrietta: 15 casks brandy (401

gallons) (CBR)
From same warehouse, imported per Eagle: 3 casks brandy (175 gallons) (CBR)
Date arrived: 26.9.1863 (DFB)
Date arrived: 25.9.1863 (SAD)
Cargo: 201 cases Austrian rifles (SAD)

10b As *Cornubia*
From: Wilmington   Date left: 5.9.1863 (DCE)
To: St George's   Date arrived: 9.9.1863 (DCE)
Date arrived: 9.9.1863 (BRG)
Cargo: 384 bales cotton, turpentine, specie

11a As *Cornubia*
From: St George's   Date left: 18.9.1863 (CBR, DCE/BRG)
To: Wilmington   Date arrived: 22.9.1863* (LLC)
Date arrived: 24.9.1863 (DCE)
Cargo: not recorded

11b As *Cornubia*
From: Wilmington   Date left: 11.10.1863* (LLC)
To: St George's   Date left: 11.10.1863 (DCE)
Date arrived: 15.10.1863 (DCE/BRG)
Cargo: "cotton, etc"

12a As *Cornubia*
From: St George's   Date left: 4.11.1863 (CBR/BRG)
To: Wilmington   Date arrived: CAPTURED
Cargo: From W. L. Penno's warehouse, imported per Harriet Pinckney: 58 cases bacon, 3 casks bacon, 19 hogsheads bacon, 3 cases cartridge paper, 1 case blankets (CBR)
From same warehouse, imported per Rover's Bride: 12 bales, 1 case (CBR)
From Hunter's warehouse, imported per Glendower, London: 15 cases caps, 36 pigs lead, 300 sacks saltpeter (CBR)
From A. J. Musson's warehouse, imported per Miriam, London: 64 cases rifles (CBR)
From Higgs and Hyland's warehouse, imported per Harkaway: 4 quarter casks brandy (CBR)
Cargo: 64 cases rifles = 1,536 Austrian rifle muskets (SAD)

References

BRC:
Cochrane, H., *Blockade Runners of the Confederacy*. Fine Art Books.

BRG:
British Royal Gazette

CCC:
Correspondence Concerning Claims Against Great Britain volume IV.

DCE:
Diary of Current Events (see below)

DFB:
Allen, Charles Maxwell, 2014. *Dispatches From Bermuda: The Civil War Letters of Charles Maxwell Allen, U.S. Consul at Bermuda, 1861–1888*. Edited by Wiche, Glen N., Kent State University Press.

LLC:
Wise, Stephen R., 1988. *Lifeline of the Confederacy. Blockade Running During the Civil War*. University of South Carolina Press.

LM:
Liverpool Mercury

MDA:
Memphis Daily Appeal 21.8.1863

NYDT:
New York Daily Times 2.7.1863

NYT:
New York Times

ORN:
Official Records of the Union and Confederate Navies in the War of the Rebellion

SAD:
Madaus, H. M., 2001. *Small Arms Deliveries Through Wilmington, NC in 1863, the Impact on Confederate Ordnance Policy*. Bulletin of the American Society of Arms Collectors No. 85 pp

WD:
Western Democrat 3.2.1863

Appendix II

"Diary of Current Events"

Private notebook kept by J. T. Gordon onboard the blockade runner Cornubia, captured November 8, 1865, by US steamers James Adger and Niphon, near New Inlet, Wilmington, North Carolina. Transcribed by the author.

Friday 4th September 1863
Attached to the CS Cornubia, now at anchor off Wilmington, N.C. At 1 o'clock hove up anchor & proceeded down the river below Fort St Phillips, opposite Ft Fisher, where we came to anchor & purpose remaining till tomorrow night, when we expect to get under way for St Georges, Bermuda, where we are bound. We have a number of passengers, among whom are . . . . [not finished]

Saturday, Sept 5th 1863
Pleasant day - at anchor off Ft Fisher, in Cape Fear river - At 25 minutes past 11 pm got underway & proceeded slowly down to the "Rip" which we crossed without grounding. The moon was then up - crossed the "Bar" at 12 minutes past 12 o'clock midnight. The moon shone very brightly - we saw one Blockader, very near - but he did not see us, although the furnaces were so hot that the flame flashed out over the tops of the funnels or smokestacks at 7 (?) past 3 o'clock saw a Yankee cruiser ahead - kept off to avoid him - he did not discover us.

Sunday 6th Sept 1863
Pleasant weather - dawn revealed several sailing vessels - some of passengers sea sick, among them Professor Bledsoe slightly - He made fun of it, & proved the most agreeable sea sick companion I ever met with - He is full of life & wit.

Monday 7th Sept 1863
Little equality in the morning - Professor Bledsoe has quite gotten over his sea sickness. Made a vessel ahead during the night & kept off to avoid her.

Tuesday 8th Sept 1863
Delightful day - made a sail on starboard beam - kept off a point to avoid her. Sighted the Bermuda light at half past five o'clock p.m. (Wilmington time) & about ½ past 6 o'clock p.m. ships time, being just 64 hours & 30 minutes from the New Inlet Bar - Came up to St Davids Head about ½ past 10 p.m. & kept off

& on till day light -

Wednesday 9th 1863 (Sept)

Came in to the harbour of St Georges, about 6 o'clock a.m. - found the vessels & Haven, steamers, from Wilmington, N. C. in safely. Quite a number of sailing vessels are in the port. A Yankee cruiser came to 5 fathoms hole & communicated with the authorities.

Thursday 10th Sept: 1863

Nothing of interest - commenced discharging cargo - The Yankee cruiser that came in yesterday has left. She is undoubtedly after vessels running the Blockade - on the Confederate Coast.

Friday 11th Sept 1863

The str "Juno" left to day for Wilmington. A very heavy North East Gale came up about 12 m (?) - & it arrived in torrents - the storm continued through the might. Many of the vessels in post dragged - but no damage done. Paid crew off.

Saturday 12th Sept 1863

Very rainy & squally in first part of the day. Cleared off about 11 o'clock. Finished discharging. Spent the evening very pleasantly with Com. Barron, Professor Bledsoe, Mr & Lieut. Whittle.

Sunday 13th

Beautiful day - Went to the Episcopal Church in St Georges, Bermuda, in company with Commodore Barron, Professor Bledsoe & Lieutenant Whittle. Dined with these gentlemen at their mess. Pleasant time & nice dinner.

Monday 14th Sept 1863

Nothing of interest - the Flora came in from Wilmington. Captain Gayle went to Hamilton.

Tuesday 15th Sept 1863

Flora came Str Phantom from Wilmington came in. I went to Hamilton in a Buggy.

Wednesday 16th Sept 1863

Nothing of interest - Capt. Gayle returned from Hamilton.

Thursday 17th Sept 1863

Coaled the Cornubia. Str St Thomas came in for freight bound to Liverpool.

Friday 18th Sept 1863

Pleasant day. Got under way at 25 minutes past 3 o'clock P. M. bound for Wilmington. Was loath to part with the pleasant party Ive brought out with us - viz - Com. Barron, Professor Bledsoe, Mr Volck & Lieut. Whittle, all of whom are very pleasant company. At 15 minutes before 4 o'clock P. M. Pilot left us off St David's Head. Machinery worked badly - very much annoying the Capt. &c.

Saturday 19th Sept 1863

Pleasant weather at sea. in afternoon breeze freshened & cloudy.

Sunday 20th Sept 1863

Fresh breeze from the south west - thick rainy weather.

Monday 21st Sept 1863

Fresh breeze - about 10 A. M. wind hauled round to N. W. several sail in sight during the day. At 10 P. M. (night) made a vessel on the port bow - Kept up N to avoid her.

Tuesday 22d Sept 22 1863

Pleasant clear weather. At day light, sighted an Hermaphrodite Brig on the starboard bow, in distance. She hoisted the Yankee flag, with the Union down, as a signal of distress - Her Fore & maintopmasts were carried away, shorn off at the cap. She was under Fore Staysail, Foresail, main staysail & new storm topsail. We went down to her to see what was the matter & if we could aid her. She proved to be the "Caroline" of East Machias, bound to New York. When we hailed her & asked what was the matter, she answered "can't you see what is the matter" - where upon we kept on our course, rejoicing. Saw a number of sails - one a three masted steamer - made Cape Lookout Light houses in the afternoon - Made land about sunset - & were up to Bogue Inlet about that time - At 10 P. M. were up to New Topsail Inlet - at ½ past two o'clock were off Fort Fisher - at six A. M. Wednesday morning crossed the Bar safely - A strong north eastern sprung up about the time we arrived off Fort Fisher - Another steamer - a propeller was off the Bar the same time.

Wednesday 23d Sept 1863

Came in over the Bar of New Inlet at 6 a.m. grounded on the Rip & then remained until next high tide, in the afternoon, when we got off & went up to Fort St Philipe, when we remained all night - & then I should say - we kept up to the Quarantine station just below Wilmington, when we anchored for the night.

Thursday 24th Sept 1863

After the visiting officer came on board we went up along side the wharf.

Friday 25th Sept 1863

Commenced unloading

Saturday 26th Sept

nothing of interest

Sunday 27th

nothing of interest

Monday 28th

nothing of interest

Tuesday 29th

Mr & Mrs Bill - Cotton press started operating Wednesday - 30th - Finished loading & also ---- down from the wharf & anchored in the stream- Dr & Mrs M - & Mrs & Miss P dined onboard.

Thursday 1st Oct 1863

Nothing of interest. Rosin oil burnt down.

Friday 2d Oct 1863

nothing of interest -

Saturday 3d

nothing of interest

Late in the evening went up to Fair Bluff with an interesting young lady - at 2 o'clock at night started back & arrived in Wilmington at 6 a.m. The Str R. E. Lee left today.

Sunday 4th Oct 1863

Pleasant day - Rcd a letter from my sister Mrs Hayes which I answered - Very sleepy all day from being up all last night.

Monday 5th Oct 1863

Nothing of interest

Tuesday 6th

Nothing of note

Wednesday 7th

"   "

Thursday 8th

"   "

Friday 9th

Finished coaling about 4pm got under way & anchored off Ft Fisher. Also Ex-President Tyler, 2 children & srt among -- passengers.

Saturday 10th

The steamer "Ad-Vance" formerly "Lord Clyde" came in at 8 o'clock A. M. under a heavy fire from the blockading squadron, which was replyed to by our guns at Ft Fisher. The "Ad Vance" came safely in, but grounded on the "Rip". I went up to Wilmington to get mail &c.

Sunday 11th Oct 1863

Came down from Wilmington & joined the "Cornubia" about ½ past 2 pm. Came down in Capt. James' Boat, the "Flora McDonald". The wind is from the Northard - the "Ad Vance" is still aground on the "Rip". At 6pm commenced heaving up the anchor - At 7pm crossed the Bar - soon discovered a "Blockader" close into the "Bar" but she did not see us.

Monday 12th Oct 1863
Heavy sea on - Saw 4 or 5 sails during the day. - all the passengers sick except little Pearl, Mrs Taylor's little daughter 3 or 4 years of age - Mrs Tyler & her little son Walter & colored nurse are very sea sick. Our passengers are Mrs John Tyler, Pearl, his daughter, Walter, her son and her nurse. Mr G. Alexander, Mr Black, Capt. Atkins, Paymaster Harwood & Paymaster Moses, both C. S. Navy.

Tuesday 13th Oct 1863
Sea quite smooth - not so much sea-sickness among the passengers - Ohio election comes off to day - Hope C. L. Vallandigham will be elected. A beautiful little bird flew outboard

Wednesday 14th Oct 1863
Weather wet & squally - saw several sailing vessels - stood off from the Land about 1 o'clock at night until 3 o'clock - then stood on for the again & made the light from the mast head at 5 o'clock. During the night again a vessel & took her for a steamer.
82 hours from the New inlet bar sighted Bermuda light

Thursday 15th Oct 1863
At seven am Island of Bermuda in full sight - at 8 took aboard the Pilot - at ½ past 11 o'clock we came into the harbour of St Georges. Found the ships Alicia, Ella & Annie, & Ella in harbour - Passengers soon went ashore.

Friday 16th Oct 1863
Went to Hamilton

Saturday 17th Oct
Flora came in from Wilmington. The Alice left for Wilmington. Heavy rain squalls in the evening & through the night.

Sunday 18th Oct 1863
Dismal day - Raining very hard & steady

Monday 19th
Rainy

Tuesday 20th
do

Wednesday 21st
Paid off

Thursday 22d
nothing of int.

Friday 23d
Went to evening party (Atwoods)

Saturday 24

Went to Hamilton
Rained very heavily. R. E. Lee arrived from Halifax.

Sunday 25
Rained all day. In Hamilton. Mail str from Halifax came in.

Monday 26th Oct 1863
Returned to St Georges from Hamilton. Str Ad-Vance arrived from Wilmington N. C.

Tuesday 27th
Nothing of interest

Wednesday 28th
I was attacked with the broken bone fever [a mosquito-borne tropical disease caused by the dengue virus].

Thursday 29th
Very sick

Friday 30th
do

Saturday 31st
got up & went ashore
Sunday 1st November 1863
pleasant day - staid onboard all day. Str Heroine came in.

Monday 2d November
Dinner party given on "Cornubia" to a Bride - & in the evening a large dancing party. It was a nice affair.

Thursday 5th Novr 1863
passed a full rigged ship early in the morning

Friday 6th Novr 1863
Nothing of interest

Saturday 7th Novr
Pleasant weather - number of sails in sight.

Appendix III

Crew Members of the *Cornubia* and the *New England*

1. SS *Cornubia* Hayle-Bristol Packet Service

Vivian	John junior		Master	Cornwall
Gill	William	46	Master	Cornwall
Rosewarne	John	32	Mate	Cornwall
Hill	John	34	2nd Mate	Cornwall
Rowe	James	37	Seaman	Cornwall
Dunn	James	33	Seaman	Cornwall
Martin	Willm	33	Seaman	Bristol
Luke	Jacob	29	Seaman	Cornwall
Probert	Thomas	32	Seaman	Bristol
Bush	George	42	Engineer	Bristol
Stevens	William	46	Engineer	Cornwall
Gall	Thomas	24	Fireman	Cornwall
Jenkins	John	40	Fireman	Cornwall
Wyatt	John	29	Fireman	Bristol
Hodge	William	38	Fireman	Bristol
Massey	Fred	23	Fireman	Cornwall
Higgens	Samuel	26	Coal trimmer	Bristol*
Woolcock	John	35	Seaman	Cornwall
Jones	Willm	28	Fireman	Cornwall
Davey	Willm	22	Sailor	Cornwall
Higgens	Samuel	26	Fireman	Bristol*
Stratton	Christn	30	Coal trimmer	Cornwall
Sprague	John	32	Fireman	Bristol
Wood	Thomas	29	Fireman	Bristol
Burt	George	58	Engineer	Bristol

*These men have the same name in the ship's register.

2 SS *Cornubia* South-West Packet Service, unknown number of crewmen

Davidson	Master
Dolphin, John	Seaman

3. CSS *Cornubia*, crew of 37 (5th June 1863)

Burroughs, James	Pilot
Burroughs, John D.	Master
Holmes, John Thomas	Master
Davidson, John	Master
Gayle, Richard H.	Captain
Gilbert, William	Carpenter
Gordon, J. T.	Purser
Gregory, Frederick W.	Signal Officer
Grissom, Thomas	Pilot
Heistand, A.	Chief Engineer
Long, Joseph Brown	Chief Mate/Chief Officer
Morfitt, John	Seaman
Morse, Christopher Columbus	Pilot
Silfversparre, Axel	Engineer
Thomas, Captain	Acting Chief Officer

4. USS *Cornubia*, crew of 76 (ORN 1 22 pXIV)

Ship name in 'Joined' column is sending vessel, name in 'Left' column is receiving vessel; below referring date.

Name	Age	Rank/position	Joined	Left
Adams, William V.	nk	Surgeon's Steward	8.3.1864	29.8.1864
Altham, George	nk	Acting 3rd Assistant Engineer	19.3.1864	13.10.1865
Anderson, Joseph	21	Landsman	20.2.1865	nk
Austin, William	24	2nd Class Fireman	11.7.1864	nk
Bailey, William H.	29	Landsman	11.7.1864	nk
Barron, Sprague S.	25	Seaman	nk	nk
Barry, Thomas	43	Seaman	16.4.1864	15.8.1864
Beecher, Charles	22	Coal Heaver	27.11.1863	22.12.1864
Behm, C. F. W.	51	Volunteer Acting Lieutenant	28.12.1863	27.11.1864 following medical
Berry, Charles	45	Cabin Cook	15.11.1861	19.6.1862
Berry, George	21	Landsman	20.2.1865	nk

Bibbles, Frank P.	nk	Acting Ensign/Sailing Master	11.1.1864	3.1.1865
			Colorado	*Donegal*
Boynton, James A.	nk	Acting 3rd Assistant Engineer	19.3.1864	10.10.1865
Brailey, George F.	nk	Acting Ensign	26.10.1864	1.10.1866
Brown, James	24	2nd Class Fireman	1.10.1863	5.11.1864
Brown, James	29	Landsman	11.7.1864	nk
Brown, John	23	2nd Class Fireman	18.1.1864	27.2.1865
Brown, John	18	2nd Class Fireman	20.1.1864	9.8.1865
Brown, Thomas	nk	Ordinary Seaman	nk	nk
Byron, Paul	44	2nd Class Fireman	2.12.1863	5.8.1864
Brummage, Samuel R.	nk	Acting 1st Assistant Engineer	3.2.1864	5.5.1865
Caiter, Harrison	23	Landsman	11.7.1864	nk
Casey, Francis	21	Landsman	6.4.1864	nk
Chaples, Albion	36	Seaman	8.3.1864	7.4.1864
Clark, Charles	26	Landsman	23.2.1864	30.5.1865
Clark, Robert	18	Coal Heaver	25.5.1863	22.12.1864
Clennon, Willis	47	Landsman	11.7.1864	nk
Cluney, James	25	Sailmaker's Mate	13.2.1864	19.12.1866
Condren, Dennis	24	Landsman	25.3.1864	6.5.1865
Counter, Arthur	21	Ordinary Seaman	21.4.1864	nk
Crane, George H.	21	Coal Heaver	24.11.1863	22.12.1864
Crockert, David	21	Coal Heaver	3.2.1864	27.2.1865
Cuddy, Edward	28	Cabin Cook	25.3.1864	9.8.1865
Dearborn, John G.	nk	Acting Assistant Surgeon	10.2.1864	9.8.1865
			Montgomery	
Deland, Charles	45	Quarter Gunner	29.3.1864	9.8.1865
Dempsey, Timothy	22	2nd Class Fireman	19.12.1863	27.2.1865
Devlin, James	37	Coal Heaver	20.11.1863	16.12.1864
Dixon, James	35	1st Class Fireman	22.1.1864	9.8.1865
Rebel prisoner when enlisted				
Eastlake, A. P.	nk	Acting Assistant Paymaster	7.3.1864	nk
Eayers, John A.	38	Quartermaster	25.3.1864	9.8.1865
Ferris, George	nk	Acting Master and Executive Officer	21.1.1864	nk
Fleming, Robert	nk	Acting 2nd Assistant Engineer	by 3.1864	nk
Floury, L. H.	nk	Acting 1st Assistant Engineer	nk	26.1.1864
			Cherokee	

Freeman, Robert C.	19	Landsman	27.2.1864	9.8.1865
Galer, John R.	18	Landsman	20.2.1865	nk
Gaskins, Richard	29	Landsman	4.11.1861	nk
Gerrish, D. F.	nk	Acting 1st Assistant Engineer	6.1.1864	nk
Goodyear, Charles H.	18	Landsman	2.2.1864	27.2.1865
Gorman, Edward	nk	Seaman	26.1.1863	10.2.1864
		Quartermaster	2.3.1864	9.8.1865
Griffin, Charles	26	Seaman	14.3.1864	8.5.1865
Hahn, Adolph	27	Gunner's Mate in Charge	28.3.1864	9.8.1865
Ham, George H.	21	Landsman	19.10.1861	26.9.1864
Ham, George W.	25	2nd Class Fireman	17.12.1863	12.12.1864
Hamston, Robert	55	Sailmaker's Mate	8.3.1864	9.8.1865
Harriman, George A.	nk	Acting Ensign	13.3.1863	nk
			Marblehead	
Hart, Daniel	23	Quartermaster	8.3.1864	15.7.1865
Hayes, James	46	Coal Heaver	28.11.1863	22.12.1864
Hayes, Patrick	22	Coal Heaver	27.11.1863	6.1.1865
Hennessey, John	21	Landsman	23.10.1863	5.8.1865
Hill, Orrin T.	nk	Acting 3rd Assistant Engineer	9.2.1864	8.8.1864
Houghton, Lewis S.	21	Coal Heaver	23.11.1863	23.12.1864
Jackson, Charles	47	Landsman	11.7.1864	nk
Jackson, William M.	18	Landsman	11.2.1864	9.8.1865
Jackson, William T.	39	Landsman	28.2.1863	nk
Jaynes, William	25	2nd Class Fireman	14.1.1864	27.2.1865
Jones, Ben	23	Landsman	11.7.1864	nk
Jones, James	21	Landsman	6.4.1864	nk
Johnson, James	23	Landsman	11.7.1864	nk
Johnstone, John A.	nk	Acting Lieutenant	27.11.1864	nk
Kingston, John	20	2nd Class Fireman	14.1.1864	27.2.1865
Lavery, Thomas L.	nk	Acting 3rd Assistant Engineer	12.2.1864	na
also Savery		Acting 2nd Assistant Engineer	23.2.1865	nk
Leary, Michael	21	Landsman	15.4.1864	30.5.1865
Lee, Joseph	19	1st Class Boy	27.2.1864	nk
Leonard, William	nk	nk	nk	nk
			from army	
Linier, Edward	42	Landsman	11.7.1864	nk
Linier, Haywood	25	Landsman	11.7.1864	nk

Linier, Peter	37	Landsman	11.7.1864	nk
Long, Joseph	nk	nk	nk	nk
Maher, John	19	2nd Class Painter	29.3.1864	9.8.1865
Malone, John	22	Ordinary Seaman	31.12.1862	30.12.1863
		2nd Class Fireman	18.1.1864	27.2.1865
Mason, Isiah	24	Ordinary Seaman	20.2.1865	nk
Marshall, Andrew	19	1st Class Fireman	19.3.1864	30.5.1865
McArdle, Patrick	36	Landsman	14.3.1864	12.3.1865
McNea, Artemus	18	1st Class Boy	6.10.1863	9.8.1865
McQuade, Thomas	23	Coal Heaver	5.2.1864	27.2.1865
Merritt, J. D.	nk	Acting Assistant 2nd Engineer	9.2.1864	4.4.1864
			detached, sick	
Millett, Frank	nk	Acting Ensign	by 3.1864	nk
			Marblehead	
Morse, Alanson W.	19	Surgeon's Steward	5.3.1864	9.8.1865
Mullen, John	21	Coal Heaver (R)	10.3.1864	26.5.1864
Murphy, Jeremiah	26	Ordinary Seaman	17.7.1863	16.7.1864
Nott, Henry	24	Landsman	11.7.1864	nk
O'Regan, Patrick H.	27	Ordinary Seaman	2.3.1864	9.8.1865
Overbaugh, Isaac R.	23	Landsman	11.7.1864	nk
Perkins, Gustavus S.	nk	Acting 2nd Assistant Engineer	12.2.1864	11.3.1864
			Colorado	*Fort Donaldso*n
Peterson, James	21	Seaman	2.4.1864	25.8.1965
Phillips, Patrick	25	1st Class Fireman	20.1.1864	9.8.1865
Rebel prisoner when enlisted				
Phillips, Thomas	36	2nd Class Fireman	14.1.1864	13.4.1865
Phinney, Ezra	18	Ordinary Seaman	2. 4. 1864	14.9.1865
Power, Elias R.	42	Landsman	11.7.1864	nk
Powers, Joseph	37	Landsman	11.7.1864	nk
Powers, George	25	Landsman	11.7.1864	nk
Pratt, Samuel S. jr	28	Coal Heaver	nk	nk
		2nd Class Fireman	12.8.1864	9.8.1865
Redwood, James	35	Landsman	11.7.1864	nk
Rench, Hezekiah	24	Ordinary Seaman	20.2.1865	nk
Robertson, James	22	2nd Class Fireman	nk	nk
		1st Class Fireman	5.1.1864	8.2.1865
Ross, William	nk	Acting Master's Mate	9.2.1864	nk

Russell, George H.	nk	Acting Master's Mate	nk	nk
Savery, Thomas L.	nk	Acting 3rd Assistant Engineer	12.2.1864	nk
Sewall, Harrison	nk	nk	nk	nk
James, nk	20	Ordinary Seaman	3.4.1864	nk
Sharp, William	24	Landsman	11.7.1864	nk
Sheridan, Daniel	35	Seaman	5.3.1864	6.9.1865
Silk, James	23	Coal Heaver	28.11.1863	22.12.1864
Smith, Abram	31	Coal Heaver	8.9.1864	nk
Smith, Charles	48	Seaman	nk	nk
		Boatswain's Mate in Charge	5.4.1864	9.8.1865
Smith, John W.	23	Coal Heaver	20.11.1863	18.12.1864
Stephens, Richard	35	Landsman	11.7.1864	nk
Taylor, David E.	24	2nd Class Fireman (R)	19.8.1864	21.1.1865
Taylor, William	21	Ordinary Seaman	nk	nk
		Seaman	6.3.1864	9.8.1865
Thomas, Richard	20	Ordinary Seaman	3.4.1863	nk
Todd, William	35	Seaman	5.3.1864	nk
Tracy, Edward	22	Landsman	nk	nk
Tripp, Theodore	nk	1st Class Fireman	19.1.1864	9.8.1865
Jotham, nk	20	Ordinary seaman	2.4.1864 *Ohio*	9.8.1865
Turner, James	31	Coal Heaver	8.9.1864	nk
Vennard, J. L.	nk	Acting Master's Mate	nk	11.2.1864 *Colorado*
Walsh, John	23	Quarter Gunner	12.3.1864	9.8.1865 *Colorado*
Warren, William	nk	Acting Master's Mate	by 3.1864	nk
Williams, Patrick	29	Ordinary Seaman	14.11.1863	nk
Williamson, nk	nk	Chief Engineer	nk	nk
Wilson, Richard	29	Ordinary Seaman	14.11.1863	nk
Wilson, Richard	18	Landsman	20.2.1865	nk
Wood, Joseph	29	Landsman	4.11.1861	nk
Wood, William H.	nk	Acting Master's Mate	28.3.1864	nk
Wyman, Samuel	21	Coal Heaver	23.11.1863	22.12.1864

5. Barquentine *New England*, crew of 8

Baxter	Obediah	Master
Hallet		Master

References

Notes

Refer to bibliography for full references

Official Records of the Union and Confederate Navies in the War of the Rebellion Series (ORN) references are Series, Volume, Page: thus 1 09 p286 refers to Series 1, Volume 9, Page 286

Boston Archives refers to documents relating to United States District Court Ma, Admiralty NS vs *Cornubia* Steamer & Cargo case file; dates of specific documents given.

Chapter 1: The Beginning: The Bristol and Hayle Packet Service

1. *Royal Cornwall Gazette* 19.2.1831
2. *Royal Cornwall Gazette* 13.8.1831
3. *Bristol Mirror* 24.9.1831
4. *Royal Cornwall Gazette* 1.10.1831
5. Carter, C., 2003
6. *Royal Cornwall Gazette* 17.1.1835
7. *Bristol Mercury* 19.3.1859
8. Carter, C., 2003
9. *Royal Cornwall Gazette* 22.4.1842
10. *Royal Cornwall Gazette* 13.5.1842
11. *Royal Cornwall Gazette* 21.4.1848
12. Carter, C., 2003
13. *Royal Cornwall Gazette* 3.6.1842
14. Carter, C., 2003
15. *Royal Cornwall Gazette* 3.12.1847
16. Fenton, R., 2003
17. Carter, C., 2003
18. Carter, C., 2003

19. *Royal Cornwall Gazette* 25.7.1851
20. *Royal Cornwall Gazette* 16.1.1852
21. *Royal Cornwall Gazette* 21.5.1852
22. Carter, C., 2003
23. *Royal Cornwall Gazette* 11.7.1856
24. *Royal Cornwall Gazette* 2.1.1857

Chapter 2: A New Ship for the Packet Service

1. *Cornish Telegraph* 1.4.1857
2. *London Daily News* 30.6.1860
3. *Cornish Telegraph* 5.3.1858
4. *Cornish Telegraph* 5.3.1858
5. *Royal Cornwall Gazette* 18.6.1858
6. *Royal Cornwall Gazette* 2.7.1858
7. *Royal Cornwall Gazette* 24.2.1854
8. *Royal Cornwall Gazette* 9.7.1858
9. *Royal Cornwall Gazette* 2.7.1858
10. *Bristol Mercury* 17.7.1858
11. *Bristol Mercury* 17.7.1858
12. *Bristol Mercury* 17.7.1858
13. National Maritime Museum document TN 32769 - C/L 19895 (1862)
14. *Royal Cornwall Gazette* 16.7.1858
15. *Royal Cornwall Gazette* 30.7.1858
16. *Royal Cornwall Gazette* 3.12.1858
17. *Western Daily Press* 1.4.1859
18. *Falmouth Packet* 26.3.1859
19. Wikipedia article: *Pilot* tug
20. *Royal Cornwall Gazette* 9.9.1859
21. *Royal Cornwall Gazette* 28.10.1859
22. *Royal Cornwall Gazette* 23.12.1859
23. *Royal Cornwall Gazette* 27.1.1860
24. Wikipedia article: Great Western Railway
25. Great Western Railway website
26. Wikipedia article: Cheltenham and Great Western Union Railway
27. Wikipedia article: West Cornwall Railway
28. *Royal Cornwall Gazette* 8.6.1860

29. *Royal Cornwall Gazette* 15.2.1861
30. *Royal Cornwall Gazette* 5.4.1861
31. *Royal Cornwall Gazette* 19.4.1861
32. *Western Daily Press* 27.4.1861
33. *Western Daily Press* 16.10.1861
34. Fenton, R., 2003
35. *Royal Cornwall Gazette* 8.9.1861
36. National Maritime Museum document TN 32769 - C/L 19895 (1862)
37. *Royal Cornwall Gazette* 1.11.1861
38. *Royal Cornwall Gazette* 8.11.1861
39. Graham, Eric J., 2006
40. Graham, Eric J., 2006
41. Carter, C., 2003
42. *Royal Cornwall Gazette* 4.11.1859 (this disaster was covered by virtually every British newspaper over a long period)
43. *Royal Cornwall Gazette* 4.11.1859
44. Carter, C., 2003

Chapter 3: A Time of Transition

1. *Western Daily Press* 18.6.1862
2. *Daily News* 8.7.1862
3. AIM25 website: www.aim25.ac.uk
4. *Morning Post* 8.7.1862
5. *Cork Examiner* 15.8.1862
6. *Morning Post* 22.7.1862
7. NHHC
8. *Western Daily Press* 11.8.1862
9. *Hampshire Advertiser* 2.8.1862
10. *The Standard* 14.8.1862
11. *Belfast News-Letter* 15.8.1862
12. *Southern Reporter and Cork Commercial Courier* 15.8.1862
13. *Southern Reporter and Cork Commercial Courier* 16.8.1862
14. Queenstown Trade Directory, 1871
15. *Liverpool Post* 25.3.1864
16. *Glasgow Herald* 26.8.1862
17. *London Evening Standard* 27.8.1862

18. *Bristol Mercury* 18.10.1862
19. ORN 1 08 p276
20. *Glasgow Herald* 4.11.1862
21. Graham, Eric J., 2006
22. *Cork Examiner* 11.11.1862
23. *Cork Examiner* 12.11.1862

Chapter 4: The Origins of the Blockade

1. Sprunt, J., 1916
2. Sprunt, J., 1916
3. NHHC
4. Graham, Eric J., 2006; Stern, Philip Van Doren, 1992
5. NHHC
6. *Liverpool Mercury* 26.9.1863
7. Graham, Eric J., 2006
8. Graham, Eric J., 2006; Philip Van Doren, 1992
9. Jones, F. I. W. 1999
10. Wikipedia article: Bermuda
11. Cochrane, H., 1958; Graham, Eric J., 2006; Stern, Philip Van Doren, 1992 Wikipedia article: *Trent* Affair
12. NHHC
13. Wikipedia article: Samuel Phillips Lee

Chapter 5: British Shipbuilders and the Rebels

1. *Punch* 30.3.1861
2. Anderson, Ben, 1962; Cochrane, Hamilton, 2005; Wise, Stephen R., 1988
3. *Executive Documents 1872-1873*
4. ORN 1 09 p80
5. Stern, Philip Van Doren, 1992; Anderson, Ben, 1962
6. NHHC
7. Anderson, Ben, 1962; ORN 1 01 p776
8. Graham, Eric J., 2006
9. ORN 1 09 p282
10. Anderson, Ben, 1962; Stern, Philip Van Doren, 1992
11. Sprunt, J.,1916, *Alabama Claims 1872*
12. Sprunt, J.,1916; *Report of the Secretary of Navy, 1864*
13. Graham, Eric J., 2006

14. Graham, Eric J., 2006; Stern, Philip Van Doren, 1992
15. Graham, Eric J., 2006; Wise, Stephen R., 1988
16. Graham, Eric J., 2006; Wise, Stephen R., 1988
17. Wikipedia article: London Armoury Company
18. Graham, Eric J., 2006; Shingleton, Royce, 1994
19. Shingleton, Royce, 1994
20. *Executive Documents 1864-1865*
21. ORN 1 08 p294
22. *Daily Post* 19.12.1862
23. *Daily Post* 13.12.1862
24. ORN 1 01 p564
25. Eaton, Clement, 1954; Wise, Stephen R., 1988
26. *Papers relating to Foreign Affairs 1864*

Chapter 6: Enigma: Captain John Burroughs

1. *The Federal Cases, 1896*
2. Hayward, Walter Brownell, 1910
3. *Bermuda Royal Gazette* 9.12.1862; ORN 1 13 p483
4. *Bermuda Royal Gazette* 30.12.1862
5. *Bermuda Royal Gazette* 28.7.1863
6. *Report of the Secretary of the Navy 1864*
7. Sprunt, J., 1902
8. National Archives document ADM 196 Admiralty: Officers' Service Records (Series III)
9. Wise, Stephen R., 1988
10. *Bermuda Royal Gazette* 5.4.1864
11. *Bermuda Royal Gazette* 10.5.1864
12. Wikipedia article: James Sprunt
13. Sprunt, J., 1920
14. Graham, Eric J., 2006
15. Graham, Eric J., 2006
16. *Houston Tri-Weekly Telegraph* 15.9.1863
17. *Belfast News-Letter* 15.8.1862
18. *Cork Examiner* 10.11.1862; *Daily Post* 19.12.1862
19. *Liverpool Daily Post* 19.12.1862; *Bermuda Royal Gazette* 9.12.1862
20. *Cork Examiner* 14.8.1862

21. *Correspondence concerning claims against Great Britain, 1870*
22. NHHC

Chapter 7: Runner! The Cornubia and the Blockade

1. Taylor, T., date not known. Excerpt from *Running the Blockade*, in *North Carolina Civil War Documentary*. University of North Carolina Press, Chapel Hill & London.
2. *The Monthly Law Reporter, March 1865*
3. ORN 1 13 p483
4. *Register of Officers of the Confederate States Navy, 1861--1865*
5. *The Federal Cases, 1896*
6. Wilson, Walter E. and McKay, Gary L. 2012
7. ORN 1 08 p246
8. ORN 1 13 p483
9. Allen, Charles Maxwell, 2014
10. ORN 1 13 p483; McKenna, Joseph, 2010
11. Boston Archives
12. ORN 1 14 p276
13. Allen, Charles Maxwell, 2014
14. ORN 1 08 p296
15. ORN 1 08 p297
16. ORN 1 08 p298
17. ORN 1 14 p726
18. McNeil, Jim, 2003
19. ORN 1 08 p612
20. *The Federal Cases, 1896*
21. Vandiver, F. E., 1947
22. *Memphis Daily Appeal 1.1.1863*
23. Allen, Charles Maxwell, 2014
24. *Daily Dispatch* 13.11.1863
25. Graham, Eric J., 2006
26. Graham, Eric J., 2006
27. Vandiver, F. E., 1947
28. ORN 1 14 p726
29. ORN 1 08 p492
30. ORN 1 08 p496
31. ORN 1 08 p423 et seq.

32. ORN 1 08 p512
33. Allen, Charles Maxwell, 2014
34. Allen, Charles Maxwell, 2014
35. ORN 1 08 p528
36. ORN 1 01 p565
37. Vandiver, F. E., 1947
38. *Correspondence concerning claims against Great Britain, 1871*
39. ORN 1 08 p563
40. ORN 1 09 p778
41. ORN 1 08 p580
42. ORN 1 08 p582
43. ORN 1 08 p581
44. ORN 1 08 p581
45. *Liverpool Mercury* 22.4.1863; ORN 1 08 p810
46. *Liverpool Mercury* 22.4.1863
47. ORN 1 08 p582
48. ORN 1 08 p810
49. 1 08 p810; *Liverpool Mercury* 22.4.1863
50. ORN 1 08 p582
51. ORN 1 08 p582
52. ORN 1 06 p3
53. McNeil, Jim, 2003; Sprunt, J., 1920
54. ORN 1 08 p630
55. Wikipedia article: Signal Corps in the American Civil War: Confederate Signal Corps
56. *Correspondence concerning claims against Great Britain, 1870*
57. ORN 1 08 p612
58. ORN 1 08 p584
59. *Wilmington Journal* 12.3.1863
60. ORN 1 08 p860
61. ORN 1 08 p72
62. ORN 1 08 p861
63. ORN 1 01 p565
64. *Bermuda Royal Gazette* 24.3.1863
65. Allen, Charles Maxwell, 2014
66. *Bermuda Royal Gazette* 24.3.1863

67. ORN 1 08 p814
68. Henderson, D. W., 1963
69. Henderson, D. W., 1963
70. Allen, Charles Maxwell, 2014
71. ORN 1 08 p630
72. Allen, Charles Maxwell, 2014
73. Vandiver, F. E., 1947
74. *Bermuda Royal Gazette* 14.4.1863
75. ORN 1 09 p285
76. Allen, Charles Maxwell, 2014
77. ORN 1 8 p810; Allen, Charles Maxwell, 2014
78. *Daily News* 16.4.1863
79. *Daily News* 16.4.1863
80. *Bermuda Royal Gazette* 20.4.1863
81. Whittle, William C. jr, 2004
82. Carr, D. W., 1998

Chapter 8: Richard Haynsworth Gayle

1. Wiggins, Sarah Woolfolk, 1995, *biography*
2. Wiggins, Sarah Woolfolk, 1995: 28.1.1857
3. Wiggins, Sarah Woolfolk, 1995, *biography*
4. Wiggins, Sarah Woolfolk, 1995: 7.6 1857
5. *Journal of the executive proceedings of the Senate of the United States of America, 1855-1858*
6. Wiggins, Sarah Woolfolk, 1995: 16.6.1858
7. Wiggins, Sarah Woolfolk, 1995, *biography*
8. Wiggins, Sarah Woolfolk, 1995, *biography*
9. *Journal of the Congress of the Confederate States of America, 1861-1865*
10. Boston Archives 6.6.1862
11. Boston Archives 25.6.1862
12. Boston Archives 22.7.1862
13. Boston Archives 20.11.1862
14. Boston Archives 13.1.1863
15. Wikipedia article: Wartrace
16. Boston Archives 15.2.1863
17. Boston Archives 22.2.1863

18. Boston Archives 24.2.1863
19. Boston Archives 6.4.1863
20. Boston Archives 12.4.1863
21. ORN 1 09 p279
22. ORN 1 09 p280
23. ORN 1 09 p280

Chapter 9: Under the Stars and Bars

1. *Daily News* 16.4.1863
2. *Correspondence concerning claims against Great Britain, 1871. Volume 7*
3. *Correspondence concerning claims against Great Britain, 1871. Volume 7*
4. Carr, D. W., 1998
5. Sprunt J., 1902
6. Vandiver, F. E., 1947
7. NHHC: USS *Niphon*; ORN 1 10 p18
8. ORN 1 09 p017
9. ORN 1 09 p019
10. ORN 1 09 p020
11. Allen, Charles Maxwell, 2014
12. Allen, Charles Maxwell, 2014
13. Allen, Charles Maxwell, 2014
14. *Bermuda Royal Gazette* 2.6.1863
15. Vandiver, F. E., 1947
16. Graham, Eric J., 2006
17. ORN 1 09 p280
18. Boston Archives 10.6.1863
19. Boston Archives 10.6.1863
20. ORN 1 09 p281
21. ORN 1 09 p281
22. Allen, Charles Maxwell, 2014
23. Wikipedia article: Gunboat Lady Davis
24. Barret, John G., 1963
25. *Bermuda Royal Gazette* 23.6.1863
26. Klement, Frank L., 1970
27. Wikipedia article: Crittenden Compromise
28. Executive Documents 1871-1872

29. NHHC: USS *James Adger*
30. ORN 1 12 p411; ORN 1 12 p624; ORN 1 12 p784; ORN 1 14 p271
31. ORN 1 02 p314; 1 09 p30
32. *Bermuda Royal Gazette* 7.7.1863
33. Klement, Frank L., 1970
34. *Bermuda Royal Gazette* 7.7.1863
35. Vandiver, F. E., 1947
36. *Semi Weekly Wisconsin* 17.7.1863
37. *Executive Documents 1871-1872*
38. ORN 1 09 p282
39. *Correspondence concerning claims against Great Britain, 1871*
40. *Bermuda Royal Gazette* 28.7.1863
41. *Correspondence concerning claims against Great Britain, 1871*
42. *Correspondence concerning claims against Great Britain, 1871*
43. Allen, Charles Maxwell, 2014
44. ORN 1 09 p141
45. ORN 1 02 p420
46. NHCC
47. *Bermuda Royal Gazette* 11.8.1863
48. *Bermuda Royal Gazette* 11.8.1863
49. ORN 1 02 p420
50. Vandiver, Frank E., 1947
51. Vandiver, Frank E., 1947
52. *New York Times* 23.12.1863
53. *Liverpool Mercury* 26.9.1863
54. *Liverpool Mercury* 26.9.1863
55. "Diary of Current Events": see Appendix II
56. Wikipedia article: Albert T. Bledsoe
57. ORN 1 09 p283
58. ORN 1 09 p283
59. *Bermuda Royal Gazette* 15.9.1863
60. *Bermuda Royal Gazette* 15.9.1863
61. *Bermuda Royal Gazette* 15.9.1863
62. Vandiver, F. E., 1947, op. cit.
63. "Diary of Current Events": see Appendix II
64. Wikipedia article: Commodore Barron

65. Wise, Stephen R., 1989
66. Vandiver, F. E., 1947
67. "Diary of Current Events": see Appendix II
68. Madaus, H. M., 2001
69. ORN 1 09 p284
70. ORN 1 09 p285
71. ORN 1 09 p285
72. *New York Times* 23.12.1863
73. NHCC
74. *New York Times* 23.12.1863
75. Anderson, Ben, 1962; Wikipedia article: Battle of Mobile Bay; Wikipedia article: *Metacomet*; *Report of the Secretary of the Navy with an Appendix containing Reports from Officers*, December 1864; NHHC
76. *New York Times* 23.12.1863
77. *New York Times* 23.12.1863
78. "Diary of Current Events": see Appendix II
79. ORN 1 09 p234
80. "Diary of Current Events": see Appendix II
81. "Diary of Current Events": see Appendix II
82. ORN 1 09 p234
83. *New York Times* 23.12.1863
84. Allen, Charles Maxwell, 2014
85. Henderson, D. W., 1963
86. Vandiver, F. E., 1947
87. Boston Archives: deposition of Thomas Patterson
88. ORN 1 09 pp673-675
89. ORN 1 09 p273
90. ORN 1 09 p273
91. ORN 1 90 p274
92. ORN 1 90 p274
93. Wikipedia article: Coston Lights
94. Boston Archives: deposition of Robert Patterson
95. ORN 1 09 p273
96. *Daily Dispatch* 13.11.1863
97. Boston Archives: depositions of William Gilbert and John Morfitt,
98. *Daily Dispatch* 13.11.1863

99. Boston Archives: deposition of Robert Patterson
100. ORN 1 09 p274
101. ORN 1 09 p279
102. ORN 1 09 p275
103. Sprunt, J., 1920
104. ORN 1 09 p274
105. ORN 1 09 p288
106. ORN 1 09 p288
107. ORN 1 09 p290
108. ORN 1 09 p290
109. Cochrane, Hamilton, 2005
110. ORN 1 02 p420
111. ORN 1 09 p290
112. ORN 1 09 p275
113. Henderson, D. W., 1963, op. cit.
114. ORN 1 09 p276
115. ORN 1 09 p276
116. ORN 1 09 p294
117. ORN 1 09 p294
118. ORN 1 09 p291; ORN 1 09 p294
119. Wyllie, Arthur, 2007
120. ORN 1 09 p291
121. ORN 1 09 p291
122. ORN 1 09 p291
123. NHHC
124. ORN 1 09 p294
125. *Royal Cornwall Gazette* 27.11.1863
126. *Bermuda Royal Gazette* 24.11.1863
127. ORN 1 09 p282
128. Wiggins, Sarah Woolfolk, 1995
129. Henderson, D. W., 1963
130. McNeil, J., 2003
131. Explore Southern History website
132. Wise, Stephen R., 1988
133. Cochrane, Hamilton, 2005
134. Wise, Stephen R., 1988; Cochrane, Hamilton, 2005, Hamilton, 2005

135. Wiggins, Sarah Woolfolk, 1995, biography
136. Wiggins, Sarah Woolfolk, 1995: 23.10.1864
137. ORN 1 11 p622
138. ORN 1 11 p621
139. Wise, Stephen R., 1988
140. ORN 1 11 p627
141. Wise, Stephen R., 1988; Silverstone, Paul H., 2006
142. Wiggins, Sarah Woolfolk, 1995, biography

Chapter 10: Poacher Turned Gamekeeper

1. *Letter from the Secretary of the Navy, 1868*
2. *New York Times* 23.12.1863
3. Stern, Philip Van Doren, 1992; Jones, F. I. W. 1991; *Glasgow Daily Herald* 7.1.1864; NHHC: Chesapeake
4. ORN 1 02 p517
5. ORN 1 02 p563
6. ORN 1 02 p523
7. Stern, Philip Van Doren, 1992; Jones, F. I. W. 1991; *Glasgow Daily Herald* 7.1.1864
8. NHHC: Chesapeake
9. *The Times* 28.11.1863
10. *The Times* 3.12.1863
11. *New York Times* 25.12.1865
12. *Boston Post* 23.1.1864

Chapter 11: Captain Charles Behm

1. New York Public Library document Mss Col 247
2. Yolles, Melanie A., 1990
3. *Public Ledger* 21.5.1867; *Evening Telegraph* 23.5.1867; *New York Tribune* 28.5.1867
4. *Evening Telegraph* 23.5.1867
5. *New York Tines* 24.5.1867

Chapter 12: Under the Stars and Stripes

1. ORN 2 01 p67
2. *Boston Post* 9.4.1864
3. New York Public Library document Mss Col 247
4. Allen, Charles Maxwell, 2014
5. Allen, Charles Maxwell, 2014

6. Cochrane, Hamilton, 2005
7. Allen, Charles Maxwell, 2014
8. ORN 1 21 p164
9. ORN 1 21 p275
10. ORN 1 21 p300
11. ORN 1 21 p304
12. ORN 1 21 p313
13. Wikipedia article: Galveston; Wikipedia article: Second Battle of Galveston; Texas State Historical Association website
14. ORN 2 01 p67
15. ORN 1 21 p369
16. ORN 1 90 p230

Chapter 13: Captain John Alexander Johnstone

1. ORN 1 21 p739
2. Malcolm Johnstone (great-grandson of J. A. Johnstone), personal communication
3. *New York Times* 8.3.1883
4. Malcolm Johnstone, personal communication
5. *Register of American Shipping*, 1876.
6. *New York Times* 27.2.1879; *New York Times* 5.9.1879; *New York Times* 5.9.1881
7. *New York Times* 20.2.1881
8. *New York Times* 15.2.1881
9. *New York Times* 10.5.1881; Malcolm Johnstone, personal communication
10. *New York Times* 8.3.1883
11. *New York Daily Tribune* 20.3.1883; *New York Tribune* 7.3.1884; *New York Times* 14.5.1884

Chapter 14: Service to the end of the War

1. Gragg, Rod, 1991
2. Gragg, Rod, 1991
3. Wise, Stephen R., 1988; Gragg, Rod, 1991; Wikipedia article: Battle of Wilmington
4. Sprunt, J., 1902
5. ORN 1 22 p137
6. ORN 1 22 p136
7. ORN 2 01 p67
8. Wikipedia article: Battle of Wilmington
9. ORN 1 22 p67; Cochrane; Wise

10. *Boston Post* 12.6.1865
11. ORN 1 22 p197
12. ORN 1 22 p197
13. ORN 1 22 pp197-198
14. ORN 1 22 p224
15. *Boston Post* 12.6.1865
16. Wikipedia article: Galveston
17. Sands, Benjamin F., 1874
18. Juneteenth website

Chapter 15: End of Service

1. *Houston Tri-Weekly Telegraph* 21.7.1865
2. Byler, Charles A., 2006; Chisholm, David, 2001; *Houston Tri-Weekly Telegraph* 19.6.1865
3. Wise, Stephen R., 1988; Cochrane, Hamilton, 2005, Hamilton, 2005; ORN 2 01 p066
4. Encyclopaedia of Greater Philadelphia website
5. *Letter from the Secretary of the Navy, May 7, 1868*
6. Boston Archives
7. *Letter from the Secretary of the Navy, May 7, 1868*
8. Sprunt, J., 1914
9. *Executive Documents 1871-1872*
10. *New York Times* 25.10.1865

Chapter 16: New England: The *Cornubia* Reborn

1. Wikipedia article: Definition of barquentine
2. Clarke, Francis E., 1965
3. *New York Times* 23.4.1875
4. Nehemiah Gibson of East Boston website
5. NHHC: USS *Penobscot*
6. NHHC: USS *Vanderbilt*
7. *New York Maritime Register*
8. *New Orleans Republican* 21.2.1872
9. *New York Maritime Register*
10. *New York Maritime Register*
11. *New York Maritime Register*
12. *New York Maritime Register*

13. Clarke, Francis E., 1965
14. Wikipedia article: Eugene Grandin
15. Clarke, Francis E., 1965
16. Historical Society of Old Yarmouth personal communication
17. *New York Maritime Register*
18. *New York Maritime Register*
19. *Shields Daily Gazette* 5.7.1873
20. *New York Maritime Register*
21. *New York Maritime Register*
22. *New Orleans Republican* 24.10.1873
23. *New York Maritime Register*
24. *New York Maritime Register*
25. *New York Maritime Register*
26. *New York Maritime Register*
27. *New Orleans Bulletin* 14.11.1874
28. *New Orleans Bulletin* 12.11.1874
29. *New York Times* 13.4.1875
30. Clarke, Francis E., 1965
31. *New Orleans Bulletin* 12.11.1874
32. *New Orleans Bulletin* 12.11.1874
33. *New York Maritime Register*
34. *New York Maritime Register*
35. *New Orleans Bulletin* 1.3.1876
36. *New York Maritime Register*
37. *New York Maritime Register*
38. *New York Maritime Register*
39. Clarke, Francis E., 1965
40. *New Orleans Daily Democrat* 8.8.1877
41. *Seamen's Journal: A Journal of Seamen, by Seamen, for Seamen*, Volume 23

Bibliography

Books and Articles

1. *Alabama Claims: Cases argued by the United States. Documents of the Tribunal of Arbitration held at Geneva, Switzerland, 1871-1872.* Dubioson & Co., Paris, 1872.
2. Allen, Charles Maxwell, 2014. *Dispatches from Bermuda: The Civil War Letters of Charles Maxwell Allen, U.S. Consul at Bermuda, 1861–1888.* Edited by Wiche, Glen N., Kent State University Press.
3. Anderson, Ben, 1962. *By Sea and by River*. The Naval History of the Civil War. Da Capo Press, New York.
4. Barret, John G. 1963. *The Civil War in North Carolina*. University of North Carolina Press.
5. Brown, R. jr, 1995. *From Cape Charles to Cape Fear. The North Atlantic Blockading Squadron during the Civil War*. University of Alabama Press.
6. Byler, Charles A., 2006. *Civil-Military Relations on the Frontier and Beyond, 1865-1917*. Praeger Security International, Westport.
7. Carr, D. W., 1998. *Gray Phantoms of the Cape Fear: Running the Civil War Blockade*. John F. Blair.
8. Carter, C., 2003. *The Cornubia and the Hayle Packet Service: A Cornish Confederate*. Journal of the Trevithick Society Number 30 pp105-123.
9. Chisholm, David, 2001. *Waiting for Dead Men's' Shoes. Origins and development of the US Navy's officer personnel system, 1793-1941*. Stanford University Press, Stanford.
10. Clark Francis E. 1965. *An Early Four-Masted Barquentine*. American Neptune volumes 21-25, 1965.
11. Cochrane, H., 1958. *Blockade Runners of the Confederacy*. Fine Art Books.
12. *Correspondence concerning claims against Great Britain, transmitted to the Senate of the United States in answer to Resolutions of December 4 and 10, 1867, and of May 27, 1868. Volume 1.* Government Printing Office, Washington.
13. *Correspondence concerning claims against Great Britain, 1870. Voume1.* Government Printing Office, Washington.

14. *Correspondence concerning claims against Great Britain, 1871. Volume 7.* Government Printing Office, Washington.

15. *Director of the Bureau of Statistics, 1916. A List of the Soldiers, Sailors and Marines of the Civil War Surviving Residents in Massachusetts on April 1, 1915.* Wright & Potter Printing Company, Boston.

16. Eaton, Clement, 1954. *A History of the Southern Confederacy.* The Free Press, New York.

17. *Executive Documents, printed by order of the House of Representatives during the second session of the thirty-sixth Congress, 1859-1860.* Government Printing Office, Washington.

18. *Executive Documents, printed by order of the House of Representatives during the second session of the thirty-seventh Congress, 1861-1862.* Government Printing Office, Washington.

19. *Executive Documents, printed by order of the House of Representatives during the second session of the thirty-eighth Congress, 1864-1865.* Government Printing Office, Washington.

20. *Executive Documents, printed by order of the House of Representatives during the second session of the thirty-eighth Congress, 1867-1868.* Government Printing Office, Washington.

21. *Executive Documents, printed by order of the House of Representatives during the second session of the fortieth Congress, 1871-1872.* Government Printing Office, Washington.

22. *Executive Documents, printed by order of the House of Representatives during the third session of the forty-second Congress, 1872-1873.* Government Printing Office, Washington.

23. *The Federal Cases: Comprising Cases Argued and Determined in the Circuit and District Courts of the United States from the Earliest Times to the Beginning of the Federal Reporter, Arranged Alphabetically by the Titles of the Cases and Numbered Consecutively, Book 28*, West Publishing Company, 1896.

24. Gragg, Rod, 1991. *Confederate Goliath. The Battle of Fort Fisher.* Louisiana State University Press, Baton Rouge.

25. Graham, Eric J., 2006. *Clyde Built. Blockade Runners, Cruisers and Armoured Rams of the American Civil War.* Birlinn, Edinburgh.

26. Gratton, John W., 1999. *Under the Blue Pennant, or Notes of a Naval Officer 1863-1865.* John Wiley & Sons, Inc.

27. Hayward, Walter Brownell, 1910. *Bermuda Past and Present, a descriptive and historical account of the Somers Islands.* Dodd, Mead & Company, New York.

28. Headley, J. L., 1867. *Farragut, and Our Naval Commanders.* Applewood's Military History Series. List of vessels captured and destroyed for violation of the blockade. Scholarly Publishing Office, University of Michigan Library.

29. Henderson, D. W., 1963. *The Private Journal of Georgiana Walker 1862-1865 with Selections from the Post-War Years 1865-1876*. Confederate Centennial Studies 25. Confederate Publishing Company.

30. Huse, Caleb, 1904. *The Supplies for the Civil War Army*. Ninety Nine Cent Publishing, printed by Amazon UK.

31. Jones, F. I. W. 1991. *Treason and Piracy in Civil War Halifax: the Second Chesapeake Affair Revisited*. The Dalhousie Review.

32. Jones, F. I. W. 1999. *This Fraudulent Trade: Confederate Blockade-Running from Halifax during the American Civil War*. The Northern Mariner/Le Marin du nord, IX, No. 4 (October 1999).

33. *Journal of the executive proceedings of the Senate of the United States of America, 1855-1858*. Government Printing Office, Washington.

34. *Journal of the Congress of the Confederate States of America, 1861-1865*. Government Printing Office, Washington.

35. Klement, Frank L., 1970. *The Limits of Dissent. Clement Laird Vallandigham and the Civil War*. University of Kentucky Press.

36. *Letter from the Secretary of the Navy, 1868, in: Executive Documents oriented by order of the House of Representatives during the Second Session of the Fortieth Congress, 1867-68*. Government Printing Office, Washington.

37. Madaus, H. M., 2001. *Small Arms Deliveries Through Wilmington, NC in 1863, the Impact on Confederate Ordnance Policy*. Bulletin of the American Society of Arms Collectors.

38. Marshall, John A., 1881. *American Bastile: A History of the Illegal Arrests and Imprisonment of American Citizens in the Northern and Border States ... During the Late Civil War*. T. W. Hartley & Company, 1881.

39. McKenna, J., 2009. *British Ships in the Confederate Navy*. McFarland & Co Inc.

40. McNeil, J., 2003. *Masters of the Shoals. Tales of the Cape Fear Pilots Who Ran the Union Blockade*. Da Capo Press.

41. *The Monthly Law Reporter, March 1865*. William Guild & Co., Boston.

42. *Papers Relating to Foreign Affairs Accompanying the Annual Message of the President to the First Session of the Thirty-Eighth Congress*. Part 1. Government Printing Office, Washington.

43. Peters, T., 1943. *Blockade-Running in the Bahamas During the Civil War*. Paper read before the Historical Association of Southern Florida, 5th May 1943.

44. Phillips, Stephen Henry, 1865. *The Monthly Law Reporter*. Volume 27; Volumes 1865-1866.

45. *Official Records of the Union and Confederate Navies during the War of the Rebellion, various volumes*.

46. *Register of Officers of the Confederate States Navy, 1861—1865. As compiled and revised by the Office of Naval Records and Library, United States Navy Department*

1931, from all available data. United States Government Printing Office, Washington, 1931.

47. *Report of the Secretary of the Navy with an Appendix containing Reports from Officers, December 1864: Prizes adjudicated from the commencement of the rebellion, &c.* Washington, Government Printing Office.
48. Sands, Benjamin F., 1874. *Reefer to Rear Admiral. Reminiscences and Journal Jottings of nearly half a Century*. Frederick A. Stokes, New York.
49. Semmes, R., 1869. *Memoirs of Service Afloat, During the War Between the States*. Kelly, Piet & Co., Baltimore.
50. SIDCO, 2002. SS Pevensey. *A Stealth Machine of the Confederacy. A preliminary archaeological assessment of the "iron steamer" wreck, sunk at Pine Knoll Shores, NC*. Surface Interval Diving Company.
51. Shingleton, Royce, 1994. *High Seas Confederate: The Life and Times of John Newland Maffitt*. University of South Carolina Press.
52. Silverstone, Paul H., 2006. *Civil War Navies, 1855-1883*. Routledge, New York.
53. Sprunt J., 1902. *Tales of the Cape Fear Blockade*. North Carolina Booklet, Vol. 1 No. 10.
54. Sprunt, J., 1914. *Events on the Lower Cape Fear, Being Some Account of Historic Events on the Cape Fear River*. Raleigh, Edwards & Broughton Printing Co.
55. Sprunt, J., 1916. *Chronicles of the Cape Fear River 1660-1916*. 2nd edition, Edward & Droughton Printing Co., Raleigh.
56. Sprunt, J., 1920. *Derelicts. An account of ships lost at sea in general commercial traffic and a brief history of blockade runners along the North Carolina coast 1861-1865*. The Lord Baltimore Press, Baltimore.
57. Stern, Philip Van Doren, 1992. The *Confederate Navy, A Pictorial History*. Da Capo Press, New York.
58. Tans, J. H., 1995. *The Hapless Anaconda: Union Blockade 1861-1865*. The Concord Review, Inc.
59. Texas State Historical Association, article on Galveston County.
60. *The United States Service Magazine*, Volume 1 (1864) to Volume 4 (1865). Government Printing Office, Washington.
61. Vale, Edmund, 2009. *The Harveys of Hayle* (revised edition). The Trevithick Society, Camborne.
62. Vandiver, F. E., 1947. *Confederate Blockade Running through Bermuda 1861-1865. Letters and Cargo Manifests*. University of Texas Press. Kraus Reprint Co. 1970.
63. Vandiver, F. E., 1952. *Ploughshares into Swords. Josiah Gorgas and Confederate Ordnance*. University of Texas Press.
64. Vandiver, F. E., 1995. *The Journals of Josiah Gorgas, 1857-1878*. University of Alabam Press.
65. Whittle, William C. jr, 2004. *The Voyage of the CSS Shenandoah: A Memorable*

Cruise. University of Alabama Press.

66. Wiggins, Sarah Woolfolk, 1995. The *Civil War Diary of General Josiah Gorgas*. University of Alabama Press.
67. Wiggins, S. W. and Truss, R. S. (eds) 2013. *The Journal of Sarah Haynsworth Gayle 1827-1835. A Substitute for Social Intercourse*. The University of Alabama Press.
68. Wilson, Walter E. and McKay, Gary L. 2012. *James D. Bulloch: Secret Agent and Mastermind of the Confederate Navy*. MacFarland & Co., Inc., Jefferson, North Carolina and London.
69. Wise, Stephen R., 1988. *Lifeline of the Confederacy. Blockade Running During the Civil War*. University of South Carolina Press.
70. Wise, Stephen R., 1989. *Greyhounds and Cavaliers of the Sea: Confederate Blockade Running during the Civil War*. Journal of Confederate History IV: Special Commemorative Naval Issue, CSS Alabama, 1864-1889. Southern Heritage Press, Tennessee.
71. Wyllie, Arthur, 2007. *The Union Navy*. Lulu.com.
72. Yolles, Melanie A., 1990. *Guide to the Charles F. W. Behm Papers, 1826-1871*. New York Public Library, Manuscripts and Archives Section.
73. Unattributed, 1984. *The Civil War. The Blockade, Runners and Raiders*. Time-Life Books.

Other publications

1. *American Lloyd's Register of American and Foreign Shipping*
2. *Belfast News Letter*
3. *Bermuda Royal Gazette*
4. *Boston Post*
5. *Bristol Mercury*
6. *Charleston Courier*
7. *Cork Examiner*
8. *Dundee Courier*
9. *Freeman's Journal and Daily Commercial Advertiser*
10. *Glasgow Herald*
11. *Houston Tri-Weekly Telegraph*
12. *Lake's Falmouth Packet*
13. *Liverpool Daily Post*
14. *Liverpool Mercury*
15. *London Standard*
16. *Memphis Daily Appeal*
17. *Morning Post*

18. *New Orleans Bulletin*
19. *New Orleans Daily Democrat*
20. *New Orleans Republican*
21. *New York Maritime Register*
22. *New York Times*
23. *Official Records of the Union and Confederate Navies in the War of the Rebellion*
24. *Record of American and Foreign Shipping*
25. *Register of American Shipping*
26. *Royal Cornwall Gazette*
27. *Shields Daily Gazette*
28. *Southern Reporter and Cork Commercial Courier*
29. *The Times*
30. *Western Daily Press*
31. *Wilmington Journal*

Websites

1. Bermuda National Library Digital Collection: www.bnl.contentdm.oclc.org
2. British Newspaper Archive: www.britishnewspaperarchive.co.uk
3. Chronicling America: Library of Congress: www.chroniclingamerica.loc.gov/newspapers
4. The Civil War: www.sonofthesouth.net
5. Civil War Talk: www.civilwartalk.com
6. Encyclopaedia of Greater Philadelphia: www.philadelphiaencyclopedia.org
7. Explore Southern History: www.exploresouthernhistory.com
8. Historic American Newspapers: www.chroniclingamerica.loc.gov/newspapers
9. Juneteenth.com: www.juneteenth.com
10. Mystic Seaport: www.mysticseaport.org
11. Nehemiah Gibson of East Boston: www.nehemiahgibson.com
12. NHHC – Naval History and Heritage Command: www.history.navy.mil
13. Portal to Texas History: www.texashistory.unt.edu

Other sources

1. Hoole Special Collections Library, University of Alabama
2. National Archives, Boston, Ma
3. National Archives, Kew
4. National Maritime Museum, Greenwich

Index